Praise for *Wild Fermentation*

"In the spirit of the great reformers and artists, Sandor Katz has labored mightily to deliver this opus magnum to a population hungry for a reconnection to real food, and to the process of life itself."

From the Foreword by Sally Fallon, author of *Nourishing Traditions*

"*Wild Fermentation* takes readers on a tour of fermented foods from around the globe—many of them delicacies available at Zabar's—and describes techniques for making them at home. For me the book was a nostalgic journey, reminding me of traditional foods I knew in my childhood, which are rarely found today. This is a book that will fascinate and inspire food lovers."

Saul Zabar, owner of Zabar's, New York City's most famous food market

"For those of us raised to believe that cleanliness is Godliness and "sterilization" the route to health, the notion that we'd sometimes be better off letting microbes have their way in our food seems. . . well, "wild." Armed with nothing more than a taste for sour flavors, and a decade of experiment that began with salted cabbage, Katz takes the reader on a tour of praise for what microbial biodiversity can do for foods and human health. A witty and enlightening romp with "mix, wait, and check" recipes for everything from brined garlic to vineagre de pina."

Joan Gussow, author *This Organic Life*

"In our mad rush to adopt newer, more technological food production, we have abandoned the fermenting, healthful wisdom of our forebears. Sandor Katz's book reclaims one of the most important, and ecologically sustainable processes of preserving and enhancing foods that humankind has discovered. *Wild Fermentation* is a significant, hands-on, journey through the miracle of fermented foods."

Stephen Harrod Buhner, author of *Sacred and Herbal Healing Beers: The Secrets of Ancient Fermentation* and *The Lost Language of Plants*

"This immensely valuable book belongs in the kitchen of anyone interested in health, nutrition and wild cultures. It is a feast of fact, fun, and creativity by a modern-wise wo-MAN."

Susun Weed, author of *Healing Wise*

"This is a very well written book, a pleasure to read, with excellent information and easy recipes for cultured and fermented foods. If you read it carefully, you will even find a recipe for gentle social activism that will help you feel you can indeed do something to improve the state of the world."

Annemarie Colbin, Ph.D., author of *Food and Healing*

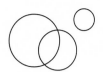

Wild Fermentation

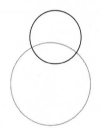

wild

ferment ation

The Flavor, Nutrition, and Craft of Live-Culture Foods

Sandor Ellix Katz

CHELSEA GREEN PUBLISHING COMPANY
WHITE RIVER JUNCTION, VERMONT
CPL

Designed by Jill Shaffer.

Printed in the United States
First printing, July, 2003
06 05 04 03 1 2 3 4

Library of Congress Cataloging-in-Publication Data
    Katz, Sandor Ellix, 1962-
      Wild fermentation : the flavor, nutrition, and craft of live-culture
    foods / Sandor Ellix Katz.
          p.   cm.
      Includes bibliographical references and index.
      ISBN 1-931498-23-7 (alk. paper)
      1. Fermented foods.   I. Title.
    TP371.44.K37 2003
    641.7—dc21

                                                    2003046207

Chelsea Green Publishing Company
P.O. Box 428
White River Junction, Vermont 05001
800-639-4099
www.chelseagreen.com

DEDICATED TO JON GREENBERG (1956–1993)

This beloved ACT UP comrade first articulated to me the idea of peaceful coexistence with microbes rather than warfare. I honor Jon and all our fellow skeptics, rebels, and iconoclasts who question prevailing wisdom and authority. Believe in the future and keep change fermenting.

CONTENTS

LIST OF RECIPES

FOREWORD
by Sally Fallon

THE PROCESS of fermenting foods—to preserve them and to make them more digestible and more nutritious—is as old as humanity. From the Tropics—where cassava is thrown into a hole in the ground to allow it to soften and sweeten—to the Arctic—where fish are customarily eaten "rotten" to the consistency of ice cream—fermented foods are valued for their health-giving properties and for their complex tastes.

Unfortunately, fermented foods have largely disappeared from the Western diet, much to the detriment of our health and economy. Fermented foods are a powerful aid to digestion and a protection against disease. And because fermentation is, by nature, an artisanal process, the disappearance of fermented foods has hastened the centralization and industrialization of our food supply, to the detriment of small farms and local economies.

The taste for fermented foods is usually an acquired taste. Few of us can imagine eating fermented tofu crawling with worms, which is relished in parts of Japan; or bubbly sorghum beer, smelling like the contents of your stomach, which is downed by the gallons in parts of Africa. But then, few Africans or Asians can enjoy the odiferous chunks of rotten milk (called cheese) that are so pleasing to Western palates. To those who have grown up with fermented foods, they offer the most sublime of eating experiences—and there are many that will appeal to Western tastes even without a long period of accustomization.

In the spirit of the great reformers and artists, Sandor Katz has labored mightily to deliver this magnum opus to a population hungry for a reconnection to real food and to the process of life itself. For fermented foods are not only satisfying to eat, they are also immensely satisfying to prepare. From the first successful batch of kombucha to that thrilling taste of homemade sauerkraut, the practice of fermentation is one of partnership with microscopic life. This partnership leads to a reverence for all the processes that contribute to the well-being of the human race, from the production of enzymes by invisible bacteria to the gift of milk and meat from the sacred cow.

The science and art of fermentation is, in fact, the basis of human culture: without culturing, there is no culture. Nations that still consume cultured foods, such as France with its wine and cheese, and Japan with its pickles and miso, are recognized as nations that have culture. Culture begins at the farm, not in the opera house, and binds a people to a land and its artisans. Many commentators have observed that America is a nation lacking culture—how can we be cultured when we eat only food that has been canned, pasteurized, and embalmed? How ironic that the road to culture in our germophobic technological society requires, first and foremost, that we enter into an alchemical relationship with bacteria and fungi, and that we bring to our tables foods and beverages prepared by the magicians, not machines.

Wild Fermentation represents not only an effort to bring back from oblivion these treasured processes but also a road map to a better world, a world of healthy people and equitable economies, a world that especially values those iconoclastic, free-thinking individuals—so often labeled misfits—uniquely qualified to perform the alchemy of fermented foods.

ACKNOWLEDGMENTS

THIS PROJECT has given my life focus and meaning at a time when I desperately needed these things. I spent 1999 and 2000 in the abyss of AIDS, accepting the idea that death could be near, living in the moment as much as possible, and trying not to dwell on a future that appeared dim. My deepest gratitude is for being alive and healthy. This project has given me back a sense of the future as expansive and full of possibilities.

I wish to thank all the people who have encouraged me in my obsession with fermentation as it has developed over the past decade. The ever-shifting cast of characters I live with, too many people to name here, but many of whom you will meet in these pages, supported my mad experimentation and tolerated my bubbling crocks and jars as they took over our kitchen. I thank everyone at Short Mountain Sanctuary, our sister communities, IDA and Pumpkin Hollow, and our beautiful extended community of neighbors for indulging my single-mindedness and showing me so much love and appreciation. I especially thank the gardeners and the milkers (and the plants and the goats) for providing us with such gorgeous abundance.

I thank my friends from the Sequatchie Valley Institute at Moonshadow, particularly Ashley and Patrick Ironwood, for inviting me to teach about fermentation at their annual Food for Life events. It has been an extraordinary pleasure to introduce simple fermentation skills to such enthusiastic groups. It was missing Food for Life in 2001 that prompted me to put together the self-published thirty-two-page precursor to this book.

I wrote the *Wild Fermentation* booklet during an extended stay at my home away from home, in Maine. I thank Edward, Caity, and Roman Curran for sharing their home with my crocks and me. Edward was my first reader and encouraged my work by becoming no less than a disciple of fermentation. As he sustained himself on a diet of nothing but kraut, kefir, pickles, miso, yogurt, and various other stray ferments, his body dramatically healed a number of chronic health problems. Edward is a true believer who helped me believe I could do this.

I thank the folks at Chelsea Green Publishing for their receptiveness to this project. I decided to look for a publisher after I put my booklet out, and I picked Chelsea Green on the basis of an Internet search. Our earliest exchanges were most auspicious. When I went to White River Junction and met with the staff, we sealed the deal eating *kimchi* I had made out of a jar with our fingers. I feel like I found a good niche.

I thank my family for giving me my love of food, and so much more. When we get together, we eat. My grandmother, Betty Ellix, lovingly prepared the foods I think of as my cultural heritage. My mother, Rita Ellix, taught me basic kitchen skills and instilled in me a sense of culinary adventure. My father, Joe Katz, is a lifelong gardener and cook. He and my stepmother, Pattie Eakin, continually inspire me with the creative use they make of their garden's bounty. My sister Lizzi Katz and my brother Jonny Katz I thank simply for their love and devotion.

I thank my fermentation mentors and fellow-travellers: Dr. Crazy Owl, James Creagh, Merril Harris, Hector Black, Patrick Ironwood, Ashley Ironwood, Sylvan Tucker, Tom Foolery, David J. Pinkerton, Justin Bullard, and Nettles for sharing their fermentation methods. I thank the following friends who read my evolving manuscript and offered feedback and suggestions: Echo, Nettles, Leopard, Scotty Heron, Lapis Luxury, Orchid, MaxZine Weinstein, Spark, Buffy Aakaash, Joel Kimmons, Ravel Weaver, Book Mark, Edge, Dee Dee, and Tanya Einhorn; Echo, Spark, Weeder, Louis, Kasha, Johnni Greenwell, Joan Scott, and Laura Harrington for referring me to books and articles; Matt and Raivo for taking me out into the ocean with them to harvest seaweed; Todd Weir for finding me German recipes for *sonnenblumenkernbrot* and Christoph Gielen for translating them for me; Ron Campbell for sharing his tales of prison fermentation and Mike for introducing us; David Ford for reciting Walt Whitman on compost for me; John Wall for computer help; Betty Stechmeyer of G.E.M. Cultures for finding me, sending me samples of some of the exotic cultures she sells, and teaching me the word *organoleptic;* Alicia Svigals for Yiddish consultations; Jai Sheronda for photography; Jay Blotcher for sharing his picture archive; Valerie Borchardt for her willingness to advise me informally; and B. Whiting for proofreading.

I thank the librarians at the Adams Memorial Library in Woodbury, Tennessee, Middle Tennessee State University in Murfreesboro, Vanderbilt University in Nashville, Bowdoin College in Brunswick, Maine, and the University of Vermont in Burlington. Libraries are glorious institutions, and this project reawakened my love of library research after a fifteen-year hiatus.

I thank *you* for your interest in my book.

Wild Fermentation

CULTURAL CONTEXT:
The Making of a Fermentation Fetish

THIS BOOK IS my song of praise and devotion to fermentation. For me, fermentation is a health regimen, a gourmet art, a multicultural adventure, a form of activism, and a spiritual path, all rolled into one. My daily routine is structured by the rhythms of these transformative life processes.

Sometimes I feel like a mad scientist, tending to as many as a dozen different bubbly fermentation experiments at once. Sometimes I feel like a game show host: "Would you like to taste what's in Crock Number One, or trade it for what lies buried in Crock Number Two?" Sometimes I feel like a Holy Roller evangelist, zealously spreading the word about the glorious healing powers of fermented foods. My friends tease me about my single-mindedness as they sample my fermented goodies. One friend, Nettles, even wrote a song about my obsession:

> Come on friends and lend me an ear,
> I'll explain the connection between wine and beer,
> And sourdough and yogurt and miso and kraut,
> What they have in common is what it's all about.
> Oh the microorganisms,
> Oh the microorganisms . . .

1

Fermentation is everywhere, always. It is an everyday miracle, the path of least resistance. Microscopic bacteria and fungi (encompassing yeasts and molds) are in every breath we take and every bite we eat. Try—as many do—to eradicate them with antibacterial soaps, antifungal creams, and antibiotic drugs, there is no escaping them. They are ubiquitous agents of transformation, feasting upon decaying matter, constantly shifting dynamic life forces from one miraculous and horrible creation to the next.

Microbial cultures are essential to life's processes, such as digestion and immunity. We humans are in a symbiotic relationship with these single-cell life-forms. Microflora, as they are often called, digest food into nutrients our bodies can absorb, protect us from potentially dangerous organisms, and teach our immune systems how to function. Not only are we dependent upon microorganisms, we are their descendents: According to the fossil record, all forms of life on Earth spring from bacterial origins. Microorganisms are our ancestors and our allies. They keep the soil fertile and comprise an indispensable part of the cycle of life. Without them, there could be no other life.

Certain microorganisms can manifest extraordinary culinary transformations. Tiny beings, invisible to us, bring us compelling and varied flavors. Fermentation gives us many of our most basic staples, such as bread and cheese, and our most pleasurable treats, including chocolate, coffee, wine, and beer. Cultures around the globe enjoy countless exotic fermented delicacies. The process of fermentation makes food more digestible and nutritious. Live, unpasteurized, fermented foods also carry beneficial bacteria directly into our digestive systems, where they exist symbiotically, breaking down food and aiding digestion.

In this book, I explain simple methods for making a variety of fermented foods and beverages. Over the past decade, I have explored and experimented widely in the realm of fermentation. I want to share what I have learned. I am not really an expert. The experts are likely to find my techniques primitive. They are. Fermentation is easy. Anyone can do it, anywhere, with the most basic tools. Humans have been fermenting longer than we've been writing words or cultivating the soil. Fermentation does not require vast expertise or laboratory conditions. You do not need to be a scientist able to distinguish specific microbial agents and their enzymatic transformations, nor a technician maintaining sterile environments and exact temperatures. You can do it in your kitchen.

The focus of this book is the basic processes of transformation, which mostly involve creating conditions in which naturally occurring wild organisms thrive and proliferate. Fermentation can be low-tech. These are ancient rituals that humans have been performing for many generations. They make me feel connected to the magic of the natural world, and to our ancestors, whose clever observations enable us to enjoy the benefits of these transformations.

When I try to conjure the origin of my fascination with this natural phenomenon, it leads me to my taste buds. I have always been crazy about brined sour pickles and sauerkraut. I am a descendent of Jewish immigrants from Poland, Russia, and Lithuania. These foods and their distinctive flavors are part of my cultural heritage. In Yiddish, these sour vegetables are known as *zoyers*. Sour flavors from fermentation are prominent in the food of Eastern Europe (as in many regions of the world), and carried over into the distinctive culinary identity of New York City, where I grew up. We lived on the Upper West Side of Manhattan, two blocks from Zabar's, an icon of New York food, and my family regularly feasted on their *zoyers*. I recently learned that Lithuanian tradition worships Roguszys, a god of pickled food. Just a few generations out of Eastern Europe, my taste buds still salivate at Roguszys' temple.

My fermentation adventures have been encouraged and aided by my live-in panel of taste-testers, critics, philosophers, and fellow fermentation enthusiasts. I am part of a community called Short Mountain Sanctuary, a rural homestead of queer folks who call ourselves faeries, nestled in the hills of Tennessee. We generally have twenty or more people in residence, eat meals together, and host twice-weekly potlucks with our extended community of neighbors.

I feel incredibly lucky to live in the woods in such a beautiful place. This land itself nourishes, nurtures, and teaches me. Every day I drink fresh spring water from deep within the earth, and feast upon wild plants, homegrown organic vegetables and fruits, and gourmet concoctions prepared in our communal kitchen with tender loving care. We are homesteaders, far from the infrastructure and service amenities of mainstream American life. No utility poles have come marching through our woods (hallelujah!), so I am typing this into a laptop computer powered by electricity we harness from the Sun.

The do-it-yourself ethic of rural homesteading and the insatiable collective appetite of our community inspired me to learn how to make sauerkraut nearly a decade ago. I found an old crock buried in our barn and harvested cabbage from our garden. I chopped it up, salted it, and waited. That first kraut tasted so alive and powerfully nutritious! Its sharp flavor sent my salivary glands into a frenzy and got me hooked on fermentation. I have made sauerkraut ever since, earning the nickname Sandorkraut, even as my repertoire has expanded. After kraut, I learned how easy it is to make yogurt and cheese with the steady supply of fresh milk from our small herd of goats. Sourdough baking, beer- and wine-making, and miso-making followed. Bubbling crocks have become a permanent feature of our kitchen. Some of these projects are finished overnight, some take years, and others are ongoing, as we feed and stir the crocks and jars, developing a symbiotic rhythm with these tiny fermenting organisms, nurturing them so that they will nourish us.

Nutrition is extremely important to me. I have AIDS and need my body to be as strong and resilient as it can be. Fermented foods make my body feel well-nourished, and I eat them regularly as a health practice. Fermented foods not only nourish, they help protect us from potentially harmful organisms and contribute to immunity. Unfortunately, nothing is a panacea, and fermented foods did not prevent me from developing AIDS. I've lived through harrowing downward spirals, but also miraculous recoveries. I feel very lucky to be alive and relatively healthy, awed by my body's recuperative powers. I take anti-retroviral drugs, but many different factors, including regular consumption of live fermented foods, contribute to my present robust and energetic state, as well as my ability to tolerate drugs notorious for intestinal upset. Tangible health benefits have only encouraged my devotion to fermentation.

A *fetish*, according to Webster's, is anything "supposed to possess magical powers" and thereby worthy of "special devotion." Fermentation is magical and mystical, and I am deeply devoted to it. I have indulged this arcane fetish (and been indulged). This book is the result. Fermentation has been an important journey of discovery for me, and I invite you to join me along this effervescent path, well trodden for thousands of years yet largely forgotten in our time and place, bypassed by the superhighway of industrial food production.

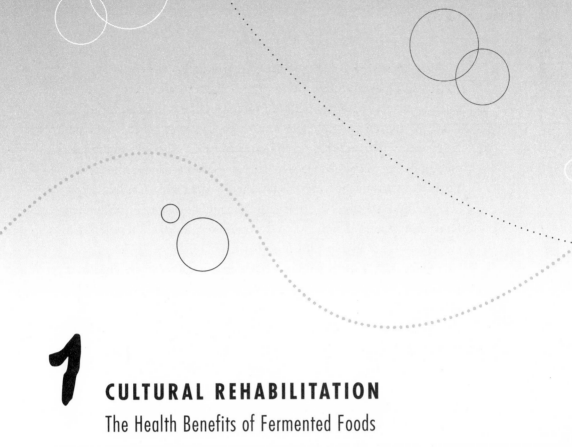

1

CULTURAL REHABILITATION
The Health Benefits of Fermented Foods

FERMENTED FOODS and drinks are quite literally alive with flavor and nutrition. Their flavors tend to be strong and pronounced. Think of stinky aged cheeses, tangy sauerkraut, rich earthy miso, smooth sublime wines. Humans have always appreciated the distinctive flavors resulting from the transformative power of microscopic bacteria and fungi.

One major benefit of fermentation is that it preserves food. Fermentation organisms produce alcohol, lactic acid, and acetic acid, all "bio-preservatives" that retain nutrients and prevent spoilage. Vegetables, fruits, milk, fish, and meat are highly perishable, and our ancestors used whatever techniques they could discover to store foods from seasons of plenty for later consumption. Captain James Cook, the eighteenth-century English explorer who extended the far reaches of the British Empire, was recognized by the Royal Society for having conquered scurvy (vitamin C deficiency) among his crews by sailing with large quantities of sauerkraut.[1] On his second round-the-world voyage, in the 1770s, sixty barrels of kraut lasted for twenty-seven months, and not a single crew member developed scurvy, which previously had killed huge numbers of the crews of long sea voyages.[2]

Among the many lands Cook "discovered" and delivered into the Crown's realm were the Hawaiian Islands (Cook called them the Sandwich Islands in honor of his patron). I find it an interesting parallel that the Polynesian people who crossed the Pacific Ocean and populated Hawaii more than a thousand years before Captain Cook also sustained themselves through the long voyage with fermented food, in this case *poi,* a thick starchy taro root porridge still popular in Hawaii and throughout the South Pacific.[3]

Fermentation not only preserves nutrients, it breaks them down into more easily digestible forms. Soybeans are a good example. This extraordinarily protein-rich food is largely indigestible without fermentation. Fermentation breaks down the soybeans' complex protein into readily digestible amino acids, giving us traditional Asian foods such as miso, tempeh, and tamari (soy sauce), which have become staples in contemporary Western vegetarian cuisine.

Milk, too, is difficult for many people to digest. *Lactobacilli* (a type of bacteria present in fermented dairy products and many other types of ferments) transform lactose, the milk sugar that so many humans cannot tolerate, into easier-to-digest lactic acid. Likewise, wheat that has undergone fermentation is easier to digest than unfermented wheat. A study in the journal *Nutritional Health* compared unfermented and fermented versions of a mix of barley, lentils, milk powder, and tomato pulp and found that "starch digestibility almost doubled in the fermented mixture."[4] According to the United Nations Food and Agriculture Organization, which actively promotes fermentation as a critical source of nutrients worldwide, fermentation improves the bioavailability of minerals present in food.[5] Bill Mollison, author of the *Permaculture Book of Ferment and Human Nutrition,* calls the action of fermenting foods "a form of pre-digestion."[6]

Fermentation also creates new nutrients. As they go through their life cycles, microbial cultures create B vitamins, including folic acid, riboflavin, niacin, thiamin, and biotin. (Ferments have often been credited with creating vitamin B_{12}, otherwise absent from plant-source foods; however, this bubble has now been burst by improved assaying techniques that show that what had been identified as B_{12} in fermented soy and vegetables are actually inactive "analogues." B_{12} is only found in foods from animal sources, suggesting that a vegan diet is deficient in B_{12} without supplementation, the efficacy of which is quite controversial.[7])

Some ferments have been shown to function as antioxidants, scavenging cancer precursors known as "free radicals" from the cells of your body.[8] *Lactobacilli* create omega-3 fatty acids, essential for cell membrane and immune system function.[9] A marketer of "cultured whole food supplements" boasts that "the culturing process generates copious amounts of naturally occurring ingredients like superoxide dismustase, GTF chromium, detoxifying compounds like glutathione, phospholipids, digestive enzymes, and beta 1,3 glucans."[10] Frankly, nutritional factoids like this make my eyes glaze over. You don't really need chemical analysis to tell you what foods are healthy. Trust your instincts and your taste buds. The data adds up to this: Fermentation makes food more nutritious.

Fermentation also removes toxins from foods. This is vividly illustrated by the case of cassava, an enormous tuber native to the tropical regions of the Americas that has also become a staple food in equatorial regions of Africa and Asia. Certain varieties of cassava contain high levels of cyanide and are poisonous until they have undergone a soaking fermentation. The fermentation process eliminates the cyanide, rendering the cassava edible and nutritious.

Not all food toxins are as dramatic as cyanide. All grains contain a compound called phytic acid, which can block absorption of zinc, calcium, iron, magnesium, and other minerals and lead to mineral deficiencies. Fermenting grains by soaking them before cooking neutralizes phytic acid, rendering the grain far more nutritious.[11] Nitrites, prussic acid, oxalic acid, nitrosamines, and glucosides are some other potentially toxic chemicals found in foods that can be reduced or eliminated by fermentation.[12]

Eating fermented foods live is an incredibly healthy practice, directly supplying your digestive tract with living cultures essential to breaking down food and assimilating nutrients. Not all fermented foods are still alive when you eat them. Certain foods, by their nature, cannot contain live cultures. Breads, for instance, must be baked, thereby killing the organisms present in them. However, many fermented foods can be consumed live, especially those involving *Lactobacilli,* and alive is the most nutritious way to eat them.

Read labels and be aware: Many commercially available fermented foods are pasteurized, which means heated to the point at which microorganisms die. Though yogurt is well known for its live cultures, many yogurt brands are pasteurized after culturing, killing the prized bacteria. Yogurt that is still alive generally includes in the small print of the label words to the effect that the yogurt "contains live cultures." Sauerkraut too is usually heat-processed and canned to extend shelf life, at the cost of its healthful live bacteria. Even miso is often dried and sold in a lifeless powdered form. If you want live-culture fermented foods in our food-security-obsessed, instant-gratification age, you have to seek them out or make them yourself.

By promoting digestive health, live fermented foods can help control digestive disease processes such as diarrhea and dysentery. Live-culture foods can even improve infant survival rates. A study conducted in Tanzania compared mortality rates between infants fed different "weaning gruels," some cultured, some not. The infants eating fermented gruels had half as many "diarrhea episodes" as the infants fed nonfermented gruels.[13] *Lactobacillus* fermentation inhibits the growth of diarrhea-related bacteria such as *Shigella, Salmonella,* and *E. coli.*[14] Another study, reported in the journal *Nutrition,* concludes that thriving microflora prevent disease because *Lactobacillus* "competes with . . . potential pathogens for receptor sites at the mucosal cell surfaces" of the intestines and proposes a treatment strategy of "ecoimmunonutrition."[15]

As eighteen-letter words go, I like the word *ecoimmunonutrition.* It recognizes that an organism's immune function occurs in the context of an ecology, an ecosystem of different microbial cultures, and that it is possible to build and develop that cultural ecology in oneself through diet. As a person living with AIDS, immune function is something always on my mind. I do not claim that fermented foods can cure AIDS. Nor do I claim that live-culture foods will cure anyone of cancer or any other disease. I am distrustful of miracle cure-alls. However, quite an awesome array of medical studies have identified specific anti-cancer and other disease-preventing properties in fermented foods. Hundreds of such studies, published in medical and scientific journals, are cited in the book *The Life Bridge: The Way to Longevity with Probiotic Nutrients.* The literature all reaffirms the idea that the organisms of fermentation play a role in protecting us, as organisms among organisms, from disease.

THE CASE FOR MICROBIAL COEXISTENCE

Our culture is terrified of germs and obsessed with hygiene. The more we glean about disease-causing viruses, bacteria, and other microorganisms, the more we fear exposure to all forms of microscopic life. Every new sensationalized killer microbe gives us more reason to defend ourselves with vigilance. Nothing illustrates this more vividly than the sudden appearance, everywhere in the United States, of antibacterial soap. Twenty years ago, mass marketing of antibacterial soap was but a glimmer in some pharmaceutical executive's eye. It has quickly become the standard hand-washing hygiene product. Are fewer people getting sick as a result? "There's no evidence that they do any good and there's reason to suspect that they could contribute to a problem by helping to create antibiotic-resistant bacteria," says Dr. Myron Genel, chair of the American Medical Association's Council on Scientific Affairs.[16] Antibacterial soap is just another exploitative and potentially dangerous product being sold by preying on people's fears.

The antibacterial compounds in these soaps, most commonly *triclosan,* kill the more susceptible bacteria but not the heartier ones. "These resistant microbes may include bacteria . . . that were unable to gain a foothold previously and are now able to thrive thanks to the destruction of competing microbes," says Dr. Stuart Levy, director of the Tufts University Center for Adaptation Genetics and Drug Resistance.[17] Your skin, your orifices, and the surfaces of your home are all covered with microorganisms that help protect you (and themselves) from potentially harmful organisms that you both encounter. Constantly assaulting the bacteria on, in, and around you with antibacterial compounds weakens one line of defense your body uses against disease organisms.

Microorganisms not only protect us by competing with potentially dangerous organisms, they teach the immune system how to function. "The immune system organizes itself through experience, just like the brain," says Dr. Irun R. Cohen of the Weizmann Institute of Science in Israel.[18] A growing number of researchers are finding evidence to support what is known as "the hygiene hypothesis," which attributes the dramatic rise in prevalence of asthma and other allergies to *lack* of exposure to diverse microorganisms found in soil and untreated water. "The cleaner we live . . . the more likely we'll get asthma and allergies," states Dr. David Rosenstreich, director of

Allergy and Immunology at the Albert Einstein School of Medicine in New York.[19]

Paranoia about germs has been magnified by the recent anthrax terror and fears of biological warfare. According to the December 2001 newsletter of *Household and Personal Products on the Internet,* "A widespread fear of disease—specifically anthrax bacteria—has caused consumers to take a more serious look at cleansing. . . . Antibacterial cleansers are expected to spike in sales."[20]

Well-informed hygiene is very important, but it is impossible to avoid exposure to microbes. They are everywhere. A 1970s made-for-TV movie called *The Boy in the Plastic Bubble* dramatized the tragic saga of a young man born with an immune disorder who could only survive in a germ-free environment. The boy, portrayed by John Travolta en route to superstardom, lived in a hermetically sealed, sterilized room and could only interact with other people through protective barriers. He periodically ventured out of his room in a spacesuit-like outfit. He grew so lonely and sad in his sterile cage that he chose to leave it and live normally for the brief time before the inevitable pathogenic organism killed him. This is a pop culture parable of the impossibility and undesirability of sequestering oneself from the biological risks of being alive.

Much of Western chemical medicine aims to eradicate pathogenic organisms. In the case of my AIDS drugs, the treatment strategy is called "highly active anti-retroviral therapy." Having benefited from the miracles of high-tech pharmaceuticals, I'm in no position to argue against the value of this approach. I firmly believe, however, that microbial warfare is not a sustainable practice. "Bacteria are not germs but the germinators—and fabric—of all life on Earth," writes Stephen Harrod Buhner in *The Lost Language of Plants.* "In declaring war on them we declared war on the underlying living structure of the planet—on all life-forms we can see—on ourselves."[21]

Health and homeostasis require that humans coexist with microorganisms. Bacteria-counting scientists have quantified this simple fact, estimating that each person's body is host to a bacterial population in excess of 100 trillion, and noting that "the interactions of these colonizing microbes with the host are nothing if not complex."[22] Humans and all other forms of life evolved from and with these organisms, and we cannot live without them. "Nature appears to maximize mutual cooperation and mutual coordination of goals," wrote ethnobotanist Terence McKenna. "To be indispensable to the organisms with which one shares an environment—that is the strategy that ensures successful breeding and continued survival."[23]

The study of symbiogenesis views evolutionary innovation as a consequence of symbiosis, tracing the source of all life to prokaryotes, which are cells distinguished by the absence of nuclear membranes. Bacteria are prokaryotes. Their genetic material is free-floating in the cell. "Genes from the fluid medium, from other bacteria, from viruses, or from elsewhere enter bacterial cells on their own," write biologists Lynn Margulis and Karlene V. Schwartz.[24] By incorporating DNA from their environment into themselves, prokaryotes assimilate genetic traits. They evolved first into eukaryotes (cells with nuclear membranes) and eventually into complex organisms such as ourselves. But they never left their progeny; they are with us always.

"Prokaryotes are the master engineers of our complexity," explains my excited scientist friend Joel Kimmons, recent recipient of a Ph.D. in nutrition from the University of California. Inside our bodies, most dramatically in the gut, prokaryotes absorb genetic information that informs our function as organisms; they are an integral part of our sentient experience. "We eat and thus we know," says Joel. Humans are in mutually beneficial and mutually dependent relationships with these and many different microbes. We are symbiotic, inextricably woven together, in a complex pattern far beyond our capacity to comprehend completely.

MICROBIODIVERSITY AND INCORPORATING THE WILD

By eating a variety of live fermented foods, you promote diversity among microbial cultures in your body. Biodiversity is increasingly recognized as critical to the survival of larger-scale ecosystems. Earth and all its inhabitants comprise a single, seamless matrix of life, interconnected and interdependent. The frightening repercussions of species extinctions starkly illustrate the impact of the loss of biodiversity all over our planet. The survival of our species depends upon biodiversity.

Biodiversity is just as important at the micro level. Call it microbiodiversity. Your body is an ecosystem that can function most effectively when populated by diverse species of microorganisms. Sure, you can buy "probiotic" nutritional supplements containing specific selected bacteria that promote healthy digestion. But by fermenting foods and drinks with wild microorganisms present in your home environment, you become more interconnected with the life forces of the world around you. Your environment becomes you, as you invite the microbial populations you share the Earth with to enter your diet and your intestinal ecology.

Wild fermentation is a way of incorporating the wild into your body, becoming one with the natural world. Wild foods, microbial cultures included, possess a great, unmediated life force, which can help us adapt to shifting conditions and lower our susceptibility to disease. These microorganisms are everywhere, and the techniques for fermenting with them are simple and flexible.

Are live fermented foods the answer to a long, healthy life? The folklore of many different cultures associate longevity with foods such as yogurt and miso. Many researchers have found evidence to support this causal connection. Pioneering Russian immunologist and Nobel laureate Elie Metchnikoff studied yogurt-eating centenarians in the Balkans early in the twentieth century and concluded that *Lacto-bacilli* "postpone and ameliorate old age."[25]

Personally, I'm not so inclined to reduce the secret of long life and good health to any one product or practice. Life consists of multiple variables, and every life is unique. But very clearly fermentation has contributed to the longevity and well-being of humanity as a whole. The methods of fermentation are many and varied; it is practiced on every continent, in thousands of different ways. As you proceed through these pages, you will see how simple it is for you to share in the nutritional and healing powers of fermented foods and drinks that humans have enjoyed for thousands of years.

2 CULTURAL THEORY
Human Beings and the Phenomenon of Fermentation

HUMAN BEINGS have recognized the magic and power of fermentation for as long as we have been human. A honey wine called mead is generally regarded as the most ancient fermented pleasure. Archaeologists believe that human collecting of honey predates our cultivation of the soil. Cave paintings in locations as geographically dispersed as India, Spain, and South Africa depict images of people gathering honey in the Paleolithic era, as long as 12,000 years ago.

Cave painting of prehistoric honey gathering

When by chance or intention honey is mixed with water, fermentation happens. Yeasts surfing through the air aboard particles of dust find their way to that sweet, nutritive honey-water. When the honey is pure, it acts as a preservative and inhibits microscopic life. But honey diluted with water becomes a stimulating medium for airborne yeast to land in, feast upon, and reproduce exponentially, bubbling and vividly alive. Within a short time, the honey-water will

13

be mead, its sugars having been converted to alcohol and carbon dioxide by the action of tiny beings invisible to the human eye.

According to Maguelonne Toussaint-Samat's vast survey, *A History of Food,* "The child of honey, the drink of the gods, mead was universal. It can be regarded as the ancestor of all fermented drinks."[1] Our hunter-gatherer forebears, at least some of them, some of the time, enjoyed mead. The production of mead does not require fire, and possibly it has been part of human life for even longer than controlled fire. Imagine the wonder and awe our ancestors must have felt as they first encountered fermenting honey-water in the hollow of a tree. Were they scared by the bubbling? Or just curious? Once they tasted it, they must have liked it and drunk more. Then they started to experience a light, giddy feeling. Surely some divine spirit granted them this substance and the state it induced.

The anthropologist and cultural theorist Claude Levi-Strauss suggests that mead-making marks the passage of humanity from nature to culture. He illustrates this distinction by describing the transitional role of a hollow tree, "which, as a receptacle for honey, is part of nature if the honey is fresh and enclosed within it, and part of culture if the honey, instead of being in a naturally hollow tree, has been put to ferment in an artificially hollowed out trunk."[2] The learning of techniques to ferment alcohol and thus enter sacred states of altered consciousness is a defining characteristic of human culture, made possible by the life cycles of humble yeast cultures. "What seems clear," writes Stephen Harrod Buhner in his *Sacred and Herbal Healing Beers,* "is that human knowledge of fermentation arose independently throughout human cultures, that each culture attributed its appearance to divine intervention, and that its use is intimately bound up with our development as a species."[3]

Fermentation-induced altered states have long been associated with oral storytelling, mythical traditions, and poetry in many different cultures. The Papago people of the Sonoran Desert region of northern Mexico and southern Arizona ferment a drink called *tiswin* from the fruit of the saguaro cactus. Buhner cites the traditional song the Papago sing as they drink *tiswin:*

> Dizziness is following me!
> Close it is following me.
> Ah, but I like it.

Yonder far, far
On the flat land it is taking me.
Dizziness I see.
High up there I see it.
Truly I like it.
Yonder they lead me.
And dizziness they give me to drink.

'Tis at the foot of little Gray Mountain
I am sitting and getting drunk.
Beautiful songs I shall unfold."[4]

This same inspirational quality is often attributed to fermented alcohol, across cultures. Inebriation is the state "of which the hymns of all primitive peoples tell us," condescended Friedrich Nietzsche.[5] Language, the most fundamental faculty that distinguishes our species, has been developed, exercised, and elaborated "under the influence." Meads, wines, and beers have been held sacred in many different traditions for thousands of years. Prohibitions notwithstanding, alcohol ferments have always been worshiped, invested with important symbolic meaning, and offered to deities.

The Sumerians, beer makers with written recipes dating back nearly five thousand years, worshiped a goddess of beer, Ninkasi, whose name means "you who fill my mouth so full."[6] Egyptians buried great ceramic casks of wines and beers with their mummified royals in the pyramids, and in *The Egyptian Book of the Dead,* prayers for the souls of the deceased are addressed to "givers of bread and beer."[7] Ancient Mayan ceremonies involved a honey ferment called *balché,* which they used in enema form to maximize its inebriating effect. Perhaps because of this unfamiliar mode of consumption, their conquerors saw the devil lurking in *balché,* in order to "turn into snakes and worms that gnawed at the souls of the Maya."[8] It was banned in the name of Christendom. Nevertheless, in the Catholic magic of transubstantiation, wine becomes the blood of Jesus Christ. In my own Jewish tradition, repeated recitations of the prayer "Blessed is the creator of the fruit of the vine" are accompanied by sacramental drinks of wine.

*Hieroglyph symbols
for bread and beer*

Other forms of fermentation seem to have developed in tandem with the domestication of plants and animals, as human cultures evolved. It is no accident that the word *culture* has such broad connotation. It derives from the Latin *colere,* "to cultivate." Fermentation cultures are cultivated no less than plants and animals are cultivated, and for that matter no less than the "socially transmitted behavior patterns, arts, beliefs, institutions, and all other products of human work and thought" that constitute the dictionary's first definition of *culture.*[9] The various cultures are inextricably intertwined.

Nomadic herding peoples domesticated various animals—yaks, horses, camels, sheep, goats, cattle—and by observing how milk soured, learned to culture it and curdle it in order to extend its usefulness. Whether by chance or intention, raw unpasteurized milk not drunk quickly ferments. *Lactobacilli* convert lactose to lactic acid, which sours and eventually causes milk to separate, curds from whey, into more stable and storable dairy products.

Eventually, people developed techniques for the cultivation of cereal grains. Grain porridges or doughs inevitably ferment. Mix flour (or any form of any grain) with water and it will attract yeast and bacteria that ferment it. Bread and beer both are born of grain fermentation, and historians debate which came first. The conventional wisdom is that humans settled into grain agriculture as a means of producing reliable, storable foodstuffs. "Are we to believe that the foundations of Western civilization were laid by an ill-fed people living in a perpetual state of partial intoxication?" asked botanist Paul Manglesdorf in a symposium on this question organized by the journal *American Anthropologist.* But an alternative hypothesis presents a cultural paradox: Is it not possible that beer provided a more compelling incentive than mere food for well-fed migratory peoples to settle?[10] Either way, fermentation is part of the story. Grain fermentation techniques evolved together with grain agriculture.

SCIENCE PUZZLES OVER A PERPLEXING PHENOMENON

Though many peoples throughout history have recognized fermentation as a mystical life force, in the Western scientific tradition it was long shrouded in confusion. Since at least Roman times, natural historians such as Pliny the Elder described what they called "spontaneous generations." The theory of spontaneous generation viewed certain forms of life as phenomena occurring independent of any reproductive process. This belief was not limited to the bubbling action of fermentation. Scientists were earnestly trying to elucidate the spontaneous generation of mice as late as the seventeenth century, when Jean Baptista van Helmont reported that "if one presses a dirty shirt into the opening of a vessel containing grains of wheat, the ferment from the dirty shirt does not modify the smell of the grain but gives rise to the transmutation of the wheat into mice after about twenty-one days."[11] He also had a recipe for creating scorpions by carving a hole into a brick, filling it with dried basil, and placing it in the full sun.

As van Helmont was generating mice from wheat and dirty shirts, a Dutchman, Anton van Leeuwenhoek, developed the microscope and first observed microorganisms in 1674:

> I now saw very plainly that these were little eels, or worms, lying all huddled up together and wriggling; just as if you saw, with the naked eye, a whole tubful of very little eels and water, with the eels a-squirming among one another: and the whole water seemed to be alive with these multifarious animalcules. This was for me, among all the marvels that I have discovered in nature, the most marvelous of all; and I must say, for my part, that no more pleasant sight has ever yet come before my eye than these many thousands of living creatures, seen all alive in a little drop of water, moving among one another, each several creatures having its own proper motion . . .[12]

Meanwhile, French philosopher René Descartes had expounded his revolutionary view that all natural phenomena could be reduced to mechanical processes. Descartes ushered in a period of scientific inquiry focused on describing natural processes by causal mechanisms. Chemistry flourished in the eighteenth and nineteenth centuries, and a sort of chemical reductionism came into vogue, which held that all physiological processes were ultimately reducible to a series of chemical reactions. Chemists of this period dismissed the idea that fermentation was caused by living organisms as "retrograde."[13]

The chemists were aware of the "animalcules" revealed by the microscope, but they stubbornly dismissed their importance and constructed elaborate theories to explain them away. The nineteenth-century chemist Justus von Liebig, a pioneer in the development of chemical fertilizers, was a major proponent of fermentation as a chemical rather than biological process. Von Liebig believed that the importance of the yeast in the fermentation process was its decomposition as dead matter. In an 1840 treatise, he wrote: "It is the dead part of the yeast, the part that is no longer alive and undergoing alteration, that acts on the sugar."[14]

LOUIS PASTEUR AND THE ADVENT OF MICROBIOLOGY

Enter Louis Pasteur, a French chemist who turned his attention to fermentation processes at the behest of a Lille industrialist, a beetroot alcohol manufacturer whose factory was experiencing inconsistent results and whose son was enrolled in Pasteur's class at the university. Pasteur's methodical study of beetroot fermentation quickly convinced him that fermentation was a biological process. His first study on fermentation, *Memoire sur la fermentation appelée lactique*, was published in April 1857: "Fermentation is a correlative of life and of the production of globules, rather than of their death or putrefaction."[15] Pasteur solved the beetroot alcohol manufacturer's problem by heating the beet juice to destroy naturally occurring lactic acid–producing microorganisms and reseeding it with alcohol-producing yeast. This was the earliest application of the heating process now credited on every carton of milk: pasteurization.

Pasteur's findings contradicted the chemistry establishment of the time, and Pasteur became a crusader. He spent the rest of his life studying the life cycles of various types of microorganisms, and spawned the whole field of microbiology. Pasteur's work features a vivid vocabulary. Citing his success at culturing specific yeasts, he challenged the idea underlying spontaneous generation, which he calls "undifferentiated panspermatism." Examining sour beer under a microscope, Pasteur observed the simultaneous appearance of butyric acid and moving microorganisms, which he called "butyric vibrios." Butyric vibrios (a great name for a band or a vibrator) is the original name Pasteur used to describe mobile bacteria when he first distinguished them from yeast.

Though the academic chemistry establishment reacted defensively to his findings, the burgeoning fermentation industries gratefully incorporated Pasteur's innovations. His discoveries gave a great boost to the mass production of fermented foods and drinks. These products had been enjoyed for thousands of years, created using processes learned from nature, often accompanied by prayers, rituals, and offerings to deities. Now, with scientific precision and without elaborate ritual, they could be reliably manufactured in mass quantities.

The advent of microbiology gave rise to a sort of colonial outlook toward microorganisms, that they, like other elements of nature and other human cultures, must be dominated and exploited. One book that expresses this attitude especially poignantly is *Bacteria in Relation to Country Life,* published in 1908, midway between Pasteur's research and the development of antibiotic drugs.

> The deepening current of human existence now forces us to study the bacteria and other microorganisms. In so far as they are dangerous to our health and happiness we must learn to defend ourselves; we must learn to destroy them or to render them harmless. In so far as they are beneficial, we must learn to control them and to make their activities widely useful to human society.[16]

Homo sapiens prone to feeling overly confident of our superiority and ability to dominate would do well to ponder a small bit of wisdom attributed to Louis Pasteur himself: "It's the microbes that will have the last word."[17]

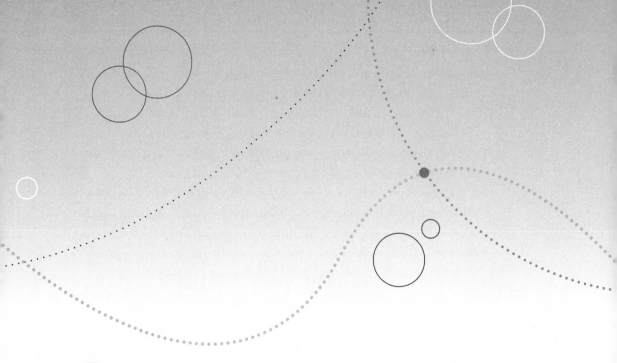

3 CULTURAL HOMOGENIZATION
Standardization, Uniformity, and Mass Production

*Part of the pleasure those [McDonald's] fries gave me was how
perfectly they conformed to my image and expectation of them—
to the idea of Fries in my head, that is, an idea that McDonald's
has successfully planted in the heads of a few billion people
around the world.*

—MICHAEL POLLAN, *The Botany of Desire*

CULTURES AROUND the world have evolved as specific localized
phenomena. This is true of both microbial cultures and human cultures. Cultural practices such as languages, beliefs, and food (including fermentation), are incredibly diverse. But that rich diversity is
threatened by the expansion of trade into a unified global market.
Where once beer, bread, and cheese were quirky local products varying from place to place, we lucky twenty-first-century consumers can
buy fermented commodities such as Bud Lite, Wonder Bread, or Velveeta that look and taste the same everywhere. Mass production and
mass marketing demand uniformity. Local identity, culture, and taste
are subsumed by the ever-diminishing lowest common denominator,

as McDonald's, Coca-Cola, and other corporate behemoths permeate minds on a global scale to create desire for their products.

This is the homogenization of culture, a sad, ugly process by which languages, oral traditions, beliefs, and practices are becoming extinct every year, while ever-greater wealth and power is concentrated in fewer hands. Wild fermentation is the opposite of homogenization and uniformity, a small antidote you can undertake in your home, using the extremely localized populations of microbial cultures present there to produce your own unique fermented foods. What you ferment with the organisms around you is a manifestation of your specific environment, and it will always be a little different. Perhaps your homemade sauerkraut or miso will conform perfectly to your image and expectation of them, as the McDonald's fries do for Michael Pollan. More likely, they will possess some quirky anomaly that will force you to adjust your image and expectation. Do-it-yourself fermentation departs from the realm of the uniform commodity. Yet some of the earliest commodities exchanged on a global scale were fermented foods. Specifically, chocolate, coffee, and tea were among the first agricultural products shipped in vast quantity around the world; and all involve fermentation in their processing.

In 1985 I spent several months traveling with my friend Todd in Africa. In Cameroon, not far from a town called Abong-Mbang, we were introduced to a couple of Pygmy people who took us on a trek through the jungle. We used bamboo poles for walking sticks as we waded through knee-high swamps. These Pygmies have carried on a long tradition of subsistence in that jungle. In the course of our hike, we came across several Pygmy settlements engaged in cacao farming. We came to understand that the government was trying to force these people to settle into cash-crop agriculture. Their migratory lifestyle was being outlawed, phased out because it was of no value to a state in desperate pursuit of tax revenue and foreign exchange to pay off debts to global financial institutions.

When traditional cultures are outlawed, that is the homogenization of culture. It's an old story, which could be told by any Native American, or by my grandparents, who fled pogroms and saw the Eastern European *Yiddishkeit* they were born into disperse and disappear in a single generation. By the time I headed home to the land of obscenely stocked supermarket shelves, I had come to the conclusion that no matter what I said or did, my presence in Africa served only to glamorize the capitalist world order, adding to the seductive allure that if you abandon your traditional culture, educate your kids in colonial languages at missionary schools, and grow cacao beans for export, maybe someday you'll accumulate the kind of excess wealth to travel to the other side of the globe, just for fun and stimulation.

FERMENTED STIMULANTS AND THE RISE OF GLOBALIZATION

Chocolate is made from the seeds of a tree native to the Amazon rain forest, *Theobroma cacao* (*theobroma* is Greek for "food of god"). After the ripe seedpods are harvested, they are allowed to ferment spontaneously, with organisms naturally present, for up to twelve days before further processing. The fermentation digests the pulp of the pod and alters the color, flavor, aroma, and chemistry of the cacao beans. The unique compelling flavor of chocolate, so universally beloved, is only achieved through fermentation. After fermentation, the cacao beans are removed from their pods, allowed to dry, then roasted, peeled, and finely ground.

Humans have enjoyed cacao for at least 2,600 years. Amazonian peoples, and the Mayan and Aztec cultures that brought the cacao tree to Central America and Mexico, used ground roasted cacao as the basis for stimulant drinks rather than for solid foods. Cacao is extremely bitter without sugar; in these cultures it was consumed unsweetened, often mixed with hot chili peppers, as thick frothy beverages. The word "chocolate" is derived from the Aztec word *xocolatl*, a compounding of *xococ* (bitter) and *atl* (water). Cacao was an important sacrament in Mayan and Aztec religious ceremonies. Cacao beans were also used as a form of currency.

Cacao beans

As soon as the Spanish encountered cacao, in 1519, they began exporting it to Spain. In Europe, too, cacao was consumed exclusively as a drink until the nineteenth century. Today, chocolate production is a $60 billion per year global industry. The major growing regions are in Africa, Southeast Asia, and Brazil.[1] Some of the cacao growers I encountered in Africa had never tasted chocolate. Talk about the alienation of labor!

Though cacao is a rainforest tree, it is generally grown commercially with "zero shading" and heavy chemical spraying, and the industry is in crisis. Cacao trees grown in this manner are prone to fungal diseases, which have already decimated plantations in many areas, and threaten others. U.S. government researchers are mapping cacao's genome and trying to genetically engineer resistant strains of this most cherished commodity, likely to appear soon at a store near you.[2]

Other globalized tropical stimulants also involve fermentation: The fresh, ripe, red fruits of the tree *Coffea arabica* are allowed to spontaneously ferment to digest the pulp and free the individual beans. After fermentation, the coffee beans are dried and roasted. Chances are you already know the rest of the process.

Coffee is indigenous to Ethiopia. From there it spread across the Red Sea to the Arabian Peninsula, and then throughout the Islamic world by the end of the fifteenth century.[3] Coffee first appeared in Europe in Venice; in Europe coffee was known as food and medicine before it became popular as a beverage. Coffee drinking was first introduced in Paris in 1643, and within thirty years there were 250 cafés there.[4] The leading coffee-producing nations in our time are Brazil, Colombia, Vietnam, Indonesia, and Mexico.[5]

Tea is another stimulant dependent upon fermentation. Green teas are the unfermented leaves of *Camellia sinensis*. Fermentation intensifies the stimulant properties of the tea leaves and is used to produce black and oolong-style teas. Tea has been used in China for at least three thousand years. It first appeared in Europe in Lisbon in the 1550s and took a hundred years to reach London, where it quickly became the rage in the 1650s, and ever since.

All tea destined for Europe (and North America) was exported from the Chinese port of Canton until the early nineteenth century. Traders were not permitted inland, and the techniques of growing and fermenting tea were guarded as trade secrets. The Chinese, self-sufficient in known resources and advanced in technology, wanted nothing the English had to offer, except gold, silver, and copper, until the British hit upon opium (another product often involving fermentation) as a profitable exchange commodity. The East India Company, the British Crown's mercantile franchise, established an opium production industry in India and introduced opium into China in exchange for tea, thus initiating the global drug trade, which has grown and flourished ever since. Only in the nineteenth century did the British learn the techniques of tea cultivation and begin to grow it in India, East Africa, and other colonies.[6] Today India is the world's largest tea producer, followed by China, Sri Lanka, Kenya, and Indonesia.[7]

The enormity of the economic and cultural changes wrought to the entire world by the mass production and global trade of chocolate, coffee, and tea cannot be overstated. These stimulants, recognized today as addictive substances, were "the ideal drugs for the Industrial Revolution," according to ethnobotanist Terence McKenna. "They provided an energy lift, enabling people to keep working at repetitious tasks that demanded concentration. Indeed, the tea and coffee break is the only drug ritual that has never been criticized by those who profit from the modern industrial state."[8]

The other related commodity that rounds out the picture is sugar. Chocolate, coffee, and tea all made their appearance in England almost simultaneously, around 1650. Though all three fermented stimulants had been consumed as unsweetened, bitter beverages in their original cultural contexts, Europe married them to sugar and they became that important new mass commodity's marketing partner. This was the birth of marketing, the first instance of the manufacture of mass demand for a hitherto obscure commodity. Today there appears to be no end to the products consumers can be convinced we cannot live without, but there was a beginning.

"The fashion for these hot drinks became a potent factor in the surge in sugar demand," notes historian Henry Hobhouse in his book *Seeds of Change*.[9] Between the years 1700 and 1800, per capita sugar consumption in Britain increased more than fourfold, from an average of 4 pounds a year to 18 pounds. "Sugar surrendered its place as luxury and rarity and became the first mass-produced exotic necessity of a proletarian working class," writes Sidney W. Mintz in *Sweetness and Power*.[10] Average people used more and more sugar, and desired more of it than they could afford, while "producing, shipping, refining, and taxing sugar became proportionately more effective sources of power for the powerful."[11] Chocolate, coffee, and tea consumption increased similarly.

Sugarcane, *Saccharum officinarum,* is native to New Guinea, and spread as long as eight thousand years ago to India, the Philippines, and other tropical regions of Asia.[12] Sugar was long known, traded, and used in the Middle East and, to a lesser extent, in Europe. Limited supplies were available, it was very expensive, and it was used as a medicine and as a spice, but not as a food as it is today.[13] First the Portuguese and then the Spanish established their earliest colonial outposts beginning in 1418 as sugar plantations on Madeira, the Canary Islands, São Tomé, and the Cape Verde Islands in the Atlantic waters off the west coast of Africa. The location of the Atlantic island sugar plantations established and institutionalized the west coast of Africa as the primary source for slave labor.

As European empires colonized Caribbean and tropical American lands, they established much larger sugar (and later other) plantation economies with African slave labor. In the tragic course of recorded human history, it seems clear that slavery has existed in many different cultural contexts and been practiced in many different ways. Slavic people gave their name to the ancient institution of *slav*ery, and contemporary accounts allege that slavery persists into the twenty-first century on the cacao plantations of the Ivory Coast.[14]

But it was the sugar trade that established the systematic global racism of African slavery. As innovations in the refinement of sugar yielded a whiter and whiter product, the system of its production dehumanized people on the basis of dark skin. In symbol and in flesh and blood, sugar gave birth to the racist world order. Sugar and its associated fermented stimulant commodities also gave birth to colonial rule on a global scale.

It does not make any kind of sense for the people (or the land) of any place to grow massive quantities of stimulants for export rather than nutritious food for local consumption. It only happens by the exercise of force and the alienation of people from the land. Initially this was accomplished through slavery and direct colonial administration. In our time, the primary mode of domination has shifted to subtler instruments of global capital such as the International Monetary Fund, the World Bank, Third World debt, transnational corporations (a more descriptive name than multinational, I think, because these behemoths have come to transcend and supersede nations), and the World Trade Organization. If the people who work the fields had any measure of control over the land they worked, they would be growing food to eat, not luxury stimulants for people on other continents.

"The first sweetened cup of hot tea to be drunk by an English worker was a significant historical event, because it prefigured the transformation of an entire society, a total remaking of its economic and social basis," writes Mintz. "We must struggle to understand fully the consequences of that and kindred events, for upon them was erected an entirely different conception of the relationship between producers and consumers, of the meaning of work, of the definition of self, of the nature of things. What commodities are, and what commodities mean, would thereafter be forever different."[15]

We consumers of the affluent West have come to take for granted a constant flow of pleasure-gratifying products from faraway lands, at great cost of precious resources such as fossil fuels (for shipping), land (which could be used to grow real food to feed people), labor (which would be better directed toward local needs), and global biodiversity. Globalized markets amount to cultural decadence. Decadence (from the word "decay") is unsustainability: behavior likely to contribute to biological or social decline or collapse.

RESISTING THE COMMODIFICATION OF CULTURE

I have no formulaic plan to offer for resisting the insidious processes of globalization, commodification, and cultural homogenization. The French sheep farmer José Bové, who became an international hero after he bulldozed a McDonald's in 1999, offers one possible model. "McDonald's is merely a symbol of economic imperialism," writes Bové. "It represents anonymous globalization, with little relevance to real food. . . . Waves of opposition to this commodification can be felt in all corners of the world." What specifically sparked his McDonald's action were the trade sanctions imposed by the United States on Europe for its ban on the import of hormone-treated beef. "We reject the global trade model dictated by the multinationals," exhorts Bové. "Let's go back to agriculture. . . . People have the right to be able to feed themselves."[16]

If you tried an action like Bové's in the United States these days, it would probably be branded as terrorism and land you in a clandestine military tribunal. We cannot resist the homogenization of culture by overpowering it. Yet we must not resign ourselves to it. Resistance is everywhere at the margins. This is where the people who manage to avoid succumbing to mainstream cultural currents come together. In the margins, we create and support diverse alternative cultures that express our various needs and desires.

Resistance takes place on many planes. Occasionally it can be dramatic and public, but most of the decisions we are faced with are mundane and private. What to eat is a choice that we make several times a day, if we are lucky. The cumulative choices we make about food have profound implications.

Food offers us many opportunities to resist the culture of mass marketing and commodification. Though consumer action can take many creative and powerful forms, we do not have to be reduced to the role of consumers selecting from seductive convenience items. We can merge appetite with activism and choose to involve ourselves in food as cocreators. Food has historically been one of our most direct links to the life forces of the Earth. Bountiful harvests have always been occasions for celebration and appreciation of the divine.

In our urbanized society, the vast majority of people are completely cut off from the process of growing food, and even from the raw products of agriculture. Most Americans are used to buying and eating food that has already been processed in a factory. "Both eater and eaten are thus in exile from biological reality," writes Wendell Berry. "And the result is a kind of solitude, unprecedented in human experience, in which the eater may think of eating as first a purely commercial transaction between him and a supplier, and then as a purely appetitive transaction between him and his food."[17] Industrially produced food is dead. It severs our connection to the life forces that sustain us and deprives us of our access to the powerful magic so abundantly present in the natural world. "The time has come to reclaim the stolen harvest," writes Indian activist Vandana Shiva, "and celebrate the growing and giving of good food as the highest gift and the most revolutionary act."[18]

Not everyone can be a farmer. But that's not the only way to cultivate a connection to the Earth and buck the trend toward global market uniformity and standardization. One small but tangible way to resist the homogenization of culture is to involve yourself in the harnessing and gentle manipulation of wild microbial cultures. Rediscover and reinterpret the vast array of fermentation techniques used by our ancestors. Build your body's cultural ecology as you engage and honor the life forces all around you.

4 CULTURAL MANIPULATION
A Do-It-Yourself Guide

There is a mystique surrounding fermented foods that many people find intimidating. Since the uniformity of factory fermentation products depends upon thorough chemical sterilization, exacting temperature controls, and controlled cultures, it is widely assumed that fermentation processes require these things. The beer- and wine-making literature tends to reinforce this misconception.

My advice is to reject the cult of expertise. Do not be afraid. Do not allow yourself to be intimidated. Remember that all fermentation processes predate the technology that has made it possible for them to be made more complicated. Fermentation does not require specialized equipment. Not even a thermometer is necessary (though it can help). Fermentation is easy and exciting. Anyone can do it. Microorganisms are flexible and adaptable. Certainly there is considerable nuance to be learned about any of the fermentation processes, and if you stick with them, they will teach you. But the basic processes are simple and straightforward. You can do it yourself. Here's an example:

T'ej (Ethiopian-style Honey Wine)

TIMEFRAME: 2 to 4 weeks

SPECIAL EQUIPMENT:

1 gallon/4 liter (or larger) ceramic crock, wide-mouth jar, or plastic bucket

1 gallon/4 liter glass jug (the kind you can buy apple juice in)

Airlock (from beer and wine supply shop, under $1; this is helpful but not necessary)

INGREDIENTS (for 1 gallon/4 liters):

3 cups/750 milliliters honey (raw if available)

12 cups/3 liters water

PROCESS:

1. Mix water and honey in the crock or jar. Stir well, until the honey is thoroughly dissolved. Cover with a towel or cloth and set aside in a warm room for a few days, stirring as often as you think of it, at least twice a day. Trust that the yeast will be drawn to the sweet honey-water from the air.

2. After 3 or 4 days (more if it's cold, less if it's hot), the brew should be bubbly and fragrant. Once it's bubbly, transfer wine into a clean glass jug. If the jug is not full, you can add water and honey in a 4:1 ratio to fill. Cork with an airlock that lets air out but not in, if you can easily find one (see fig. on page 128). If not, cover the bottle with a balloon, or any jar lid that can rest on it loosely and keep air out without holding pressure in.

3. Leave for 2 to 4 weeks, until bubbling slows. This is "instant" gratification wine. Drink it now, or age it (see page 129).

Delicious, intoxicating wine can be as simple as that. For variations involving the addition of fruit or herbs to this basic recipe, see page 129.

DO-IT-YOURSELF

Do-it-yourself is an ethic that is practiced by many different people. It is an attitude of self-empowerment and openness to learning. Do-it-yourselfers include folks who garden, cook "from scratch," make clothes and handcrafts, build and fix things, and practice healing arts, to give just a few examples. Anarchist punk culture uses do-it-yourself, or d.i.y., as a slogan to live by. Publishing a "zine," being in a band, dumpster diving perfectly good food, squatting, activism, and skill-share events are all manifestations of the d.i.y. attitude.

So is rural homesteading. At Short Mountain, where I live, we create and maintain all our own infrastructure, including solar electricity, phone lines, and water systems. We raise goats and chickens, grow much of our food, and build and maintain the structures we inhabit. Among us are folks who make music, spin and dye yarn,

wild

knit, crochet, sew, and fix cars. Rural homesteads are havens for those who wish to develop their breadth as generalists. Moving "back-to-the-land" involves a long process of acquiring skills that are themselves at risk of extinction. I find it tremendously satisfying and empowering to learn techniques for doing just about anything.

Do-it-yourself fermentation is a journey of experimentation and discovery. Rediscovery really, because, like fire or simple tools, these are some of the most basic transformative processes that our ancestors used and that form the basis of human culture. Every ferment yields unique results, influenced not only by ingredients but by environment, season, temperature, humidity, and any other factors affecting the behavior of the microorganisms whose actions make these transformations possible. Some fermentations are complete in a few hours. Some require years.

Fermentation generally requires only a little preparation or work. Most of the time that elapses is spent waiting. Do-it-yourself fermentation is about as far as you can get from fast food. Many ferments get better the longer you leave them. Use this time to observe and ponder the magical actions of invisible allies. The Charoti people of South America view the time of fermentation as "the birth of the good spirit."[1] They attract the good spirit with music and singing, exhorting the spirit to come settle into the home they have prepared. You too can prepare a comfortable environment for the spirit, the organisms, the process, however it suits you to think about it. The force is with you. It will come.

I get so excited every time my crocks start bubbling and the life forces make themselves known. Inevitably, even after a decade of experience, sometimes the process doesn't go as I'd planned: wines sour, yeasts become exhausted, maggots infest aging crocks. Sometimes it's just too hot or too cold for the organisms whose flavors we're after. We are dealing with fickle life forces, in some cases over long periods of time, and though we are making an effort to create conditions favorable to desired outcomes, we do well to remember that we are not, by any measure, in complete control. When your experiments go awry, as some inevitably will, learn from them and try not to be discouraged. Feel free to e-mail me with truobleshooting questions (sandorkraut@wildfermentation.com). And remember that the prized cultures of a San Francisco sourdough or the finest bleu cheese have their roots in wild fermentations that took place in someone's kitchen or farmhouse long ago. Who knows what compelling healing flavors could be floating around in your kitchen?

"Our perfection lies in our imperfection" is one of my mantras in this life. I learned it from my friend Triscuit as we and a couple of other novice carpenters built our house together at the end of Sex Change Ridge, about a quarter-mile through the woods from "downtown" Short Mountain. We used wood that we salvaged from deconstructing an old Coca-Cola bottling plant, resting on piers of black locust wood that we harvested from our land. We learned as we built. If uniformity was what we were after, we would have done better to shop for a double-wide trailer. Luckily, we wanted to live in something funky and woodsy, and that's what we ended up with. Our mantra certainly holds true in the realm of fermentation, and I repeat it often. "Our perfection lies in our imperfection." If your desire is for perfectly uniform, predictable food, this is the wrong book for you. If you are willing to collaborate with tiny beings with somewhat capricious habits and vast transformative powers, read on.

ANY FOOD CAN BE FERMENTED

I know of no food that is without some tradition of fermentation. Though I am currently omnivorous, I have in the past been vegetarian and vegan. I am part of a demographic wave, reflecting period and generational trends, that I think of as post-vegetarians. My experience is with vegetarian cooking and vegetarian fermentation. Fermentation processes involving meat or fish are beyond the scope of this book, though the world is full of them. Sausages, pickled herrings, and fish sauces are three prominent ones, among many. A fermented fish sauce called *liquamen* was the predominant condiment of ancient Rome, not much different from Vietnamese *nuoc mam,* Thai *nam pla,* and other fermented fish sauces widely used in contemporary Southeast Asian cuisines. People of the Arctic regions dig deep pits in the ground and fill them with whole fish to ferment for months, until they reach a cheesy consistency. The word *sushi* derives from a Japanese tradition of fermenting fish and rice together.

Hungry people everywhere have innovated fermentation techniques not only to preserve food but also to turn otherwise inedible parts of animals into nutritious food. Hamid Dirar has identified eighty distinct fermentation processes in *The Indigenous Fermented*

Food of the Sudan, a book describing an incredible array of ferments that result in consumption of every bit of animal flesh and bone. *Miriss* is made by fermenting fat; *dodery* by fermenting chopped up bones in water. You won't find the recipes here, but perhaps some readers will be inspired to experiment in this vein.

SLIPPERY BOUNDARIES

Pondering fermenting meat reminds me that the distinction between a food that is fermented to perfection and one that is rotten is highly subjective. After a goat slaughter, I fermented some of the meat for a couple of weeks. I placed the meat in a gallon jar, then filled it with a mixture of all the other live ferments I had around: wine, vinegar, miso, yogurt, and sauerkraut juice. I covered the jar and left it in an unobtrusive corner of our basement. It bubbled and smelled good. After two weeks I poured the meat and its marinade into a covered pot and roasted it in the oven.

As it cooked, an overwhelming odor enveloped the kitchen. It smelled like a very strong cheese suited to only the bravest gastronome. There was some swooning and near fainting, and several folks were nauseated and had to leave the room. Lots of people complained about the smell. It was a notorious evening that immediately entered our homegrown folklore.

We had to open the windows, in spite of the December cold. Perhaps a half dozen of us tried the meat. It was quite tender for goat meat, and its taste was much milder than its smell. My fellow communard Mish absolutely loved it. He hovered over the pan for a long time picking at the meat, praising its strong cheesy aroma, and gloating over the rarefied "acquired taste" that only he and a few others could fully appreciate.

Many cultures have favorite fermented dishes with such strong flavors and aromas, or such unusual textures, that they become important symbols of distinctive cultural identity, all the more so because people outside the group generally find them repulsive. My father, an intrepid eater, once spent a Christmas visiting friends in Sweden. Forty years later he still winces when he describes tasting the traditional Swedish Christmas Eve feast of *lutfisk,* fish treated with lye and fermented for several weeks before cooking. Though many Asian soy ferments have gained widespread popularity in the West, slimy Japanese *natto* seems to have more limited appeal; and the Chinese treat known as "hundred-year eggs" actually only need to ferment in horse urine for a couple of months before the egg solidifies, the yolk turns green, and the white turns smoky black.[2]

Food scientists use the word *organoleptic* to describe the qualities of how food feels in the mouth (as well as subjective feels of the other sensory organs). Fermentation often transforms the organoleptic qualities of foods, and sometimes it is an organoleptic quality more than flavor that influences what we like or dislike. One culture's greatest gastronomic pride is another's worst nightmare. "The concept of 'rottenness' therefore belongs to the cultural rather than the biological sphere," notes Annie Hubert, the director of France's National Scientific Research Center in an essay in *Slow,* the magazine of the international Slow Food movement. "The term defines a point where a food becomes unsuitable for consumption according to criteria associated with taste, presentation, and the concept of hygiene in different human societies."[3]

This boundary is fluid, and fermented foods have a way of making boundaries in general somewhat fluid. Take the dualism of life and death. Fermentation is the action of life upon death. Living organisms consume dead food matter, transforming it and in the process freeing nutrients for the further sustenance of life. Many fermentation recipes mysteriously instruct you to ferment "until the flavor is ripe." You will have to be the judge of that. I advocate tasting your ferments at frequent intervals as the process progresses so you can learn about the spectrum of fermentation, discover what degree of ripeness you find most appealing, and experience the flavors of the other side of the elusive and slippery subjective boundary of rottenness.

Sometimes people ask me whether improperly fermented foods can cause food poisoning. I have never experienced this, nor heard any reports of it from other fermentation enthusiasts. In general, the acidic or alcoholic environments created by fermentation are inhospitable to bacteria associated with severe types of food poisoning such as salmonella. However, I cannot state in any absolute or authoritative way that food poisoning could not result from something going wrong in a fermentation process.

If it looks or smells disgusting, feed it to the compost. Usually I find that the funkiness is limited to the top layer, which is in contact with the microbe-rich air. Underneath that, the ferment is fine. If in

MANIPULATION

doubt, trust your nose to be your guide. If you're still in doubt, taste just a little bit. Mix it with your saliva and swish it around your mouth like they do at wine tastings. Trust your taste buds. If it doesn't taste good, don't eat it.

EQUIPMENT AND INGREDIENT BASICS

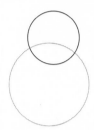

The basic pieces of equipment required for most ferments are vessels to contain them. Gourds have been a traditional favorite for this, as have animal membranes and ceramic containers. A cylindrical shape is easiest for most fermentations. I like to use old-fashioned heavy ceramic crocks. Unfortunately, they are expensive, fragile, and increasingly hard to come by. If you buy used ones, check them carefully for cracks. Maybe you'll luck out and find some in an old-timey local hardware store. Try to find crocks locally, because they are heavy and expensive to ship. Some mail-order crock sources are listed in the Cultural Resources section.

I ferment many things in wide-mouth glass jars, the only drawback being that they are not cylindrical in shape. As I experimented in the course of preparing this book, I abandoned my anti-plastic purism and had fine results fermenting in 5-gallon plastic buckets that I got from a delicatessen. I can easily believe that chemicals from the plastic leach into the food, but we live in a plastic world and there really is no escaping exposure to those chemicals. Most food you buy, even from health food sources, is wrapped in the stuff. If you use plastic, make sure it is food-grade. Do not use plastic buckets that once contained building materials. And do not ferment in metallic containers, which can react with salt as well as the acids produced by fermentation.

Another piece of equipment that gives you a good deal of versatility when using grains and legumes in fermentation processes is a grain grinder. Grinding your own ensures that your ingredients are fresh, alive, and capable of germination until you are ready to use them, in contrast to pre-ground grains, which lose nutrients through oxidation and can become rancid. Grinding your own also gives you control over texture. Coarse is beautiful and delicious. I use our grinder when I make bread, porridges, tempeh, and some beers. Check local hardware and kitchen supply stores. A good selection of grinders, starting at under fifty dollars, is available from Lehman's Hardware, 877-438-5346, www.lehmans.com. Other equipment needs will be addressed as we go along.

The measurements for recipes in this book are expressed in both the U.S. system and the metric system employed by most of the rest of the world. Since I live in the U.S. and my kitchen tools and familiar references are of this system, I created the recipes according to its conventions. In converting recipes to metric, I learned that solid ingredients are expressed and measured in the metric system by weight, rather than volume as in the U.S. system (for home as opposed to professional kitchens). Rather than weigh out volumes of flour, beans, and grains, I have converted U.S. volumes into metric volumes. Thus the metric conversions contained herein are more transliterations than translations. Nonetheless, I hope they prove helpful to fermenters outside the U.S.

The most common ingredient called for in the recipes in this book is water. Do not use water that is heavily chlorinated for fermentation projects. Chlorine is used in water precisely because it kills microorganisms. If you can smell or taste the chlorine in tap water, either boil it to evaporate the chlorine before using the water for fermenting, or use water from another source.

Another frequent ingredient is salt. Salt inhibits many organisms, but up to a point it is tolerated by *Lactobacilli,* a type of bacteria important in many food fermentation processes. I like to use sea salt. It's fine to ferment with either sea salt or pickling salt, but don't use the standard supermarket table salt with added iodine and anti-caking agents. Iodine is antimicrobial, like chlorine, and could inhibit fermentation. Coarse kosher salt is another option, but be aware that because of its larger grains, the same weight of salt will occupy greater volume, so you'll need more of it: about one and one-half times as much in volume measurement as you would use of finer salts, which the recipes in this book assume. Because of the size of the grains, you may also need to boil the water to get the coarse kosher salt to dissolve.

Other ingredients will be discussed as we come to them. In general, I would encourage you to use organic foods for your fermentation, because organic food is more nutritious, tastier, and much more ecologically sustainable. I would point out, however, that much of the organic food available in supermarkets and the big health food chains is the product of large-scale corporate monoculture. I know an organic grower in Tennessee who used to sell produce to the health food store in Nashville. After it was bought out by a national chain, they would

MANIPULATION

no longer buy his vegetables, or, for that matter, any other locally grown produce, unless it could be delivered, in sufficient quantity for national distribution, to an out-of-state central warehouse.

I think it is important to support local growers. As much as you can, eat locally and seasonally. Shop at farmers' markets and farm stands. Join a community-supported agriculture (CSA) project. These are farms with a limited number of subscribers, which distribute their harvest among the subscribers over the course of the growing season. The Robin Van En Center for CSA Resources maintains a national directory of CSA farms at www.csacenter.org, 717-264-4141 extension 3352.

Best of all, grow your own. Then you know it's as fresh as could be, and you have the joy of participating in the miracle of plant life. But don't fret too much over the source of the ingredients for your ferments. The microorganisms are not especially picky. They'll work fine with whatever you can get.

NEW FRONTIERS OF EXPERIENCE AND KNOWLEDGE

As I am writing this do-it-yourself guide, I am learning another new back-to-the-land skill. After many years of enjoying the luscious, nutritious, fresh, raw milk of our herd of goats, without getting involved in their maintenance and care, I am learning to milk the goats for the first time. It is teaching me to relate to Sassy, Lydia, Lentil, Lynnie, Persephone, Luna, and Sylvia as individuals. Milking is building my hand strength. Ultimately, the technique seems to be about finding a rhythm.

Fermentation techniques are not so very different. You get to know the microorganisms as you work with them, and find a rhythm with them. Until the time of the Industrial Revolution, fermentation processes were all household, or at least local, practices. They were sacred traditions, performed communally and often ritualistically. By reviving these fermentation practices in your home, you can bring not only extraordinary nutrition but life and magic to the food you eat and share.

This is a process-oriented cookbook. That is, the techniques I describe are what is important. The specific ingredients are in a way arbitrary and meant to be varied. Many of the recipes for fermented delicacies from faraway places are re-created from written descriptions. Two sources that merit general acknowledgment are Bill Mollison's *Ferment and Human Nutrition* and Keith Steinkraus's *Handbook of Indigenous Fermented Foods*. Each of these authors has amassed a tremendous collection of practical information. I have also consulted many ethnic cookbooks, Web sites, anthropological and historical texts, and have credited them as appropriate. The problem with written information is that it is often vague, and once you start to consult more than a single source, often it is conflicting. I cannot guarantee the authenticity of many of these culinary reconfigurations, only that they work and taste delicious. Deviate from the recipes; incorporate your own favorite ingredients, or those most abundantly available to you, whether from your garden, an irresistible sale, or dumpster-diving resource recovery missions. Happy fermenting!

5 VEGETABLE FERMENTS

FERMENTED VEGETABLES complement any meal. Their tangy flavors accent the rest of the food, cleanse the palate, and improve digestion. In many cuisines, they are routine elements. Koreans are so devoted to *kimchi* that they eat it with every meal. I like to eat some fermented vegetable every day. A half-hour of chopping or shredding fills a crock that can ferment and feed you for weeks. Nutritious and delicious fermented vegetables are then available whenever you want them, with no additional work required. Keep a few crocks of different types of ferments going for variety. It's really easy.

BASIC BRINING TECHNIQUE

The main difference between vegetables left to rot and those destined for delicious fermentation is usually salt. Vegetables ferment best under the protection of brine. Brine is simply water with salt dissolved in it. In some ferments, such as sauerkraut, the salt is used to draw water out of the vegetables, thus creating intense vegetable juice brine. In other ferments, such as cucumber pickles, a brine solution is mixed and then poured over the vegetables. Brine serves as protection against the growth of putrefying microorganisms and favors the growth of the desired strains of bacteria, *Lactobacilli*. The amount of salt used in brine can vary considerably. The more salt you use, the slower the fermentation will be and the sourer (more acidic) the resulting ferment. With too much salt, however, no microorganisms can survive and fermentation will not occur.

Fermenting vessels are discussed in the previous chapter. Once you fill your crock with whatever ingredients you wish to ferment, you need to find a cover that fits inside of it. Left to their own devices, the vegetables would float to the top, where exposure to the air would make them mold. To keep them submerged under the protection of brine, they need a cover and a weight. For a cover, I generally use as large a plate as I can find that will fit inside the crock. It's okay if there's a little space between the edge of the plate and the side of the crock. You could also cut a wooden circle of just the right diameter; if you do, use hardwood and definitely not plywood or particleboard, which are held together by glues you would not want to eat. For a weight, I usually use a 1-gallon (4-liter) glass bottle filled with water, though a scrubbed and boiled rock works just as well.

Another method I sometimes use is to ferment vegetables in a wide-mouth jar and use a smaller jar that fits inside the mouth, filled with water, to weigh down the ferment. You can even use a zip-lock bag filled with brine (in case it leaks) to weigh down a ferment in a jar. Innovate with materials close at hand. Recycling centers can be excellent sources of jars and other fermentation vessels.

Wide-mouth jar with smaller jar inside weighting down contents

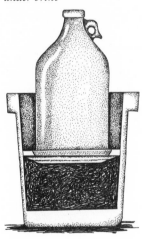

Crock with cover and weight pressing ferment under brine

Sauerkraut

For me, it all started with sauerkraut. I'd always loved it as a kid in New York City, frequently chowing down on street vendor hot dogs, always with mustard and kraut. I also loved it on Reuben sandwiches—corned beef with Thousand Island dressing, sauerkraut, and cheese melted over it all. When I stopped eating meat, I ended up not eating much sauerkraut.

That is, until I hooked up for a couple of years with macrobiotics, a dietary movement with its roots in Japanese Zen

Buddhist cuisine. The regime is fairly restrictive, mostly grains and vegetables and legumes, prepared in simple ways. The macrobiotic diet emphasizes regular consumption of miso, live unpasteurized sauerkraut, and other brine pickles to aid digestion. I started eating sauerkraut nearly daily and have been making crock after crock of the stuff ever since I learned how.

As I was completing my final revisions on this text and preparing to send it off into production, new research was published establishing sauerkraut's cancer-preventing properties. Cabbage and other *Brassicaceae* family vegetables (broccoli, cauliflower, Brussels sprouts, mustard, kale, collards, bok choi, and many more) have long been recognized as rich in anti-carcinogenic nutrients. According to a new Finnish study, published in the *Journal of Agricultural and Food Chemistry,* fermentation breaks down glucosinolates in cabbage into compounds called isothiocyanates, which are already known to fight cancer. "We are finding that fermented cabbage could be healthier than raw or cooked cabbage, especially for fighting cancer," says Eeva-Liisa Ryhanen, one of the paper's authors.[1]

Sauerkraut is generally believed to have been brought to Europe by nomadic Tartars, who are said to have encountered fermented cabbage in China, which has an extremely ancient and varied fermentation tradition. Sauerkraut is the German name; the French call it *choucroute*. It is prepared in any number of regional styles across Europe. In the war-torn lands of Serbia, Bosnia, and Herzegovina, cabbage is generally soured whole, in great barrels. A Russian variation uses apples to sweeten the kraut. Germans are so strongly associated

with sauerkraut that they are known, in derogatory slang, as "Krauts," and when the United States was at war with Germany, sauerkraut was temporarily dubbed "liberty cabbage," the precursor of "freedom fries."

In the United States, immigrants from Germany who settled in Pennsylvania became known as "Sauerkraut Yankees." William Woys Weaver, author of *Sauerkraut Yankees: Pennsylvania-German Foods and Foodways,* recounts a Civil War episode revolving around sauerkraut. "When Confederate troops captured Chambersburg [Pennsylvania] in the summer of 1863, one of the first things the famished rebels demanded from the inhabitants were barrels of sauerkraut." Unfortunately for the rebel troops, they arrived at the wrong time of year. The Pennsylvania Germans made kraut from the autumn cabbage harvest and enjoyed it during winter and spring. "No one in his right mind made sauerkraut in the summer."[2] (Here in Tennessee, we harvest spring cabbage in June or July and do indeed enjoy summer krauts.)

The fermentation of cabbage into sauerkraut is not the work of a single microorganism. Sauerkraut, like most fermentation processes, involves a succession of several different microbial species, not unlike the life of a forest, in which a series of different trees follow each other as the dominant species, each succeeding type altering conditions to favor the next. Bacteria called *Coliform* start the fermentation. As the *Coliform* produces acid, the environment becomes more favorable for *Leuconostoc* bacteria. The *Coliform* population declines as the population of *Leuconostoc* builds. As acids continue to be produced and the pH continues to drop, *Lactobacillus* succeeds the *Leuconostoc*. The fermentation involves a succession of three different types of bacteria, determined by the increasing acidity.

Do not be deterred by the biological complexity of the transformation. That happens on its own once you create the simple conditions for it. Sauerkraut is easy to make.

TIMEFRAME: 1 to 4 weeks (or more)

SPECIAL EQUIPMENT:
Ceramic crock or food-grade plastic bucket, 1-gallon/4-liter capacity or greater
Plate that fits inside crock or bucket
1-gallon/4-liter jug filled with water (or a scrubbed and boiled rock)
Cloth cover (such as a pillowcase or towel)

INGREDIENTS (for 1 gallon/4 liters):
5 pounds/2 kilograms cabbage
3 tablespoons/45 milliliters sea salt

PROCESS:

1. Chop or grate cabbage, finely or coarsely, with or without hearts, however you like it. I love to mix green and red cabbage to end up with bright pink kraut. Place cabbage in a large bowl as you chop it.

2. Sprinkle salt on the cabbage as you go. The salt pulls water out of the cabbage (through osmosis), and this creates the brine in which the cabbage can ferment and sour without rotting. The salt also has the effect of keeping the cabbage crunchy, by inhibiting organisms and enzymes that soften it. About 3 tablespoons (45 milliliters) of salt is a rough guideline for 5 pounds (2 kilograms) of cabbage. I never measure the salt; I just shake some on after I chop up each cabbage. I use more salt in

summer, less in winter. It is possible to make kraut with less salt or with no salt at all; several salt-free kraut variations follow this recipe for those who wish to avoid salt.

3. Add other vegetables, if you like. Grate carrots for a coleslaw-like kraut. Other vegetables that I've added include onions, garlic, seaweed, greens, Brussels sprouts, small whole heads of cabbage, turnips, beets, and burdock roots. You can also add fruits (apples, whole or sliced, are classic), and herbs and spices (caraway seeds, dill seeds, celery seeds, and juniper berries are classic, but anything you like will work). Experiment.

4. Mix ingredients together and pack into crock. Pack just a bit into the crock at a time and tamp it down hard using your fists or any (other) sturdy kitchen implement. The tamping packs the kraut tight in the crock and helps force water out of the cabbage.

5. Cover kraut with a plate or some other lid that fits snugly inside the crock. Place a clean weight (such as a glass jug filled with water) on the cover. This weight is to force water out of the cabbage and then keep the cabbage submerged under the brine. Cover the whole thing with a cloth to keep dust and flies out.

6. Press down on the weight to add pressure to the cabbage and help force water out of it. Continue doing this periodically (as often as you think of it, every few hours), until the brine rises above the cover. This can take up to about 24 hours, as the salt draws water out of the cabbage slowly. Some cabbage, particularly if it is old, simply contains less water. If the brine does not rise above the plate level by the next day, add enough salt water to bring the brine level above the plate. Add about 1 tablespoon (15 milliliters) of salt to 1 cup (250 milliliters) of water and stir until it's completely dissolved.

7. Leave the crock to ferment. I generally store the crock in an unobtrusive corner of the kitchen where I won't forget about it, but where it won't be in anybody's way. You could also store it in a cool basement if you want a slower fermentation that will preserve for longer.

8. Check the kraut every day or two. The volume reduces as the fermentation proceeds. Sometimes mold appears on the surface. Many books refer to this mold as "scum," but I prefer to think of it as a bloom. Skim what you can off of the surface; it will break up and you will probably not be able to remove all of it. Don't worry about this. It's just a surface phenomenon, a result of contact with the air. The kraut itself is under the anaerobic protection of the brine. Rinse off the plate and the weight. Taste the kraut. Generally it starts to be tangy after a few days, and the taste gets stronger as time passes. In the cool temperatures of a cellar in winter, kraut can keep improving for months and months. In the summer or in a heated room, its life cycle is more rapid. Eventually it becomes soft and the flavor turns less pleasant.

9. Enjoy. I generally scoop out a bowl- or jarful at a time and keep it in the fridge. I start when the kraut is young and enjoy its evolving flavor over the course of a few weeks. Try the sauerkraut juice that will be left in the bowl after the kraut is eaten. Sauerkraut juice is a rare delicacy and unparalleled digestive tonic. Each time you scoop some kraut out of the crock, you have to repack it carefully.

Make sure that the kraut is packed tight in the crock, the surface is level, and the cover and weight are clean. Sometimes brine evaporates, so if the kraut is not submerged below brine just add salted water as necessary. Some people preserve kraut by canning and heat-processing it. This can be done; but so much of the power of sauerkraut is its aliveness that I wonder: Why kill it?

10. Develop a rhythm. I try to start a new batch before the previous batch runs out. I remove the remaining kraut from the crock, repack it with fresh salted cabbage, then pour the old kraut and its juices over the new kraut. This gives the new batch a boost with an active culture starter.

Choucroute Fromage Roulades

These are a fun way to serve sauerkraut at a party, as finger food wrapped with cheese in soured whole cabbage leaves. I gave them this French name because I love the French word for sauerkraut, *choucroute* (pronounced shoo-kroot), and because I first created them for my French expatriate friend Jocelyn's annual Bastille Day party.

Make sauerkraut with the following modification: Preserve intact the central cores, about softball size, of 1 or 2 heads of the cabbage. Place the cabbage cores in the crock, pack with shredded and salted cabbage all around and above them, and ferment as directed in the preceding recipe. After 1 to 2 weeks, remove the heads of cabbage. Carefully peel off individual cabbage leaves. In each leaf place a small portion of sauerkraut and crumble some feta or other cheese, then roll the leaf and insert a toothpick to hold.

Salt-Free or Low-Salt Sauerkrauts

Even people who wish to avoid refined salt can enjoy sauerkraut. Sauerkraut is possible with little or no salt. I have tried three different methods for saltless krauts. One ferments the cabbage in wine. Another substitutes caraway, celery, and dill seeds for the salt, and the third uses seaweed instead of the salt. Seaweed contains sodium as well as other ocean minerals, but not in the refined concentration of the sodium chloride we know as table salt. My personal feeling about the salt-free krauts is that they taste better with salt. By restricting which kinds of organisms can survive in an environment, salt really helps develop sour flavors during fermentation. Salt also preserves the crunchiness of the cabbage, and salt-free krauts, other than the savory seed kraut, are soft. If you are trying to consume less salt but are not absolute about *no* salt, I would suggest adapting these as low-salt variations, with 1 to 2 teaspoons (5 to 10 milliliters) of salt per quart.

Salt-free kraut has a shorter lifespan than salted kraut, so I've given ingredients for smaller, quart-size quantities. A quart of kraut takes about 1¼ pounds (600 grams) of cabbage (about 1 medium-sized cabbage). You can ferment these in quart-size (liter) glass jars, ideally wide-mouthed ones, using a smaller jar (or even a zip-lock bag) filled with water to submerge the cabbage under liquid (see illustration on page 39). Since fermentation goes faster without salt, be sure to taste salt-free kraut frequently to monitor its progress, and refrigerate it after a week or so.

Wine Sauerkraut: Wine gives sauerkraut a pleasant, sweet flavor. Chop up cabbage, mix in any other vegetables or seasonings you like, and pack tightly into a jar. Then add a cup (250 milliliters) or so of wine, any kind, enough so the level rises above the cabbage like a brine. Then weight as described above and proceed as for basic sauerkraut from step 7.

Savory Seed Sauerkraut: This is my favorite of the saltless krauts, mostly because the large quantity of savory seeds keeps the cabbage crunchy as salt does. I heard about this method from my friend and neighbor Johnnie Greenwell, who read about it in a book by health guru Paul Bragg.

Chop the cabbage. Mix about 1 tablespoon (15 milliliters) each of caraway, celery, and dill seeds, and grind them with a mortar and pestle or other grinder. Mix the seeds with the cabbage and tamp it tightly into a jar. Add a little water (about 1 cup/250 milliters) to bring the brine above the cabbage level, then weight as described above and proceed as for basic sauerkraut from step 7.

Seaweed Sauerkraut: Replacing salt with seaweed is another way to make salt-free kraut. Dulse is a flavorful reddish seaweed that I like, but any variety would do. Take a good handful of dried seaweed, about an ounce (28 grams), cut it into small pieces with scissors, then soak it in hot water to rehydrate it. Let it soak a half hour or longer. Mix the soaked seaweed with the chopped cabbage, along with any other vegetables or seasonings you like, and pack it tightly into the jar. Add the seaweed soaking water as necessary until the water rises above the level of the cabbage like brine. Then weight as described above and proceed as for basic sauerkraut from step 7.

Sauerrüben

A traditional German variant of sauerkraut is *sauerrüben,* made from turnips. The turnip is a much maligned and under-appreciated vegetable. Our local greengrocers, Andy and Judy Fabri, are sometimes left with baskets of unsold softening turnips. Our community is always glad to take aging produce off their hands. It is a valuable scavenger mission to rescue food that is past its glorious prime, but still edible and nutritious, before it gets relegated to the compost. Fermenting is a great way to make use of a sudden bounty like this.

I love the sharp, sweet flavor of turnips. Fermentation only intensifies their distinctive flavor. My fellow communards have rarely been as enthusiastic about any of my ferments as they were the night I first served *sauerrüben.* They went on about it as if it were a rich chocolate dessert. Good thing they like it, because as I write, our garden is overflowing with a bumper crop of turnips. *Sauerrüben* can also be made from turnip's cousin rutabaga. You can also sour cabbage and turnips together, of course. Mix 'n match is allowed.

TIMEFRAME: 1 to 4 weeks

INGREDIENTS (for ½ gallon/2 liters):
5 pounds/2 kilograms turnips and/or rutabagas
3 tablespoons/45 milliliters sea salt

PROCESS:

1. Grate turnips coarsely or finely, as you prefer.

2. Sprinkle grated turnips with salt as you go. The process will work with more or less salt, so salt to taste.

3. As with sauerkraut, add any other vegetables, herbs, or spices you like. Or don't, and enjoy the strong flavor of the turnips unadulterated.

4. Cover and weight the grated turnips as for sauerkraut. Turnips contain more water than cabbage, so it does not take as much pressure or time for the brine to be expressed.

5. Check after a few days. Wipe away any surface mold and rinse the cover and weight. Taste the *sauerrüben.* As time passes, the flavor will get stronger. Enjoy its evolving flavor over weeks in warm weather and over months in cold weather.

Sour Beets

Another variation on the sauerkraut theme is sour beets.

TIMEFRAME: 1 to 4 weeks

INGREDIENTS (for ½ gallon/2 liters):
5 pounds/2 kilograms beets
3 tablespoons/45 milliliters sea salt
1 tablespoon/15 milliliters caraway seeds

PROCESS:

Proceed as for *sauerrüben,* above, using beets and adding some caraway seeds, whole or crushed. The juice expressed by beets when salted is dark and thick, like blood. As it ferments, evaporation may cause the brine to reduce. Be sure to keep the brine level above the plate. If necessary, add some brine, salted with about 1 tablespoon (15 milliliters) salt per cup (250 milliliters) of water. Sour beets can be enjoyed raw or used to make borscht.

Borscht

The Eastern European culinary tradition that gave us borscht makes extensive use of fermented sour foods, and very tasty sour borscht can be made with sour beets.

TIMEFRAME: 1 hour (or longer)

INGREDIENTS (for 6 to 8 servings):
2 to 3 onions, chopped
2 tablespoons/30 milliliters vegetable oil
2 carrots, chopped
2 cups/500 milliliters diced potatoes
2 cups/500 milliliters soured beets
6 cups/1.5 liters water
1 tablespoon/15 milliliters caraway seeds

PROCESS:

1. Chop onions, and sauté in vegetable oil in a soup pot, until browned.

2. Add carrots, potatoes, soured beets, and water, and bring to a boil.

3. Roast caraway seeds in a dry skillet for a moment, grind them, and add to soup.

4. After the soup comes to a boil, lower heat and simmer for ½ hour.

5. The longer this soup sits, the more thoroughly its flavors will blend. Prepare it in the morning, or the day before you want to serve it.

6. Reheat borscht and serve hot, with sour cream, yogurt, or kefir (see chapter 7).

KIMCHI

Kimchi is a spicy Korean pickle, made in an impressive variety of styles. It is prepared by fermenting Chinese cabbage, radishes or turnips, scallions, other vegetables, and often seafood, with ginger, hot red chili pepper, garlic, and often fish sauce.

Kimchi is a national passion in South and North Korea. The Korean Food Research Institute estimates that the average adult Korean consumes more than a quarter pound (125 grams) of kimchi every day. Day after day, that adds up to a lot of kimchi. Though factory-manufactured kimchi is gaining in popularity and making it at home is on the decline, according to the same source, three-quarters of all kimchi consumed in South Korea is still made in the home. It is customary practice for employers to give their employees an annual "kimchi bonus" in the autumn so they can purchase the ingredients to make their annual supply.

I recently served kimchi to my friend MaxZine's father, Leon Weinstein. Leon served in the U.S. Army during the Korean War. The smell of the kimchi reminded him of that time. Smells are powerfully evocative, and the kimchi's assertive essence brought him right back to the front lines fifty years ago.

A recent international trade dispute between Korea and Japan focused on kimchi authenticity. It seems that many people in Japan have developed a taste for the Korean-style pickle. Japan has become Korea's biggest export market for kimchi. But Japanese manufacturers developed a kimchi-like product that replaces the fermentation process with flavor additives such as citric acid. The Japanese pseudo-kimchi is cheaper than kimchi, since the element of time is removed from manufacturing. It also appears to have somewhat broader appeal because of its less sharp flavor.

South Korea appealed to the Codex Alimentarius, an international food standards commission, to establish a definition of kimchi as a fermented food. "What the Japanese are selling is nothing more than cabbage sprinkled with seasonings and artificial flavorings," said Robert Kim, of Doosan Corporation, which operates the world's largest kimchi factory in Korea.[3] Japan counters that its product is simply an innovative variation on traditional kimchi, arguing that Korea has no more of an exclusive claim to kimchi than India to curries or Mexico to tacos. After more than five years of deliberation and diplomacy, the Codex process rendered a decision, establishing the fermented Korean version as the international standard for kimchi.

In certain respects, making kimchi is like making sauerkraut. One difference is that kimchi recipes generally call for soaking the cabbage and other vegetables in very salty brine for several hours to soften them quickly, then rinsing them and fermenting them with less salt. Kimchi is also distinguished by the generous use of ginger, garlic, scallion, and hot chili peppers. Kimchi generally ferments faster than sauerkraut. You can certainly make it in a crock like sauerkraut, but these recipes are for smaller quantities using quart-size (liter) jars.

Baechu (Cabbage) Kimchi

This is a basic kimchi.

TIMEFRAME: 1 week (or longer)

INGREDIENTS (for 1 quart/1 liter):
Sea salt

1 pound/500 grams Chinese cabbage (napa or bok choi)

1 daikon radish or a few red radishes

1 to 2 carrots

1 to 2 onions and/or leeks and/or a few scallions and/or shallots (or more!)

3 to 4 cloves of garlic (or more!)

3 to 4 hot red chilies (or more!), depending on how hot-peppery you like food, or any form of hot pepper, fresh, dried, or in a sauce (without chemical preservatives!)

3 tablespoons/45 milliliters (or more!) fresh grated gingerroot

PROCESS:

1. Mix a brine of about 4 cups (1 liter) of water and 4 tablespoons (60 milliliters) of salt. Stir well to thoroughly dissolve salt. The brine should taste good and salty.

2. Coarsely chop the cabbage, slice the radish and carrots, and let the vegetables soak in the brine, covered by a plate or other weight to keep the vegetables submerged, until soft, a few hours or overnight. Add other vegetables to the brine, such as snow peas, seaweeds, Jerusalem artichokes, anything you like.

3. Prepare spices: Grate the ginger; chop the garlic and onion; remove seeds from the chilies and chop or crush, or throw them in whole. Kimchi can absorb a lot of spice. Experiment with quantities and don't worry too much about them. Mix spices into a paste. (If you wish, you can add fish sauce to the spice paste. Just check the label to be sure it has no chemical preservatives, which function to inhibit microorganisms.)

4. Drain brine off vegetables, reserving brine. Taste vegetables for saltiness. You want them to taste decidedly salty, but not unpleasantly so. If they are too salty, rinse them. If you cannot taste salt, sprinkle with a couple of teaspoons (10 milliliters) salt, and mix.

5. Mix the vegetables with the ginger-chili-onion-garlic paste. Mix everything together thoroughly and stuff it into a clean quart-size (liter) jar. Pack it tightly into the jar, pressing down until brine rises. If necessary, add a little of the reserved vegetable-soaking brine to submerge the vegetables. Weight the vegetables down with a smaller jar, or a zip-lock bag filled with some brine. Or if you think you can remember to check the kimchi every day, you can just use your (clean!) fingers to push the vegetables back under the brine. I myself like the tactile involvement of this method, and I especially enjoy tasting the kimchi by licking my fingers after I do this. Either way, cover the jar to keep out dust and flies.

6. Ferment in your kitchen or other warm place. Taste the kimchi every day. After about a week of fermentation, when it tastes ripe, move it to the refrigerator. An alternative and more traditional method is to ferment kimchi more slowly and with more salt in a cool spot, such as a hole in the ground, or a cellar or other cool place.

Radish and Root Kimchi

I have a strong affinity for roots. I am awed by their strength, growing deep into the earth. Some roots are gnarled, turning this way and that around rocks in their relentless search for water and nutrients in the soil. Others exhibit glamorous curves and showy colors. Their flavors are varied and in some cases extreme.

One root vegetable, the simple radish, changed my life with a mystical plant communication. It happened while I was hospitalized during February of 2000. Earlier that winter, one balmy sunny January day full of the promise of spring, I had decided to plant some radishes. Sowing seeds out of doors that early is largely a symbolic gesture, performed for the sheer life-affirming joy of seeing germination and growth in the winter, since any vegetables that might result are likely to be puny. Predictably enough, the weather turned cold and gray after this sunny day, and I didn't notice any seedlings emerge, so I gave up on the poor radishes and forgot about them. Meanwhile, I was feeling a bizarre internal pressure in my abdomen, went through some diagnostic testing, and landed in the hospital.

Such a contrast to my life in the woods, outdoors most of the time, the hospital is a totally denatured environment. The windows are sealed shut, everything is white and antiseptic, the food is all ultra-processed, and they fed me chemicals through my mouth, my veins, and my anus. I was feeling scared and just wanted to go home, when one

Radishes

night in my dreams the radishes came to comfort me and I woke up with a vivid image of the radishes I had planted germinating. It was very real. I felt like I had received a plant communication.

The day I was released from the hospital, I arrived home late in the afternoon and didn't make it out to the garden. I asked my garden co-conspirators whether they had noticed the radishes up, and they hadn't. Oh well, it was just a dream, I thought. The next morning, I made it out to the garden and, lo and behold, the radishes had germinated. Delicate, pert, tiny seedlings defied the elements to reach toward the Sun with their potent life force. As I recuperated, and to this day, radishes became one of my plant totems: so easy to grow, sharp, tangy, in so many different colors and shapes. Radishes came to offer me hope at a frightening time, and to remind me how versatile plant allies can be.

Back to the kimchi: Koreans have a tradition of radish *(moo)* kimchi. Turnips are also found in Korean recipes. But the addition of other root vegetables makes this a reinterpretation; you can make kimchi by fermenting any vegetables you like with the classic kimchi quartet of ginger, hot pepper, garlic, and onion (in any of its forms). In this kimchi, I add grated horseradish roots, which blends with and complements the traditional heating spices.

Some of the roots in this recipe may be unfamiliar. Burdock *(Arctium lappa)* grows as a weed in most of the United States. It is a powerful medicinal plant, stimulating lymphatic and other glandular flows, cleansing the blood, and tonifying the organs of elimination: skin, kidneys, and liver. Burdock is deeply nourishing, rich in trace minerals, and associated with stamina, longevity, and sexual vitality. "Burdock nourishes the most extreme, buried, and far-reaching aspects of ourselves," writes herbalist Susun S. Weed. "Burdock breaks the ground for deep transformation."[4]

Burdock has a flavor I think of as earthy. To me, no plant better embodies the Earth it grew in. Burdock is found in Japanese cuisine, where it is known as *gobo*. Many health food stores sell fresh burdock roots. Burdock is a common weed. The first wild burdock I harvested was from New York's Central Park. The idea of eating urban weeds horrifies many people. It does give me pause to eat plants subjected to the kind of pollution that all urban dwellers live amidst. But I also find myself in awe of the tenacity of weeds that find their way into the urban landscape and survive. A weed that can push itself up through cracks in the concrete possesses qualities that I want to share. If you do harvest your own burdock, make sure you dig first-year roots. The plant is biennial, and the second year, when it grows tall and develops the notorious burrs that cling to dogs and people, for which the plant is named, the roots become woody and unappetizing.

Jerusalem artichokes *(Helianthus tuberosus)* are nothing like artichokes. They are knobby tubers in the sunflower family, native to the eastern United States, with a fresh, crunchy taste reminiscent of water chestnuts. Jerusalem artichokes are not widely available in stores; farmers' markets

are probably your best bet. They are one of the easiest things you can grow. Once you plant them, they keep coming back year after year.

TIMEFRAME: 1 week

INGREDIENTS (for 1 quart/1 liter):
Sea salt
1 to 2 daikon radishes
1 small burdock root
1 to 2 turnips
A few Jerusalem artichokes
2 carrots
A few small red radishes
1 small fresh horseradish root (or a tablespoon of prepared horseradish, without preservatives)
3 tablespoons/45 milliliters (or more!) fresh grated gingerroot
3 to 4 cloves of garlic (or more!)
1 to 2 onions and/or leeks and/or a few scallions and/or shallots (or more!)
3 to 4 hot red chilies (or more!), depending on how hot-peppery you like food, or any form of hot pepper, fresh, dried, or in a sauce (without chemical preservatives!)

PROCESS:

1. Mix a brine of about 4 cups (1 liter) of water and 3 tablespoons (45 milliliters) of salt.

2. Slice daikons, burdock, turnip, Jerusalem artichokes, and carrots, and let them soak in the brine. If the roots are fresh and organic, leave the nutritious skins on. Slice the roots thin so the flavors will penetrate. I like to slice roots on a diagonal; you could also cut them into matchsticks. Leave the small red radishes whole, even with their greens attached, and soak them, too. Use a plate or other weight to keep the vegetables submerged until soft, a few hours or overnight.

3. Continue with the basic kimchi process from the previous recipe (*Baechu* Kimchi), at step 3, page 47, adding grated horseradish to the spice mixture.

Fruit Kimchi

I recently met a Tennessee neighbor, Nancy Ramsay, and when the conversation inevitably turned to fermentation, I learned that she loves to eat and make kimchi. She knows kimchi well, having spent 13 years living in Korea as a missionary (though her perspectives have changed radically since that time, and she now is busy writing a book critical of missionaries and the negative impact they have on the cultures they attempt to convert).

Nancy talked about fruit kimchi as her favorite variety, which she has never seen in the U.S. The next day I went to town, bought a bunch of fruit, and improvised. The sweet fruit melds beautifully with the sharp kimchi flavors, and makes for a surprising and memorable taste sensation, different from anything else I've ever eaten.

TIMEFRAME: 1 week

INGREDIENTS (for 1 quart):
¼ pineapple
2 plums, pitted
2 pears, cored
1 apple, cored
1 small bunch grapes, stemmed
½ cup/125 milliliters cashews (or other nuts)
2 teaspoons/10 milliliters sea salt
Juice of 1 lemon
1 small bunch cilantro, chopped
1 to 2 fresh jalapeno peppers, finely chopped

1 to 2 hot red chilies, or any form of hot red pepper, fresh or dried
1 leek or onion, finely chopped
3 to 4 cloves garlic (or more), finely chopped
3 tablespoons/45 milliliters (or more) grated ginger

PROCESS:

Chop fruit into bite-size pieces. Peel if you wish. Leave grapes whole. Add in any other fruit you want to try. Add nuts. Mix fruit and nuts together in a bowl.

Add salt, lemon juice, and spices, and mix well.

Stuff kimchi mixture into a clean quart-size jar. Pack it tightly into the jar, pressing down until the brine rises. If necessary, add a little water. Weight down and ferment as described in the first kimchi recipe on page 47, step 5. As this sweet kimchi ages, it will develop an increasingly alcoholic flavor.

Sour Pickles

Growing up in New York City, experiencing my Jewish heritage largely through food, I developed a taste for sour pickles. Most of what is sold in stores as pickles, and even what home canners pickle, are preserved in vinegar. My idea of a pickle is one fermented in a brine solution.

Pickle-making requires close attention. My first attempt at brine pickle-making resulted in soft, unappealing pickles that fell apart, because I abandoned it for a few days, and perhaps because the brine was not salty enough, and because of the heat of the Tennessee summer. And and and. "Our perfection lies in our imperfection."

There are, inevitably, fermentation failures. We are dealing with fickle life forces, after all.

I persevered though, compelled by a craving deep inside of me for the yummy garlic-dill sour pickles of Guss's pickle stall on the Lower East Side of Manhattan and Zabar's on the Upper West Side and Bubbie's in upscale health food stores elsewhere. As it turns out, brine pickles are easy. You just need to give them regular attention in the summer heat, when cucumbers are most abundant.

One quality prized in a good pickle is crunchiness. Fresh tannin-rich grape leaves placed in the crock are effective at keeping pickles crunchy. I recommend using them if you have access to grape vines. I've also seen references in various brine pickle recipes to using sour cherry leaves, oak leaves, and horseradish leaves to keep pickles crunchy.

The biggest variables in pickle-making are brine strength, temperature, and cucumber size. I prefer pickles from small and medium cucumbers; pickles from really big ones can be tough and sometimes hollow in the middle. I don't worry about uniformity of size; I just eat the smaller ones first, figuring the larger ones will take longer to ferment.

The strength of brine varies widely in different traditions and recipe books. Brine strength is most often expressed as weight of salt as a percentage of *weight* of solution, though sometimes as weight of salt as a percentage of *volume* of solution. Since in most home kitchens we are generally dealing with volumes rather than weights, the following guideline can help readers gauge brine strength: Added to 1 quart of water, each tablespoon of sea salt (weighing about .6 ounce) adds 1.8% brine. So 2 tablespoons of salt in 1 quart of water yields a 3.6% brine, 3 tablespoons yields 5.4%, and so on. In the metric system, each 15 milliliters of salt (weighing 17 grams) added to 1 liter of water yields 1.8% brine.

Some old-time recipes call for brines with enough salt to float an egg. This translates to about a 10% salt solution. This is enough salt to preserve pickles for quite some time, but they are too salty to consume without a long desalinating soak in fresh water first. Low-salt pickles, around 3.5% brine, are "half-sours" in delicatessen lingo. This recipe is for sour, fairly salty pickles, using around 5.4% brine. Experiment with brine strength. A general rule of thumb to consider in salting your ferments: more salt to slow microorganism action in summer heat; less salt in winter when microbial action slows.

TIMEFRAME: 1 to 4 weeks

SPECIAL EQUIPMENT:
Ceramic crock or food-grade plastic bucket
Plate that fits inside crock or bucket
1-gallon/4-liter jug filled with water, or other weight
Cloth cover

INGREDIENTS (for 1 gallon/4 liters):
3 to 4 pounds/1.5 to 2 kilograms unwaxed cucumbers (small to medium size)
⅜ cup (6 tablespoons)/90 milliliters sea salt
3 to 4 heads fresh flowering dill, or 3 to 4 tablespoons/45 to 60 milliliters of any form of dill (fresh or dried leaf or seeds)
2 to 3 heads garlic, peeled

1 handful fresh grape, cherry, oak, and/or horseradish leaves (if available)

1 pinch black peppercorns

PROCESS:

1. Rinse cucumbers, taking care to not bruise them, and making sure their blossoms are removed. Scrape off any remains at the blossom end. If you're using cucumbers that aren't fresh off the vine that day, soak them for a couple of hours in very cold water to freshen them.

2. Dissolve sea salt in ½ gallon (2 liters) of water to create brine solution. Stir until salt is thoroughly dissolved.

3. Clean the crock, then place at the bottom of it dill, garlic, fresh grape leaves, and a pinch of black peppercorns.

4. Place cucumbers in the crock.

5. Pour brine over the cucumbers, place the (clean) plate over them, then weigh it down with a jug filled with water or a boiled rock. If the brine doesn't cover the weighed-down plate, add more brine mixed at the same ratio of just under 1 tablespoon of salt to each cup of water.

6. Cover the crock with a cloth to keep out dust and flies and store it in a cool place.

7. Check the crock every day. Skim any mold from the surface, but don't worry if you can't get it all. If there's mold, be sure to rinse the plate and weight. Taste the pickles after a few days.

8. Enjoy the pickles as they continue to ferment. Continue to check the crock every day.

9. Eventually, after one to four weeks (depending on the temperature), the pickles will be fully sour. Continue to enjoy them, moving them to the fridge to slow down fermentation.

Mixed Vegetable Crock

The brining process described above is not limited to cucumber pickles. Pretty much any vegetable you have in abundance, except for ripe tomatoes, which get soft and lose their form, can be fermented in this way. One memorable crock I made as the first frost was predicted and we were scurrying to harvest the last of our summer garden, included small yellow summer squash, whole red hot peppers, baby eggplants, green tomatoes, and beans. I also used lots of basil, which gave the pickles and the brine a really unusual, sweet flavor. I especially enjoyed the pickled baby eggplants. They lost some of their dark color to the brine, and were left with a beautiful streaked appearance. Green tomatoes pickle well, especially the fleshy plum varieties. In this particular batch, I made the brine a little too strong, meaning the pickles tasted saltier than I like, so I simply added water to dilute the brine. These pickles kept summer garden vegetables on our dinner table well into the holiday season.

Brined Garlic

I am a garlic fanatic. I believe that raw garlic is potent medicine, and I try to eat it every day. As you get to the bottom of your pickle crocks, the garlic and other seasonings that you used will be left, either floating at the top or sunk to the bottom.

I like to collect the whole garlic cloves from the crock in a jar, cover them with brine, and keep them, either in the fridge or continuing to ferment on the kitchen counter. The garlic is still pungent, and flavored by all the other delicious vegetables and spices it's been fermenting with. I use this garlic for cooking (or eat it raw). I also like to use the brine, which quickly takes on a strong garlicky flavor, for salad dressings, or straight up in a small glass as a healthful digestive tonic. If this appeals to you, you could also skip the initial vegetable crock and simply brine peeled garlic cloves.

Brine as Digestive Tonic and Soup Stock

Brine serves not only to provide a salty, watery environment for vegetables to ferment, but as a medium to meld the flavors of the various spices and vegetables you include in your pickles. The brine itself becomes full of complex flavor as it bubbles. It is also full of *Lactobacilli*. Like sauerkraut juice or garlic brine, it is an excellent digestive tonic.

Chances are, there is more brine left in your crock after you finish your pickles than you could consume raw. It is strong, salty stuff, and there is lots of it. Try using it as a soup stock. In Russian, brine is called *rassol* and soup with *rassol* as its base is *rassol'nik*. Dilute brine with water to the level of saltiness you like, and add vegetables (including pickles) and a little tomato paste. Serve hot, with a dollop of sour cream.

Milkweed/Nasturtium Seedpod "Capers"

Capers are the seedpods of a Mediterranean shrub known as the caper bush *(Capparis spinosa)*, which I have not personally encountered. But the delicious savory flavor of commercially available capers is largely a result of the brining process, and certain other seedpods have the same texture.

Milkweed

Nasturtium

My friend Lisa Lust and I were eating capers and talking about how much we like them. In food as in fashion, the small accessories make all the difference. Lisa noticed that pods were developing on the abundant milkweed plants and had the idea to try brining them. So we mixed up a batch and they were *so* good; better than capers from caper bushes, I daresay. You can't buy milkweed pods in a store, but it's a weed that seems to grow everywhere. The seedpods you want appear in high summer, after the big flowers fall away. The smaller the pods are when you pick them, the better.

Nasturtium seedpods are another good caper alternative, using this same process. They appear in late summer after the flowers fade, and look like little green brains, all crinkled and folded. Their flavor, like the nasturtium's leaves and flowers, is peppery and slightly hot.

TIMEFRAME: 4 to 7 days

INGREDIENTS (for 1 pint/500 milliliters):

1½ cups/375 milliliters small milkweed or nasturtium seedpods
Sea salt
1 to 2 heads garlic

PROCESS:

1. Harvest seedpods. Try to catch them when they are small and tender. Milkweed pods get very large, fibrous, and bitter.

2. Dissolve salt in water, about ¾ tablespoons (12 milliliters) salt in about 1 cup (250 milliliters) of water, to create a brine solution.

3. Fill a pint (500 milliliter) jar with seedpods and garlic, as many cloves as you have patience to peel.

4. Pour the brine over the pods and garlic to cover them. If you don't have enough brine, add a little more water and salt.

5. Weight down pods and garlic in the brine. Use a smaller jar that fits inside the mouth of the jar that contains the pods and brine, or a small zip-lock bag filled with brine. Improvise. The important thing is to keep the pods, which want to float to the top, under the protection of the brine.

6. Taste the "capers" daily. Ours tasted good, but were not quite ripe, after 4 days. After a week, a film of mold appeared on the surface. I skimmed it off, tasted the capers, and they were perfect.

7. Keep in refrigerator and use as needed.

Japanese Nuka Bran Pickles

Nuka pickles are a traditional Japanese ferment, where vegetables are packed in a crock filled with absorbent rice bran mixed with salt, water, seaweed, ginger, miso, and sometimes beer or wine. In this rich medium, whole vegetables can be pickled in just days, or continue to ferment for long periods. I usually pickle vegetables whole and then slice them up. Sharp sour flavors quickly permeate the vegetables. These pickles receive frequent compliments.

I've had an easier time finding wheat bran than rice bran. Bran is the fibrous outer layer of grains, what the white processed versions seek to eliminate. Fortunately, *nuka* pickling works great with wheat bran, too. The bran pickling medium takes a few days to get going. But once you start a *nuka* crock, you can keep adding and harvesting vegetables indefinitely.

TIMEFRAME: Days, then ongoing

SPECIAL EQUIPMENT:

Ceramic crock or food-grade plastic bucket
Plate that fits inside crock or bucket
1-gallon (4-liter) jug filled with water, or other weight
Cloth cover

INGREDIENTS (for a 2-gallon/8-liter crock):

2 pounds/1 kilogram wheat or rice bran
3 4-inch/10-centimeter strips kelp or other seaweed
⅜ cup/90 milliliters sea salt
½ cup/125 milliliters miso
1 cup/250 milliliters beer or saké
1-inch/2.5-centimeter piece of gingerroot, cut into a few chunky pieces
2 to 3 turnips, carrots, radishes, peas or beans, cucumbers, or other seasonal vegetables

PROCESS:

1. Dry-roast the bran in a cast-iron or other heavy skillet. Use a low flame and stir frequently to avoid burning it. The roasting brings out the flavor of the bran, but it is not essential to the process. Roast until the bran feels hot and you can smell a pleasant toasted aroma.

2. Pour 1 cup (250 milliliters) boiling water over the seaweed and allow it to hydrate for about ½ hour.

3. Mix brine: Dissolve salt in 5 cups (1.25 liters) water. Stir well to completely dissolve.

4. Place about 1 cup (250 milliliters) of the brine in a cup or bowl and mix it with the miso. Smooth any chunks of thick miso into a paste. Once well blended, add the miso paste to the larger quantity of brine and stir well. Add beer or saké to the brine.

5. Strain the seaweed-soaking water into the brine.

6. Place the toasted bran in the crock. Add the seaweed and the ginger. Add the brine and mix well, making sure the liquid is evenly distributed, without pockets of dry bran.

7. Bury whole vegetables in the briny bran so they are not touching one another.

8. Cover and weight the bran. If, by the next day, the brine does not rise above the level of the cover over the bran, add a bit more brine, with about 1 tablespoon (15 milliliters) of salt per cup (250 milliliters) of water. If the brine rises 1 inch (2.5 centimeters) or more above the cover, remove some liquid and discard, or use less weight so more liquid is held by the bran.

9. For the first few days, remove the vegetables each day and add fresh ones. The bran and brine medium is just developing, and fresh vegetables help it establish a *Lactobacillus* culture. Mix the bran well with each change of vegetables. The vegetables you remove at this early stage may taste good or not. Some recipes say to discard them, but I've enjoyed them. Taste them and see. Keep replacing the vegetables daily until they taste good and sour. Then you can start leaving them for longer periods. *Takuwan* pickles are daikon radishes fermented in *nuka* for as long as three years.

10. Remove vegetables by reaching into the crock with your hands. Use your fingers to brush as much bran as possible off the vegetables back into the crock. Rinse the vegetables for a moment, or soak them if you find the pickles too salty. Then slice and serve. The vegetables will contain hints of all the flavors in the crock: seaweed, ginger, miso, and beer or saké, subtle enough that people will wonder about that Japanese flavor.

11. Your *nuka* bran fermenting medium can be used in perpetuity. If it gets too liquid as it absorbs water from fresh vegetables, press a cup or bowl into the bran to drain off some of the liquid. If the volume of bran seems to be reducing too far, add some more toasted bran. Salt migrates out with the vegetables, and needs to be replenished to maintain a pickle-friendly environment. Add more salt, just a little at a time, each time you add vegetables. Enjoy the ginger and seaweed as pickles. Add more ginger, seaweed, miso, beer, and saké, occasionally and in small amounts. If you go away, store the crock in a cool place, such as a cellar or a refrigerator.

wild

Gundru

Gundru, also known as *kyurtse,* is a strong and delicious pickle made from vegetable greens. This is a traditional fermenting method of the Newar people of Nepal. I learned it from a Tibetan cookbook, Rinjing Dorje's *Food in Tibetan Life.* What distinguishes this ferment is that the sole ingredient is the vegetable itself, greens. No salt or any other ingredient is required. I made *gundru* with turnip greens. A quart (1 liter) required the greens of about eight plants. Radish greens, mustard greens, kale, or collards—any type of hardy green in the *Brassica* family (not lettuce) would work.

TIMEFRAME: Weeks

SPECIAL EQUIPMENT:
Quart-size (liter) jar
Screw top for jar
Rolling pin

INGREDIENTS (for 1 quart/1 liter):
Greens, about 2 pounds/1 kilogram

PROCESS:

1. Start on a sunny day. Set greens in the sun for a few hours so they wilt.

2. Use a rolling pin on a cutting board or other hard surface to smash and crush the wilted greens. This is to encourage the juices out of the leaves, but you don't want to lose any of the potent juice.

3. Stuff the leaves and any juice oozing out into a jar. Use whatever implements are at hand, including your fingers, to compress the greens into the jar. Use pressure to force more crushed greens in, and this will force water out of them. You may be surprised how great a volume of greens can be squeezed into a small jar. Keep stuffing greens in until the jar is full and the greens are covered with liquid. The liquid will be strongly pungent vegetable juice.

4. Screw the lid on the jar and place it in a warm sunny place for at least 2 to 3 weeks. Longer is fine.

5. After a couple of weeks, open the jar and smell the greens. They should be pungent and sharp. *Gundru* packs a lot of flavor. Taste them. You can cut them up and serve them as pickles, just like this.

6. Or you can dry them and use *gundru* to flavor soups, as it is used throughout winter in Nepal. To dry *gundru,* remove fermented leaves from the jar and hang them from a line or spread them in the sun. Make sure the greens are good and dry before putting them into storage, or they'll mold.

FURTHER READING

Coultrip-Davis, Deborah, and Young Sook Ramsay. *Flavors of Korea: Delicious Vegetarian Cuisine.* Summertown, Tenn.: Book Publishing Company, 1998.

Terre Vivante. *Keeping Food Fresh: Old World Techniques and Recipes.* White River Junction, Vt.: Chelsea Green Publishing Co., 1999.

Ziedrich, Laura. *The Joy of Pickling.* Boston: The Harvard Common Press, 1998.

6 BEAN FERMENTS

BEANS, ALSO KNOWN as legumes and pulses, are important sources of protein. The soybean, in particular, has received much attention for the quality and quantity of protein it contains. Soybeans are known throughout East Asia as "the meat of the fields." Unfortunately, this dense bean can be difficult to digest. Plain cooked soybeans are notorious for the flatulence and indigestion they cause. Fermentation pre-digests the beans, breaking down complex proteins into amino acids that the human body can more easily absorb. Fermentation is the most effective way to realize the powerful nutritive potential of legumes. In addition, when beans are fermented together with grains, as they frequently are, the ferment is a complete protein, containing all the amino acids essential to human nutrition.

The United States is the world's largest grower of soybeans. Very little of it becomes nutritious food for humans. Most of it is processed into livestock feed and fry oil. Soybean byproducts also wind up in plastics, adhesives, paints, inks, and solvents. The soybean has become a potent symbol in debates about world hunger. "Enormous quantities of the highest-quality food sources are fed to animals," objects Frances Moore Lappé in *Diet for a Small Planet*.[1] She calculates that cattle are fed 21 pounds of protein to produce a single pound of meat protein for human consumption, a shameful and unconscionable waste in a world where thousands die of starvation each day.

Diet for a Small Planet helped to popularize vegetarianism in the United States a generation ago, and the vegetarian subculture adopted a range of traditional Asian soy ferments, such as miso, tempeh, and tamari (or soy sauce). Actually, vegetarianism and fermented soy foods have a long-standing connection. The earliest bean ferments were pioneered more than a thousand years ago by Buddhists in China seeking alternatives to a meat-based diet. They were reinterpretations of a much older Chinese fermentation tradition of *jiangs*. *Jiangs* were condiments fermented primarily from fish and meat, in a complex and meaningful array of styles. The Analects of Confucius (c. 500 B.C.) direct that "Foods not accompanied by the appropriate variety of *jiang* should not be served. Rather than using only one to season all foods, you should provide many to ensure harmony with each of the basic food types."[2]

Buddhism and its soy foods spread to other parts of Asia, including Japan. Japan had its own ancient fish fermentation tradition, a condiment called *hishio*. Soybean fermentation was again reinterpreted; by the year 901 the Japanese word *miso* was recorded in documents.

In Japan, the consumption of miso spread beyond the Buddhist monasteries during the Kamakura period, 1185 to 1333, which started with a samurai coup against an inattentive royalty living it up in luxurious splendor. The new rulers stressed simplicity, including a diet based on rice, complemented by vegetables, soy, and seafood. It was during this period that miso soup was first developed and became popular. According to William Shurtleff and Akiko Aoyagi's *The Book of Miso*, "It came to be a symbol of the food of the common people."[3] To this day, miso soup is a staple of Japanese cuisine.

MAKING MISO

Miso is a uniquely grounding food, often the product of years of fermentation. It embodies the contractive energy of *yang* in the yin-yang energetics that underlie Chinese philosophy and medicine (and the macrobiotic diet). In Japanese folk wisdom, miso has long been associated with good health and longevity.

One specific health benefit of miso is the protection it provides against exposure to radiation and heavy metals. The research that verified this was conducted in Japan in the wake of the nuclear bombings of Hiroshima and Nagasaki, and grew out of the observations of a Nagasaki physician, Dr. Shinichoro Akizuki. Dr. Akizuki was out of town the day of the bombing, and the hospital where he worked was destroyed. He returned to Nagasaki to treat survivors of the bombing. He and his staff ate miso soup together every day and never experienced any radiation sickness, despite their proximity to the fallout. Dr. Akizuki's anecdotal account of this experience led to the finding that miso contains an alkaloid called dipicolinic acid that binds with heavy metals and carries them out of the body.[4] In our radioactive world, we could all do with some of that healing.

Dr. Crazy Owl made the first homemade miso I tried. Dr. Owl is a friend now in his mid-seventies, who dropped out of a career in statistical analysis thirty-some years ago to devote himself to the study of Chinese medicine. He's a quirky practitioner, emphatic about his beliefs. Miso is among the healing foods he advocates most vociferously. Dr. Owl has been making miso for many years, and brought some to Short Mountain.

Owl's homemade miso was chunky and rich. Its aliveness inspired me to learn how to make miso, and I have made crocks of it every winter since. Of all the foods I have fermented, this is the one that has met with the greatest appreciation over time. So few people make their own miso, and the people who use miso at all are very passionate about it. Making your own miso to share with the people you love is a way to nourish them deeply.

Making miso requires great patience. Most varieties ferment for at least a full year. But waiting is the hardest part of the process. Making it is really quite simple. Miso is traditionally made and decanted during cool seasons, when relatively few airborne microorganisms are active, but I've made miso in the heat of summer with fine results.

Though miso is classically made with soybeans, it can be made with any legume or combination of legumes. I've made miso using chickpeas, lima beans, black turtle beans, split peas, lentils, black-eyed peas, kidney beans, adzuki beans, and more. The distinctive color and flavor of each bean carries over into the miso it produces. Use what is abundantly available to you, and be bold in your fermentation experimentation!

wild

FINDING KOJI

Koji is grain, most often rice, inoculated with spores of *Aspergillus oryzae,* a mold that starts the miso fermentation. This is the first ferment that I've covered that is not strictly speaking a wild fermentation. It can be done as a wild fermentation in an environment where *Aspergillus* is well established, such as a traditional miso shop, or perhaps your basement in a couple of years. Until then, you need to obtain a starter. Some Asian markets or health food stores carry koji. Check with local commercial miso manufacturers, where they exist, to see if they will sell you koji. Two sources I can recommend, South River Miso Company and G.E.M. Cultures, are listed in the Cultural Resources section. You can also make your own koji by inoculating rice with spores of *Aspergillus oryzae,* also available from G.E.M. Cultures.

Red Miso

This miso is strong and salty, and it requires at least a full year of fermentation. It is a style traditionally known as red miso when made with soybeans, though its color can vary, especially using different beans. A shorter-term "sweet" miso recipe follows this one.

TIMEFRAME: 1 year or more

SPECIAL EQUIPMENT:

Ceramic crock or food-grade plastic bucket, at least 1-gallon/4-liter capacity

Lid that fits snugly inside (plate or hardwood disk)

Heavy weight (scrubbed and boiled rock)

Cloth or plastic (to cover the crock and keep dust and flies out)

INGREDIENTS (for 1 gallon/4 liters):

4 cups/1 liter dried beans

1 cup/250 milliliters sea salt, plus ¼ cup/60 milliliters more for the crock

2 tablespoons/30 milliliters live unpasteurized mature miso

5 cups/1.25 liters koji (about 1¾ pounds/850 grams)

PROCESS:

1. Soak beans overnight and cook until soft. Take care not to burn the beans, especially if you're using soybeans, which take a long while to cook.

2. Place a colander over a pot and drain beans, saving bean cooking liquid.

3. Take 2 cups (500 milliliters) of the bean cooking liquid (or boiling water) and dissolve 1 cup (250 milliliters) of salt in it to make a strong brine. Stir until the salt is completely dissolved. Set the brine aside to cool.

4. Mash beans to desired smoothness, using whatever tools are available. I generally use a potato masher and leave the beans fairly chunky.

5. Check the temperature of the brine. You don't need a thermometer. Stick your (clean!) finger in it. Once it's comfortable to the touch, take about 1 cup (250 milliliters) of it out and mash the mature miso into it. Then return the miso mash to the brine, and add the koji. Finally, add this mixture to the mashed beans and mix until the texture is uniform. If it seems thicker than miso you've had, add some more bean cooking liquid or water to desired consistency. This is your miso; the remaining steps involve packaging it for its long fermentation.

6. Salt the bottom and side surfaces of your fermenting vessel with wet fingers dipped in sea salt. The idea is to have higher salt content at the edges to protect the miso from unwanted wild organisms.

7. Pack the miso tightly into the crock, taking care to expel air pockets. Smooth the top and sprinkle a layer of salt over it. Don't be timid about salting the top. You'll scrape away the top layer and discard it when you dig out the miso.

8. Cover with a lid. A hardwood lid cut to exactly the size and shape of the crock is ideal, but I usually use the biggest plate I can find that fits inside the crock. Rest a heavy weight on the lid. I find a rock, scrub it clean, and boil it. The weight is important because, as with sauerkraut, it forces the solid ferment under the protection of the salty brine. Finally, place an outer cover over the whole thing, to keep dust and flies out. Heavy woven plastic sacks are most durable, but cloth or heavy paper are fine, too. Tie or tape the cover over the crock.

9. Label clearly with indelible markers. Labeling is especially important once you have multiple batches going from different years. Store in a cellar, barn, or other unheated environment.

10. Wait. Try some the fall or winter after the first summer of fermentation.

This is called one-year miso. The years are counted as the summers, periods of most active fermentation, that have passed. Repack it carefully, salting the new top layer. Then try it a year later, even a year after that. The flavor of miso will mellow and develop over time. I tried some nine-year-old miso recently, and it was sublime, like a well-aged wine.

11. A note on decanting: When you open a crock of miso that has been fermenting for a couple of years, the top layer may be quite ugly and off-putting. Skim it off, throw it in the compost, and trust that below the surface the miso will be gorgeous and smell and taste great. I usually dig out a whole 5-gallon (20-liter) crock of miso at once. I pack the miso into thoroughly clean glass jars. If the tops are metal, I use a layer of wax paper between the jar and the lid, as miso causes metal to corrode. I store the jars in the basement. Since fermentation continues, the jars build up pressure, which needs to be periodically released by opening the jars. Occasionally, mold will form on the surface of a jar of miso. As with the crock, scrape it away, and enjoy what remains beneath it. To avoid these inconveniences, you can store miso in the fridge.

Sweet Miso

Miso is made many different styles. In addition to various types of beans and grains, different proportions of salt and koji, and length of fermentation can distinguish misos. Sweet miso is radically different from the more widely known saltier and much longer fermented misos. Sweet miso is actually sweet. It contains about half as much salt in proportion to the beans, and

wild

twice as much koji, as the red miso described above. It ferments for a much shorter time, up to about two months, at higher temperatures.

TIMEFRAME: 4 to 8 weeks

SPECIAL EQUIPMENT:
Same as miso process described above

INGREDIENTS (for 1 gallon/4 liters):
4 cups/1 liter dried beans
½ cup/125 milliliters sea salt
10 cups/2.5 liters koji (about 3½ pounds/1.5 kilograms; see "Finding Koji," p. 60)

PROCESS:
Follow the steps detailed for miso, above, with the following modifications:

1. Use only ½ cup (125 milliliters) of salt rather than a full cup, and 10 cups (2.5 liters) of koji rather than 5 cups.

2. Sweet miso does not use mature miso from an earlier batch. Mature miso contains biodiverse organisms, including acid-creating *Lactobacilli*. Sweet miso is sweet because it is fermented primarily with koji molds and decanted before *Lactobacilli* have an opportunity to proliferate.

3. There is no need to salt the crock for this shorter-term miso.

4. Store the crock in an unobtrusive corner of your kitchen, or any other *warm* place where it won't be in your way. Sweet miso ferments quickly in a warm environment. Try some after a month. Decant some to eat young, store it in the refrigerator, and carefully repack the crock, leveling the miso surface, and replacing the lid, weight, and outer cover.

5. Continue fermenting for another few weeks to a month. When you decant the miso, you will notice that the koji grains are still intact and crunchy. Purée the miso in a food processor with a little water to make it into a smooth paste. Pack the miso into thoroughly clean glass jars. If the tops are metal, use a layer of wax paper between the jar and the lid, as miso causes metal to corrode. In contrast to the saltier miso that can store well at basement temperatures, sweet miso is best refrigerated. If mold forms on the surface of a jar of miso, scrape it away, and enjoy what remains beneath it.

Miso Soup

The classic way to enjoy miso is in the form of miso soup. The comfort and healing that Jewish grandmothers have proverbially offered in the form of chicken soup, I have more often found in miso soup. No food I know is more soothing.

When you make miso soup, miso is the last thing you add. In its simplest form, miso soup is just hot water with miso, about 1 tablespoon (15 milliliters) of miso per cup (250 milliliters) of water. Add the hot water to the miso and blend it thoroughly. Boiling miso will kill it.

On the other hand, miso soup can be as elaborate as you want. Adding seaweed is generally where I start. Seaweeds have deep, complex flavors. Some people think it makes them sound more appealing to call them sea vegetables. But I like to honor their wildness by calling them weeds. They carry the essence of the sea. They are rich in nutritional and healing properties. One of their specific benefits is a compound called alginic acid, which binds with heavy metals, such as lead and mercury, and radioactive elements like strontium 90, and carries them out of your body (much like the dipicolinic acid of miso). Seaweeds also nourish the cardiovascular system, improve digestion, help regulate metabolism and glandular and hormonal flows, and calm the nervous system.[5] I love to throw seaweed into pretty much anything I cook. Miso soup is almost always prepared with seaweed. Japanese recipes for *dashi,* or soup stock, traditionally call for *kombu,* a Pacific Ocean seaweed. I get my seaweed from small-scale seaweed harvesters on the Maine coast, where *kombu* is not found. The North Atlantic equivalent is called *Laminaria digitata.* Digitata is a thick and hardy variety of kelp. Each stalk's growth splits off into several digits of wavy greenbrown flesh, hence the name digitata.

I had a memorable experience harvesting digitata, guided by seaweed harvesting partners Matt and Raivo of Ironbound Island Seaweed, off the Schoodic Peninsula in "Downeast" Maine. We woke up at 4:00 A.M., squeezed ourselves into skintight wet suits, and drove down to the harbor. We got into a wooden boat that Matt had built himself, and towed a smaller wooden boat, which he had also built. Do-it-yourself has no limits. We glided through the calm bay waters into the foggy dawn for a long time. I wondered how my guides could possibly navigate in the dense grayness where the sea, sky, and land all blended into one. We saw seagulls and seals. The water got choppier. We were headed beyond the harbor to the turbulent ocean waters where digitata thrives.

We arrived at our destination just as the tide was getting low enough to give us access. Seaweed harvesting is ruled by the tides. Matt and Raivo do almost all of

Laminaria digitata

their harvesting during the week each month when the tides are at their lowest. We anchored the big boat and got into the smaller boat, then aimed for a large stand of digitata growing from an underwater rock ledge. When we got near the digitata, we jumped out of the boat into the cold, choppy water. Matt and Raivo took turns staying in the boat to keep it from drifting away, continually rowing back to near where we were, so we could toss the digitata that we harvested into the boat.

There I was in the ocean, with a sharp knife in my hand. The idea was to stand on the rock ledge from which the digitata was growing and cut the stalk to harvest it. Sounds straightforward enough. And it would have been, had the waves been kind enough to stop. But every time a wave came rolling rhythmically in, suddenly the water over the rock ledge I was standing on was about five feet deep instead of two feet. Reaching down to the digitata stalk in the deeper water involved dunking my entire body, head included, into the ocean. And half the time the wave would knock me right off the rock ledge.

I spent a lot of that morning flailing around, knife in one hand, seaweed in the other, feeling like Lucy Ricardo in another madcap misadventure. When I'd actually get a handful of digitata, the goal was to throw it into the rowboat, another challenge intensified by the rough water. It was crazy, and incredibly fun, regardless of how little I managed to harvest. As my body was pushed around by the waves, I identified with the seaweeds, whose lives are a continual push and pull of tidal influences. Several small rowboat loads later, the tide was rising too high for us to continue, so we boated back in the mid-morning sun to the South Gouldsboro harbor, nestled in a bed of slippery digitata.

When we got back to Matt and Raivo's place, we shed our wet suits and ate, then got down to the business of hanging all the seaweed to dry. Each plant requires individual handling. After hours of hanging digitata, our hands were covered with gooey gelatinous slime. Another time when I helped Matt and Raivo hang wet seaweed, I had just been in an auto accident. I found that the flexible slimy seaweed absorbed the shock from my body. Eating seaweed brings this soothing absorptive quality into your digestive tract.

Most of the seaweed available in the United States is imported from Japan, where it is a popular staple ingredient and is farmed intensively. I want to make a plug for seaweed bioregionalism and urge readers to support small seaweed harvesters along America's coastal waters. Matt and Raivo sell seaweed as Ironbound Island Seaweed. Other seaweed harvesters I can recommend are Larch Hanson in Maine and Ryan Drum in Washington. Contact information for these suppliers is listed in the Cultural Resources section.

We were making miso soup. Use whatever is in your refrigerator or your garden that needs to get used up. Here's how I do it:

1. Start with water. One quart (1 liter) of water makes soup for 2 to 4 people. Quantities of the other ingredients are in proportion to a quart of water. Start heating the water to a boil, while you add other ingredients; once it boils, lower the heat and simmer.

2. Add the seaweed first. As it cooks, its flavors and qualities melt into the broth. I use scissors to cut up dried seaweed into small pieces, easier to fit in a spoon. Cut up a 3- to 4-inch (8- to 10-centimeter) strip of digitata, kombu, or another variety of seaweed, or more than one type. Add the small pieces of seaweed to the water. Once this boils for a few minutes, you have a traditional Japanese *dashi,* or stock. Make your miso soup from this, or make it more elaborate.

3. The next thing I add is root vegetables. Burdock root (*gobo* in Japanese) gives a hearty, earthy flavor to soup, as well as its tonifying and cleansing powers. Use about half a burdock root. Slice it lengthwise, then into thin half-moons. Also cut up a carrot and/or part of a daikon root. Add the root vegetables to the pot of soup stock.

4. Next I add mushrooms if I have them around. Shiitakes are my favorite, but any kind goes well in soup. I never wash mushrooms because they are so absorptive and I would rather have them absorb soup than plain water. Just wipe away any visible dirt. Slice 3 or 4 mushrooms into pieces small enough for a spoon and add them to the soup stock.

5. Cabbage is good in miso, just a little bit, chopped finely and added to the stock.

6. If you want heartier soup, you can add tofu. Take about half a pound (250 grams) of tofu, rinse it, slice it into small cubes, and add it to your stock. If you have any leftover cooked whole grains around, add a scoop of them to the stock. Break up any clumps with a spoon. Soups are an excellent opportunity for recycling leftovers.

7. Peel and chop four (or more!) cloves of garlic and prepare any green vegetables. Cut small pieces of florets from a stalk of broccoli, or chop up a few leaves of kale, collards, or other greens.

8. Check to make sure the root vegetables are tender and the tofu is hot. When they are, turn off the flame. Remove a cup of the stock and add the garlic and green vegetables to the pot. Cover the pot. Mash about 3 tablespoons (45 milliliters) of miso into the cup of stock you removed. For a hearty soup, you can also add 2 tablespoons (30 milliliters) of tahini. Once it's well blended, return it to the pot of stock and stir. Taste the soup. Add more miso, if needed, using the same technique.

9. Garnish the soup with chopped scallions, wild onions, or chives. Enjoy. Soup like this is a one-dish meal.

10. When you heat leftover soup, heat it gently, trying not to boil the miso.

Miso-Tahini Spread

Another great way to enjoy miso is as a spread. In a small bowl, combine 1 tablespoon (15 milliliters) of miso, 2 tablespoons (30 milliliters) of tahini, the juice of half a lemon, and a finely chopped clove of garlic. Mix until well blended. Enjoy on bread or crackers. You can liquefy this basic delicious combination by adding more lemon juice, water, or "pot liquor," the water left over from cooking vegetables. Create a sauce for grains or vegetables this way, or a salad dressing. Miso and tahini are a versatile pair. One of my fellow communards, Stv, invented a wonderful variation on miso and tahini using sweet miso and almond butter. Experiment and vary!

Miso Pickles and Tamari

Miso is an excellent medium for pickling vegetables. In a small crock or jar, layer miso with root vegetables and whole garlic cloves. You can pickle the roots whole or sliced. Try to keep the vegetables from touching one another, so each piece will be surrounded by miso. Cover the top layer of vegetables with miso and weigh it down. Leave it to ferment in a cool place for a couple of weeks. The vegetables will absorb flavor and salt from the miso, and the miso will absorb flavor and water from the vegetables. Both miso and vegetables are transformed by the process. Dark liquid will rise to the top of the crock; this is sweet, rich tamari. Pour it off and savor its complex flavor. Enjoy the vegetables as pickles, and the miso as soup or spread. Be aware that this miso now has a higher proportion of water and a lower proportion of salt, so its keeping potential will be somewhat diminished.

Tempeh

Tempeh is a soybean ferment from Indonesia that has become a popular vegetarian food in the United States. It is really worth the trouble of making tempeh yourself. I have nothing against the frozen version available in stores, but it is what I call a vehicle food, only as good as the flavors you smother it with. Freshly fermented tempeh, on the other hand, has a rich, unique, delicious flavor and texture.

I learned how to make tempeh from my friend and neighbor Mike Bondy, who learned it from another friend, Ashley Ironwood, at "Food for Life," a food skills, information, and politics gathering held every summer at the Sequatchie Valley Institute (S.V.I.) near Chattanooga, Tennessee. I've taught miso-making and sauerkraut-making at Food for Life, and others have offered various other fermentation workshops (among many other interesting topics). I highly recommend this event. It draws an eclectic crowd of activists, gardeners, and cooks. For information, you can contact S.V.I. at Route 1, Box 304, Whitwell, TN 37397, (423) 949-5922, www.svionline.org. Incidentally, Moonshadow, the community where S.V.I. is located, has some of the most beautiful rustic handcrafted buildings I've seen.

Tempeh-making involves the most sustained temperature control of anything in this book, but it is well worth the effort. Tempeh also requires spores of a mold called *Rhyzopus oligosporus*. Spores are available inexpensively from the Tempeh Lab or G.E.M. Cultures; contact information is listed in the Resources section.

The Tempeh Lab is located at the Farm, another Tennessee intentional community. When I meet people and tell them that I live in a community in Tennessee, they often ask if it's the Farm. The Farm was the most famous of the hippie communes of the 1970s. At one time it had 1,200 people, and it became a media sensation. Beacon of counter-cultural tastes, the Farm was instrumental in popularizing soy foods in the United States. *The New Farm Vegetarian Cookbook,* edited by Louise Hagler and Dorothy Bates, is now a classic text in vegetarian circles. It is still in print and contains detailed tempeh-making directions, from which my own are adapted.

Maintaining a temperature around 85 to 90 degrees Fahrenheit (29 to 32 degrees Celsius) for twenty-four hours can be tricky. Making tempeh when the weather is hot is the easiest method. Other times, I generally use the oven of our propane stove with just the pilot light on, with a Mason jar ring propping the door open just enough so that it doesn't get too hot. I've also incubated larger quantities of tempeh in the greenhouse on a sunny day, then in a small room somewhat overheated by a wood stove at night. Be sure to maintain good air circulation around the incubating tempeh. Innovate, make it work.

TIMEFRAME: 2 days

SPECIAL EQUIPMENT:

Grain grinder

Clean towels

Zip-lock bags (3 large ones) or a baking tray and aluminum foil

INGREDIENTS (for about 3 pounds/1.5 kilograms of tempeh):

2½ cups/625 milliliters soybeans

2 tablespoons/30 milliliters vinegar

1 teaspoon/5 milliliters tempeh spore

PROCESS:

1. Crack the soybeans in a grain mill, coarsely so that every bean is broken but in just a few large pieces. This makes the hulls fall off the beans when they are cooked, and gives more surface area for the spore to grow on. Removing the hulls is the critical part. In the absence of a grain grinder, you can soak the beans overnight or until they are soft, cook them a little, then knead them with your hands to loosen the hulls before cooking them the rest of the way.

2. Boil beans, without salt, until they are just barely soft enough to eat. For soybeans, 1 to 1½ hours should do it. Do not cook them as soft as you would want them to be for eating. The fermentation will continue to soften the beans. As you cook and stir the soybeans, their hulls will rise to the surface of the pot in a foamy froth. Skim off the froth with the hulls and discard.

3. As the beans boil, take a few zip-lock bags and poke holes in them with a fork, every couple of inches. The bags provide a form for the tempeh to fill, and the holes ensure good air circulation, which is necessary for the spore to thrive. You can reuse the bags by cleaning them after use, drying them thoroughly, and storing them in a special place. Alternatively, you can

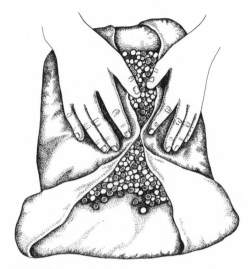

Towel-drying cooked soybeans

form tempeh in a baking tray with a lip of at least ¾ inch (1.5 centimeters), then cover it with foil with fork holes punched every couple of inches.

4. When the beans are ready, strain them and spread them, or a portion of them at a time, on a clean towel. Use the towel to dry them. The most common problem with tempeh is excess moisture, which yields a foul, inedible product. Swaddle and pat the cooked soybeans until most of the surface moisture has been absorbed into the towel. Use a second towel if necessary. It is rare that we have the opportunity to be so intimate with soybeans. Enjoy it.

5. Place the cooked and dried soybeans in a bowl. Make sure they are no warmer than body temperature, which they are not likely to be after the towel-drying. Add the vinegar and mix. Add the spore and mix well so the spore is evenly distributed around the soybeans. The acidity of the vinegar gives the spore a competitive edge over bacteria that are present in the air.

Tempeh forming methods using zip-lock bags and baking pans

6. Spoon the mixture into the bags with holes, spreading it evenly, sealing the bags, and placing them on oven racks or wherever they will incubate. Likewise, if you're using a baking pan, spread the mixture evenly and cover with foil with holes.

7. Incubate at about 85 to 90°F (29 to 32°C) for about 24 hours. No dramatic changes occur during the first half of the fermentation period. I like to start the process in the afternoon, let it spend the night unattended, then watch the exciting drama of the later period. What happens is that hairy white mold begins to form in all the space between the soybeans. It begins to generate heat, as well, so keep an eye on the temperature and adjust the incubation space as necessary. The mold gradually thickens until it forms a cohesive mat holding the beans together. The tempeh should have a pleasant, earthy odor, like button mushrooms or babies. The process generally takes 20 to 30 hours, considerably longer at cooler temperatures. Eventually, the mold will start to show patches of gray or black coloration, originating near the air holes. Once it has large patches of gray or black, it is ready.

8. Remove the tempeh from your incubator and from its forms. Allow it to cool to room temperature before refrigerating, then refrigerate without stacking. If you stack tempeh before it is cool, the mold will continue to grow and generate heat, even in the refrigerator.

9. Tempeh is generally not eaten raw. Sauté slices of it plain to discover its unique flavor. Try "Sweet and Spicy Glazed Tempeh" (page 69) or "Tempeh Reuben Sandwiches" (page 70). Or prepare it however you like it.

Black-eyed Pea/Oat/ Seaweed Tempeh

The tempeh recipe above is the most basic variety. You can incorporate any kinds of legumes, as well as grains and other goodies, into your tempeh. Here's a recipe for black-eyed pea/oat/seaweed tempeh.

TIMEFRAME: 2 days

INGREDIENTS (for about 3 pounds/ 1.5 kilograms of tempeh):

2 cups/500 milliliters black-eyed peas

1 cup/250 milliliters whole oat groats

2 4-inch/6-centimeter strips digitata kelp or kombu

2 tablespoons/30 milliliters vinegar

1 teaspoon/5 milliliters tempeh spore (see Resources for sources)

PROCESS:

1. Soak the black-eyed peas and oat groats (separately) overnight.

2. Before cooking, knead and crush the softened beans with your hands to loosen the hulls.

3. Cook the black-eyed peas in a good deal of water so hulls will float to the top and be easy to skim off. Do not cook beans long. For soaked black-eyed peas, about 10 minutes of boiling should suffice. They do not need to be soft enough for a pleasant eating experience; the mold will further soften them. If they lose their form, there will not be air spaces between beans and the tempeh process will be impeded. The general rule of thumb is to cook beans to the point where they are just barely edible, meaning you can sink your teeth through them. Figure no more than 25 percent of normal cooking time.

4. Meanwhile, cook the oats separately, in just 1½ cups (375 milliliters) of water per cup (250 milliliters) of grain. Add the seaweed, cut up with scissors, to the grain. Bring to a boil, then lower heat and cook until the water has been absorbed, about 20 minutes. You can add any kind of grain to tempeh; just cook it on the dry side so it maintains its form and doesn't add excess moisture to the tempeh. Cool the grain with the lid off.

5. Strain the beans and towel-dry them, as explained in the tempeh recipe above. Alternatively, you can simply cool the beans in a colander, stirring periodically to release steam (and with it moisture).

6. When the beans and grains are around body temperature, mix them together, add the vinegar, mix some more, add the spore, and mix yet again. Then proceed with incubation as detailed in the previous recipe, starting with step 6.

Sweet and Spicy Glazed Tempeh with Broccoli and Daikon

My housemate Orchid is a truly amazing cook. One of the tangible benefits of communal living is good food. Orchid has explored a number of different culinary traditions in depth and always manages to bring them together in inventive fusions. This is an extraordinary dish that he created with tempeh I made.

TIMEFRAME: Less than 1 hour

INGREDIENTS (to serve 3 to 4 as main dish, 4 to 6 as side dish):
½ pound/250 grams tempeh
1 cup/250 milliliters broccoli florets
½ cup/125 milliliters daikon radish (cut into half-moon slices)
¼ cup/60 milliliters orange juice
2 tablespoons/30 milliliters honey
1 tablespoon/15 milliliters arrowroot powder
1 teaspoon/5 milliliters sesame oil
1 tablespoon/15 milliliters rice vinegar
1 tablespoon/15 milliliters wine
2 teaspoons/10 milliliters chili paste
3 tablespoons/45 milliliters tamari, divided
1 tablespoon/15 milliliters miso
2 tablespoons/30 milliliters vegetable oil
2 tablespoons/30 milliliters minced fresh gingerroot
3 tablespoons/45 milliliters minced garlic
½ teaspoon/2 milliliters ground white pepper

PROCESS:

1. Cut tempeh into bite-size pieces and steam for about 15 minutes, in a steamer basket in a saucepan filled with ½ inch (1 centimeter) of water and covered. In the last 2 minutes, add the broccoli and daikon.

2. While tempeh is steaming, mix together the orange juice, honey, arrowroot, sesame oil, rice vinegar, wine, chili paste, and 2 tablespoons (30 milliliters) of tamari in a bowl. Stir well, making sure that the honey and arrowroot are thoroughly dissolved.

3. In another small bowl, blend the miso with the remaining tablespoon (15 milliliters) of tamari.

4. In a hot wok, heat the oil. Fry the ginger for about a minute, add the garlic, and fry 2 minutes or until light brown, then add the white pepper and fry for another 30 seconds. Stir the juice mixture again, add it to the wok, and cook for a few minutes, stirring constantly, until the sauce thickens.

5. Remove the wok from the flame, add the steamed tempeh and veggies, and stir. Add the miso-tamari mixture, and stir again.

6. Serve with rice.

Tempeh Reuben Sandwiches

My favorite way to enjoy tempeh is in a tempeh Reuben sandwich. This sandwich incorporates four different ferments: bread, tempeh, sauerkraut, and cheese.

1. Sauté slices of tempeh in a lightly oiled pan.

2. Spread Thousand Island dressing (made of ketchup, mayonnaise, and relish) on slices of bread (rye is best), then place sautéed tempeh slices on the dressing.

3. Cover tempeh with a generous portion of sauerkraut.

4. Cover sauerkraut with a thin slice of Swiss cheese (or your favorite).

5. Broil or bake for a minute or so, until the cheese is melted.

6. Serve open-faced, with sour pickles (page 50).

Dosas and Idlis

Dosas are South Indian fried breads, and *idlis* are South Indian steamed breads, both made from the same fermentation process. They have a wonderful flavor, mildly sour. I saw *idlis* compared to matzo balls in one cookbook, but I think they have a distinctive spongy texture all their own. I'm including them here as bean ferments, rather than in the bread section, because they are made with lentils. *Dosas* and *idlis* are much easier and faster than any of the other bean ferments I've covered. They do not require

Idli *steamer*

special mold cultures. They are truly wild fermentations, transformed by organisms present on the rice and lentils.

TIMEFRAME: Days

SPECIAL EQUIPMENT:

Idlis need forms in which to steam. I bought a simple, stainless-steel four-tiered steamer designed for this purpose at an Indian market in Nashville for about $12. It steams sixteen *idlis* at a time. It worked so much better than the muffin tin that I used the first time I tried to make *idlis;* the chief difference is that the steamer has tiny holes in it to permit the steam access to the *idlis.* In the absence of an *idli* steamer, use any steaming implement (the Chinese-style bamboo ones would work), making bigger *idlis* if necessary, and cutting them into pieces to serve.

Dosas require only a well-seasoned or non-stick frying pan.

INGREDIENTS (for 32 *dosas* or *idlis*):

2 cups rice/500 milliliters (I've tried it with brown rice and liked it fine, but my friend River, who spent time in southern India, felt the white Basmati rice *dosas* and *idlis* were more authentic)

1 cup/250 milliliters lentils (most recipes call for *urad daal*, white lentils, available in Indian groceries; I've also used red lentils, more widely available in the United States, which yield a gorgeous pink batter, and lima beans)

1 cup/250 milliliters yogurt or kefir (optional)

1 teaspoon/5 milliliters salt

1 small bunch parsley and/or cilantro (for *dosas*, not *idlis*)

1 inch/2.5 centimeters gingerroot (for *dosas*, not *idlis*)

Vegetable oil (for *dosas*, not *idlis*)

PROCESS:

1. Soak the rice and lentils in water for at least 8 hours or overnight. The lentils and rice swell and soften during this soak. If you leave them to soak a bit longer and they begin to sour, that's fine.

2. Strain the rice and lentils.

3. Grind the rice and lentils into a batter, with yogurt or kefir or water, in a food processor or other grinding implement. Put the batter in a bowl or jar with plenty of room for it to expand, because it will. The batter should be fine, not chunky, and thick, just barely pourable. If necessary, add a little water and stir.

4. Ferment 24 to 48 hours, or longer. Once it has risen substantially, you can make this batter into *idlis* or *dosas*. You can leave it for a number of days, and the sour flavor intensifies, if you're into that sort of thing.

FOR IDLIS:

5. Add salt and stir.

6. Spoon batter into molds. Leave room for batter to expand during steaming.

7. Steam about 20 minutes, covered, until *idlis* are firm.

8. Remove *idlis* from molds and cool.

9. Clean molds between batches.

10. Serve *idlis* with coconut chutney (recipe follows) and/or *sambar*, a delicious spicy vegetable *daal* soup (beyond the scope of this book).

FOR DOSAS:

5. Add 1 cup (250 milliliters) of lukewarm water to thin the batter. The batter should be liquid, to produce thin, crêpe-like pancakes.

6. Chop the parsley and/or cilantro. Grate the ginger. Add seasonings, along with salt, to the batter. Stir well.

7. Heat a well-seasoned frying pan, with oil. Use a ladle to pour batter into the center of the pan, then use the bottom of the ladle to spiral the batter from the center out toward the edges of the pan. Cook as a pancake, flipping after bubbles appear on the surface. *Dosas* should be thin. If necessary, thin the batter by adding a little more water, yogurt, or kefir. Lightly oil the pan between *dosas*.

8. Enjoy *dosas* plain, with a little yogurt or kefir, or stuffed with savory vegetable fillings. To stuff a *dosa,* place a scoop of filling in the center of it and fold it in half.

Coconut Chutney

Chutneys are the condiments of Indian food, made in infinite variety. This coconut chutney, from southern India, is an excellent accompaniment to *idlis* or *dosas*. It is sweet and sour simultaneously, and can be eaten fresh or fermented for a few days. This recipe is inspired by Shanta Nimbark Sacharoff's *Flavors of India: Vegetarian Indian Cooking.*

TIMEFRAME: 20 minutes to 4 days

INGREDIENTS (for 2 cups/500 milliliters):

1 cup/250 milliliters shredded coconut

3 tablespoons/45 milliliters *chana daal* or coarsely
  ground chickpeas

2 tablespoons/30 milliliters vegetable oil

2 tablespoons/30 milliliters tamarind paste or juice
  of 1 lemon

1 teaspoon/5 milliliters salt

1 teaspoon/5 milliliters cumin

1 teaspoon/5 milliliters coriander seed

1 tablespoon/15 milliliters honey

½ teaspoon/2 milliliters mustard seeds

A pinch of asafoetida powder (also called *hing*)

¾ cup/185 milliliters kefir or yogurt

PROCESS:

1. Soak shredded coconut in ½ cup
(125 milliliters) warm water to hydrate.

2. Fry *chana daal* (split chickpeas) in
oil for just a moment, until it begins to
darken (but don't let it burn).

3. In food processor or blender, combine fried *chana daal* with tamarind paste
or lemon juice, salt, cumin, coriander
seed, honey, and soaked coconut. Process
until well blended and puréed.

4. Fry mustard seeds in oil, briefly.
When they start popping, add asafoetida
and half of the yogurt or kefir, and stir to
combine as the mixture sizzles. Remove
from heat.

5. Add the mustard seed–asafoetida
mixture and the remaining uncooked yogurt or kefir (microorganisms still alive
and ready) to the coconut-spice mixture in
the food processor or blender, and blend
until well combined.

6. Enjoy chutney fresh, or ferment for
Lactobacilli and sour accent. To ferment,
transfer to a jar and leave in a warm spot,
covered with cheesecloth and open to air
circulation, about 2 to 4 days, until you
can see pockets of air in the chutney from
microorganism action. After that, store in
refrigerator.

FURTHER READING

Shurtleff, William, and Akiko Aoyagi. *The Book of Miso*. Berkeley: Ten
    Speed Press, 2001.

Shurtleff, William, and Akiko Aoyagi. *The Book of Tempeh*. Berkeley: Ten
    Speed Press, 2001.

7

DAIRY FERMENTS
(AND VEGAN ALTERNATIVES)

It's 8:00 A.M. and my day to milk. I take the milking pail and a dish of warm water down to the barn. The goats are waiting for me. It's feeding time as well as milking time, and they look forward to it. Sassy's usually the first one in. She's the alpha-goat, the queen of the herd. She often bullies the other goats, and eating first seems to be a way of asserting her dominance. I scoop some feed into a dish and give it to her. As she devours it, I milk. Her teats are nice and big, easy to grasp. I squeeze the teats firmly between my thumbs and the base of my index fingers, to prevent the milk from going back up into the udder, then use my remaining fingers against my palm to squirt the milk out. This action forces out a concentrated stream that froths in the pail. I relax my grip so the teat can fill with more milk, and repeat. With a teat in each hand, I rhythmically alternate.

I try to go fast, because as soon as Sassy is done with her food, she isn't so content to stay still. She squirms and tries to leave the milking platform. Worse than that, she lifts her hind legs to try to knock over or step into the pail of milk. Goats are quite intelligent and purposeful. From this point on, milking her is a battle of wills. I pour the milk I've gotten so far into a larger collecting pail, so if her sabotage efforts succeed, the loss will be minimal. I stroke her and whisper sweet nothings into her ear. "Sassy, you beautiful goat, you've been so good this morning. I'm sorry I'm so slow. Won't you please, please, please let me finish?" I negotiate, offering her more food if she'll cooperate. I milk with one hand, holding the pail with my other hand to protect it. As each squirt yields less milk, I knead her udder, trying to get all the milk out. When Sassy is done, there are three more still to go, and three who don't get milked but still need to be fed and tended.

I've only recently started milking the goats, after nearly nine years of enjoying their milk. I have deep ambivalence about the domestication of animals. At some level it seems inherently cruel to bring animals into the world for the pleasure of humans. And yet, contradictory being that I am, I drink milk and eat meat, and now I'm getting to know the goats and loving my interactions with them.

I have always felt lucky to be drinking their milk. These are not mass-bred animals treated as commodities and manipulated with growth hormones. Our goats are fenced out of our garden areas, rather than into a small grazing range. They roam the mountainside, feasting on wild vegetation. Today I watched Lentil eating the bark off a fallen tree. Actually, I believe it was the lichen growing on the bark that she was after. Through their ruminant digestive tracts, the goats extract nutrition from sources like this, which we get to share in via their milk. They even eat poison ivy; the milk with traces of poison ivy phytochemicals is said to help desensitize people to the effects of the plant.

We milk twice a day, and each milking yields 1 to 2½ gallons (4 to 10 liters) of milk. The quantity varies with the seasons, and its continued flow requires that we breed part of the herd each year. We have limited refrigeration here on our mountain homestead, powered not by electricity but by propane. I try to imagine 5 gallons (20 liters) of milk a day prior to the advent of refrigeration, not so very long ago. Milk does not stay fresh for long at room temperatures. Luckily, the earliest people who domesticated animals for milking thousands of years ago observed that, once fermented, milk becomes much more stable and long-lasting. Fermented dairy products remain edible, even improve over time, without refrigeration.

Refrigeration has become the norm in American life. Many households have more than one refrigerator. We have become used to keeping a variety of prepared perishable foods on hand, to be available immediately, whenever we want them. Entering a big supermarket, you feel the chill of the open coolers and hear their constant hum. Though refrigeration renders the original preservation benefit of fermented milk obsolete, supermarket coolers are full of fermented dairy products. Consumers are devoted to cheese, yogurt, sour cream, buttermilk, and other dairy ferments. We love cultured milk products for their flavors, textures, and, in many cases, their health benefits.

Vegans and other non-milk drinkers, do not despair. You do not need to forego the benefits and pleasures of these fermentations. Yogurt and kefir are versatile cultures, adaptable to many substances besides milk. A special section at the end of this chapter addresses vegan adaptations of these fermentations. If you avoid milk because of a lactose-intolerance, you might give cultured milks a chance. *Lactobacilli* consume lactose in milk and transform it into lactic acid that may be easier for you to digest.

Yogurt

No cultured food is better known or acknowledged for its health benefits than yogurt. Perhaps you know some of the famous and fetishized yogurt *Lactobacillus* organisms by name, such as *acidophilus* or *bulgaricus*. These *Lactobacilli,* known to improve intestinal cultural ecology, are often marketed as "probiotic" nutritional supplements. Frequently, yogurt is used to accompany or follow a regime of antibiotics, to restore the damage the drugs cause in the digestive tract. Yogurt is extremely high in calcium and confers many other health benefits. "Yogurt is especially recommended for those at high risk of cancer, as it is superb at blocking cellular changes that initiate the cancer cascade," writes Susun S. Weed.[1]

Yogurt is delicious, too. In the United States, it is mostly consumed sweet, though my favorite ways to enjoy yogurt are savory. Savory flavors complement and accent its sourness rather than try to cover it up. (See recipes following this for savory yogurt sauces).

In addition to *Lactobacilli,* yogurt generally contains an organism called *Streptococcus thermophilus* that makes yogurt thicken and coagulate. This *thermophilus* culture is most active at above body temperature, around 110°F (43°C). Many contraptions are on the market to help

(AND VEGAN ALTERNATIVES)

you maintain that temperature range. If you have one, great; but it is easy to create an incubator with an insulated cooler.

You need a starter culture to make yogurt. You can buy specialized cultures for this, or use any commercial live-culture yogurt. Make sure the yogurt you use for starter says "Contains live cultures" on the label; if not, it has probably been pasteurized after culturing, as many commercial yogurts are, killing the bacteria. Once you make yogurt from the starter culture, save a little yogurt from each batch to start the next. With regular attention, a starter culture can keep on going indefinitely. Yonah Schimmel's Knishes on Houston Street in New York City makes delicious yogurt using the same starter culture the store's founders brought over from Eastern Europe more than one hundred years ago.

TIMEFRAME: 8 to 24 hours

SPECIAL EQUIPMENT:
Quart/liter jar
Insulated cooler

INGREDIENTS (for 1 quart):
1 quart/1 liter whole milk
1 tablespoon/15 milliliters fresh live-culture plain yogurt for starter culture

PROCESS:

1. Preheat the jar and insulated cooler with hot water so they will not drain heat from the yogurt and it can stay warm to ferment.

2. Heat the milk until bubbles begin to form. If you use a thermometer, heat milk to 180°F (82°C). Use gentle heat, and stir frequently, to avoid burning the milk. It does not need to come to a full boil. The heating is not absolutely necessary, but it results in a thicker yogurt.

3. Cool the milk to 110°F (43°C), or the point where it feels hot, but it is not hard to keep your (clean!) finger in it. You can speed the cooling process by setting the pot with the hot milk into a bowl or pot of cold water. Don't let the milk get too cool; the yogurt cultures are most active in the above-body-temperature range.

4. Mix starter yogurt into the milk. Use just 1 tablespoon (15 milliliters) per quart. I used to use more starter, assuming that more is better, until I consulted my number one kitchen reference book, *The Joy of Cooking* (1964 edition), known affectionately as "Joy" in our kitchen. "You may wonder why so little starter is used and think that a little more will produce a better result. It won't. The bacillus, if crowded, gives a sour, watery product. But if the culture has sufficient *Lebensraum* [German for 'room to live'], it will be rich, mild and creamy."[2] Mix the starter thoroughly into the milk, and pour the mixture into the preheated jar.

5. Cap the jar and place it in the preheated insulated cooler. If much space remains in the cooler, fill it with bottles of hot water (not too hot to touch) and/or towels. Close the cooler. Place the cooler in a warm spot where it will not be disturbed. "Yogurt has the added idiosyncrasy that it doesn't care to be jostled while growing," notes *Joy*.

6. Check the yogurt after 8 to 12 hours. It should have a tangy flavor and some thickness. If it isn't thick (hasn't "yoged"), warm it up by filling the insulated cooler with hot water around the jar of yogurt, adding more starter, and leaving it 4 to 8 more hours. You can leave it to ferment longer if you wish. It will become more sour, as more of the milk's lactose is converted into lactic acid. A longer fermentation period can often make yogurt digestible even for lactose-intolerant individuals.

7. Yogurt can store in the refrigerator for weeks, though its flavor will become more sour over time. Save some of your yogurt to use as starter for the next batch.

Labneh (Yogurt Cheese)

In many of the cuisines where yogurt is most popular, it is strained into a thicker cheese form. The process is simple. Line a colander with a couple of layers of cheesecloth. Gently pour yogurt into the lined colander, and let it drain into a bowl, covered to keep flies away. The liquid that drains out is whey. Use the whey for other fermentation adventures (see page 88), or in place of water in other cooking or baking.

Straining yogurt in a cheesecloth-lined colander

After a couple of hours you will be left with a much more solid yogurt cheese. Add herbs for a beautiful dip or spread.

Savory Yogurt Sauces: Raita and *Tsatsiki*

Raita is a frequent condiment in Indian cuisine, *tsatsiki* in Greek cuisine. They both mix yogurt with cucumber, salt, and garlic, then diverge just a little in other ingredients. If these sauces have a chance to sit, the flavors will infuse and meld, so if you can, make them at least a few hours (or a day) in advance.

TIMEFRAME: 1 hour

INGREDIENTS (for 4 cups/1 liter):
1 large or 2 small cucumbers
1 tablespoon/15 milliliters salt, or to taste
2 cups/500 milliliters yogurt
4 to 6 cloves garlic, crushed or finely chopped

FOR *RAITA*:
1 teaspoon/5 milliliters cumin, dry-roasted then ground (or pre-ground)
¼ cup/60 milliliters chopped fresh cilantro

FOR *TSATSIKI*:
2 tablespoons/30 milliliters olive oil
1 tablespoon/15 milliliters lemon juice
Ground white pepper
¼ cup/60 milliliters fresh chopped mint and/or parsley

PROCESS:

1. Grate cucumber into a colander, sprinkle with salt, mix well, and leave in a sink or over a bowl to drain excess water for about 1 hour (or longer).

(AND VEGAN ALTERNATIVES)

2. Mix other ingredients with cucumber in a bowl. Try varying these standbys with other herbs (fresh dill, oregano, chives, thyme, bee balm and other flower petals) or grated vegetables (kohlrabi, radishes, burdock).

3. Taste. Much of the salt will have dripped away with the water. If desired, add more salt as well as other seasonings.

4. Refrigerate until ready to serve.

Kishk

Kishk, a Lebanese ferment of yogurt mixed with bulgur wheat, is one of my favorites of the new fermented foods that I've discovered in the course of preparing this book. *Kishk* is also found in Iranian and other Middle Eastern cuisines. In Greece, it is known as *trahanas.* The flavor of *kishk* is unique and distinctive, and I love it. During its fermentation it can smell almost sweet, like coconut. But ultimately it tastes like a strong, musky cheese. *Kishk* is traditionally dried after fermentation, then used to flavor and thicken soups and stews.

TIMEFRAME: About 10 days

INGREDIENTS (for about 1 1/2 cups/ 375 milliliters):

1/2 cup/125 milliliters bulgur wheat

1 cup/250 milliliters yogurt

1/2 teaspoon/2 milliliters salt

PROCESS:

1. Mix yogurt and bulgur in a bowl, cover, and leave overnight.

2. When you look in the morning, the bulgur will have absorbed much of the moisture of the yogurt. Knead the mixture with your hands. Mix it well. If it seems dry, as though it could absorb more moisture, add a little more yogurt and knead it in. Cover it and leave to ferment for about 24 hours more.

3. Check it again the next day, and knead. Continue to knead the bulgur-yogurt dough every day for about 9 days. (If you neglect to knead it, it may develop surface mold; if so, just scrape off of the mold, knead, and proceed.)

4. At the end of this period (a few days more or fewer would not be significant), knead salt into the *kishk.* Spread *kishk* on a baking sheet and leave in a sunny spot, or in the oven with the pilot light on, to dry. As it dries, crumble it into smaller bits to create more surface area.

5. Once the *kishk* is completely dry, use a mortar and pestle or a food processor to crush it into powder and crumbs for storage. Kept dry, it should store for several months in a jar at room temperature.

6. To cook with *kishk,* fry the crumbs with butter, then add water and boil to desired consistency. Cooking will thicken it, as in a flour-based gravy or sauce. *Kishk* cooked with just water is flavorful and delicious; it also enhances soups and stews. Use about 2 tablespoons of *kishk* per cup of water.

Shurabat al Kishk (Lebanese Kishk Soup)

Traditionally, this soup would feature lamb or goat. This is a vegetarian adaptation.

TIMEFRAME: 1/2 hour

INGREDIENTS (for 6 to 8 servings):

2 to 3 onions

2 tablespoons/30 milliliters vegetable oil

3 potatoes

2 carrots

6 cloves garlic

2 tablespoons/30 milliliters butter

1 cup/250 milliliters *kishk*

Salt and pepper to taste

3 tablespoons/45 milliliters fresh parsley

PROCESS:

1. Dice onions and sauté in oil in a soup pot.

2. Once the onion is translucent, add 2 quarts (2 liters) of water, and bring to a boil.

3. Add diced potatoes and carrots (and any other ingredients you like). Cook until soft.

4. Mince garlic and sauté it in butter in a separate skillet. Add *kishk,* and sauté a minute or so. Then take about 1 cup (250 milliliters) of liquid from the soup pot and add it to the *kishk* and garlic. Stir until well blended, then add the liquefied *kishk*-garlic mixture to the soup. Add salt and pepper to taste.

5. Cook 5 to 10 minutes, then serve, garnished with parsley.

Tara and Kefir

As I embarked upon this project, I attended a workshop with herbalist Susun S. Weed, whose books have inspired me for years. Susun raises goats and served delicious homemade goat cheese. I told her about our goats, and we bonded talking about making yogurt and cheese. When I left, she gave me a plastic bag containing curds of a culture called *tara,* which she likes to use in goat milk.

Susun was given *tara* by some Tibetan monk friends, who brought the culture from Tibet. I mix it with milk, leave it in a jar at room temperature for about 24 hours, and love the fizzy light drink it produces.

Tara is a Tibetan cousin of a ferment more widely known as *kefir,* which originates in the Central Asian Caucasus mountains. Some readers may recall a Dannon yogurt commercial from the 1970s, which correlated the longevity of people from "Soviet Georgia" with yogurt consumption. Georgia is in the Caucasus mountains, and the healthful fermented

Kefir grains

milk associated with this region is actually *kefir.* *Kefir* and *tara* are distinguished from yogurt by both the method of fermentation and the types of organisms that the fermentation involves. *Kefir* and *tara* are made with "grains," actually colonies of yeast and bacteria that look like curds, which you strain out of the milk after fermentation, then use to start the next batch. The presence of yeast in addition to *Lactobacilli* gives *kefir* a bubbly effervescence and a small alcohol content (about 1 percent). On the Internet, I found an e-group of *kefir* enthusiasts eager to share their grains, and started fermenting *kefir* alongside *tara.*

For a while, I managed to keep *tara* and *kefir* going in separate jars, maintaining each one's cultural purity. But I really couldn't tell them apart, and eventually I confused the jars and ended up mixing them together. Now my curds are a bastard love child of impure culture, and no less delicious or nutritious for the confusion.

I have not been able to learn much about the history of the *tara* side of the family. I have found exactly two references

(AND VEGAN ALTERNATIVES)

to it in my searching. One was on the menu of a Tibetan restaurant called Tsampa in New York, where a yogurt smoothie was listed as *thara*; the other was in Rinjing Dorje's *Food in Tibetan Life,* where it is transliterated as *dara* as an ingredient in a recipe for buckwheat pancakes called *Drawoe Kura,* which follows this one.

The *kefir* story is full of intrigue. The first *kefir* grains are said to have been a gift from Allah, delivered by his prophet Mohammed. The grains were treasured by the people who possessed them, passed down from generation to generation, and definitely not shared with strangers.

Early in the twentieth century, the "All-Russian Physicians' Society" became interested in obtaining the mysterious source of this healthful drink. Since the keepers of the grains did not wish to share them, this required deception and culture thievery. The scheme involved a young Russian woman named Irina Sakharova, whom the physicians hoped would be able to charm a Caucasus prince, Bek-Mirza Barchorov, into giving her some *kefir* grains. He refused, she tried to leave, he had her kidnapped, she was rescued, and he was charged in the Czar's courts. For reparations, the young woman was awarded the treasure she sought; the court ordered the prince to give her some of his cherished *kefir* grains. In 1908, she brought the first *kefir* grains to Moscow. *Kefir* became, and remains to this day, a popular drink in Russia. In 1973, at age 85, Irina Sakharova was formally recognized by the Soviet Ministry of Health for her role in bringing *kefir* to the Russian people.[3]

Tara or *kefir* is especially easy to make because it requires no temperature con-

trol. The hard part is coming by the grains to get started. I recommend two sources in the Cultural Resources section. One is www.egroups.com/group/Kefir_making. The computer age has brought together this e-group of *kefir* lovers eager to provide grains to new converts. The group's Web master, Dominic Anfiteatro, the source of the story I've just recounted, also has a Web site (www.chariot.net.au/~dna/kefir page) full of interesting fermentation variations you can try with *kefir*. My other recommendation is G.E.M. Cultures, which also sells other delicious and easy-to-use milk cultures such as *Viili* from Finland and *Fil Mjölk* from Sweden.

TIMEFRAME: Days

INGREDIENTS (for 1 quart/1 liter):
1 quart/1 liter milk
1 tablespoon/15 milliliters *kefir* grains

PROCESS:

1. Fill a jar with milk, no more than two-thirds full. Add *kefir* grains, and cap.

2. Leave at room temperature for 24 to 48 hours, agitating jar periodically. Milk will become bubbly, then coagulate and separate. You can remix it by shaking.

3. Strain out the grains with any straining implement. You may need to use a spoon or chopstick (or your clean finger) to stir and keep the strainer from clogging up with grains. Grains will grow and multiply in number over time. You only need a tablespoon (15 milliliters) or so of grains to keep your *kefir* going. You can eat the extras, toss them in the compost, give them away to your friends, or use them to try culturing other things. *Kefir* grains are very versatile.

4. Enjoy your *kefir*, and use the grains to start another batch. *Kefir* can stay out at room temperature and continue to develop, or it can be refrigerated. If you tighten the lid on a jar of fermenting *kefir*, it will develop effervescence.

SOUR CREAM AND WHEY:

5. If you leave your *kefir* to ferment for a few days at room temperatures after removing the grains, it will curdle and separate. When the thick creamy *kefir* floats above the whey, gently spoon it out and enjoy it like sour cream. Use the whey for other fermentation adventures (see page 88), or in place of water in other cooking or baking.

6. Grains can be stored in the fridge in milk for a couple of weeks, or frozen for a couple of months, or dried for a couple of years.

For people who do not drink milk, this same process can be done with soy or rice or nut milk or juice or honey water. See vegan adaptations on page 88 for details.

Drawoe Kura (Tibetan Tara-Buckwheat Pancakes)

These simple buckwheat and *tara/kefir* pancakes are delicious. I cook them for breakfast and love them savory, with *tara/kefir* poured over them, and a little salt and pepper. Some other folks eat them with maple syrup. This recipe is adapted from a recipe in Rinjing Dorje's *Food in Tibetan Life*.

INGREDIENTS (for about 8 large pancakes):
1 cup/250 milliliters buckwheat flour
1 cup/250 milliliters *tara/kefir*
½ teaspoon/2 milliliters sea salt
1 cup/250 milliliters water
Vegetable oil

PROCESS

1. Pour flour and salt in a bowl and add *tara*. Mix well.

2. Add a little water at a time until a thin batter forms that can be poured with a ladle.

3. Heat a well-seasoned pan or griddle, lightly oiled.

4. Ladle batter into the center of the hot pan. Cook the pancake for a moment or two, until brown but not burnt, then flip and cook on the other side.

5. Lightly oil the pan between pancakes.

Buttermilk

Buttermilk is great for pancakes, biscuits, and other baking projects. Its acidity reacts with alkaline baking soda to make things rise. You can use *kefir* in place of buttermilk with fine results. You can also make your own buttermilk easily. Add about ½ cup (125 milliliters) of commercial live-culture buttermilk to 1 quart (1 liter) of milk, leave it at room temperature for about 24 hours, and it will all become buttermilk, which can be stored in a refrigerator for months.

CHEESE MAKING

Cheesemaking involves many different variables. Milk can be transformed into a hard Cheddar cheese, a runny Camembert, a moldy bleu cheese, or, for that matter, Velveeta. Cheese exists in thousands of variations. Traditionally, the variations have been highly localized. A particular cheese is the product of the particular milk of particular animals grazing in particular pastures, subjected to particular temperatures and particular microorganisms, and aged in a particular environment.

An aging cheese is often host to a succession of different organisms, each influencing flavor and texture. Burkhard Bilger recently waxed poetic in the pages of *The New Yorker* on the molds that age the cheese *Saint-Nectaire,* which he had observed through a microscope: "Like a continent evolving in rapid motion, the ripening rind would be invaded by wave after wave of new species, turning from gold to gray to a mottled brown. The cat hairs [a type of mold] would sprout up like ancient ferns, then topple and turn to a velvet compost for their successors. The *penicillium* molds would arrive, their stalks too fine to be seen under a standard microscope, and put down pillowy patches of the palest gray. Then, at last, a faint-pink blush would spread across the surface like a sunset: *Trichothecium roseum,* the flower of the molds."[4]

The local particulars of traditional cheesemaking are being supplanted by the uniformity that global markets demand. In the anthropology journal *Food and Foodways,* Pierre Boisard explored the cultural clash between traditional and industrial methods of cheesemaking in an article called "The Future of a Tradition: Two Ways of Making Camembert, the Foremost Cheese of France." The article quotes Michel Waroquier, a cheesemaker from Carel, France, as he describes the subjective rigors of his art: "Human intervention has to be precisely right; it is limited in scope but its parameters cannot be exactly determined. Experience, the nose, the glance of an eye are the only guides a cheesemaker has; his knack is his only measure. It is up to him to consider a multitude of variables that affect his craft: weather conditions, aspects of the milk, season of the year, amount of rennet required, time needed for optimal coagulation of the milk."[5]

One approach to home cheesemaking is to try to reproduce a specific cheese, buying a commercially available culture and following exact instructions. My approach to cheesemaking has been more experimental, varying the various variables, and seeing what happens. In my experience, every homemade cheese is one-of-a-kind, and every homemade cheese is delicious. Here are a few different simple cheese recipes, to get you started. Vary the process and participate in the creation of the incredible range of textures and flavors that cheeses can embody.

The only special equipment that you need for cheesemaking is cheesecloth. Check in fabric stores, because cheesecloth by the yard is cheaper than the small packages you can buy in supermarkets. In the cloth store in the small town nearest to us, we have a selection of many different densities of weave, from extremely tight to extremely loose. I usually go for a fairly tight weave.

Farmer Cheese

This is the most basic process for making cheese. In its simplest manifestation, it is not even a fermented food. Aging it will introduce cultures.

TIMEFRAME: 20 minutes to several hours

SPECIAL EQUIPMENT:
Cheesecloth

INGREDIENTS (for 3 to 4 cups/750 milliliters to 1 liter of cheese):
1 gallon/4 liters whole milk
½ cup/125 milliliters vinegar

PROCESS:

1. Heat milk to a slow boil, taking care to stir frequently to avoid burning. Remove from heat.

2. Add vinegar, a little at a time while stirring, until the milk curdles.

3. Strain curdled milk through a cheesecloth-lined colander. Collect the curds in the cheesecloth into a ball by lifting the corners of the cheesecloth out of the colander; then join the corners together, and twist the cheesecloth to tighten the ball and force water out. (See illustration on the next page.) You can hang the ball from a hook and let it drip into a bowl for a while. This is farmer's cheese, similar in consistency to ricotta, and great for lasagna or blintzes or Italian-style cheesecake.

For a more solid cheese that holds its form:

4. After you collect curds in cheese-cloth (but before you lift it into a ball), sprinkle about 1 tablespoon (15 milliliters) of salt onto the curds and mix it in thoroughly. The salt pulls moisture from the curds and results in a more solid cheese. At this point you can also add other herbs and spices; their flavors quickly infuse into cheeses. The most beautiful cheeses I've made used red flowers of bergamot or bee balm (*Monarda didyma*), and their gorgeous color bled.

5. Collect cheese into a ball and hang it from a hook to drip. Or you can use

(AND VEGAN ALTERNATIVES)

Collecting cheese into a ball and hanging

Weighted cheese

weight to force moisture out: Place the ball of cheese on a sloped surface (such as a cutting board with something under one end), then place a second flat surface on top of the curds, weighted down. After a couple of hours (or more), the cheese will hold its form when you unwrap the cheesecloth. Indian recipes often call for cubing this cheese, called *paneer,* coating it with spices, frying it, then adding it to spinach *(saag paneer)* or other delicious stews. Or you can serve this cheese on a plate with crackers.

Rennet Cheese

Rennet is a curdling agent containing an enzyme called rennin. Rennet produces very different curds than vinegar or other acids that curdle milk, and rennet cheeses have smoother textures. The other great advantage of rennet is that it curdles milk at lower temperatures, so you can curdle cultured milks into cheese without killing the cultures as boiling would.

Rennet is traditionally obtained from the stomach linings of milk-producing animals, where microorganisms that produce the enzyme reside. Many animal-herding cultures used stomachs to hold milk, and the curdling effect did not go unnoticed. Many cheeses are still made using rennet from animal sources; the rennet I have worked with is cultured in laboratories using vegetable-source nutrients. New England Cheesemaking Supply Co., the source we use, carries rennet from both animal and vegetable sources. Contact information is listed in the Cultural Resources section.

The step-by-step rennet cheesemaking process that follows is the method I learned from David J. Pinkerton, or Pinkie, Short Mountain's most accomplished cheesemaker, a true iconoclast, a peaceful and loving soul whose guiding motto is "Peace, Love, and all that shit."

TIMEFRAME: Days-weeks-months

INGREDIENTS:

1 gallon/4 liters whole milk

1 cup/250 milliliters yogurt and/or *kefir*

3 to 10 drops rennet (source information in Resources section)

3 tablespoons/45 milliliters sea salt

PROCESS:

1. "Ripen" the milk by adding live cultures: Frequent cheesemakers often simply collect milk each time in the same wooden barrel, whose walls become covered with cultures that go on to develop in each batch of milk. The easiest method for the occasional home experimentalist is to pour the milk into a stainless steel pot. Add the yogurt and/or *kefir,* mix well, and gently heat to just above body temperature, around 100°F (38°C). Maintain it at that temperature for 1 to 2 hours to allow the *Lactobacilli* to proliferate. This step is not essential, but adds flavor and health benefits to your cheese. You can maintain the temperature by removing the pot from the heat, covering it, and wrapping it in a blanket, or by periodically rewarming the pot over gentle heat. If the temperature fluctuates between about 90° and 110°F (32° to 43°C), that's fine. Thermometers are fragile and never last long in our chaotic communal kitchen. It's easy to use your body temperature as a gauge; just think of a gentle warm bath.

2. Add rennet, with milk still around 100°F (38°C). The rennet we buy comes in a small plastic container with a dropper. You need just a tiny amount, between 3 and 10 drops per gallon (4 liters) of milk. Three drops will yield a softer cheese and 10 drops a harder cheese. Dilute the rennet in about ¼ cup (60 milliliters) of water before you add it, and stir the milk while you pour the rennet-water solution into it. Once you've added the rennet, stop stirring. It is important to leave the milk still while the rennet works its coagulating magic. Within ½ hour or so, the milk will coagulate. The milk solids will draw together in a mass of curd, and you will notice it pull away from the sides of the pot.

3. Once the milk has coagulated, use a long knife or spatula to gently cut the curd. Reheat over a gentle heat to restore the tem-

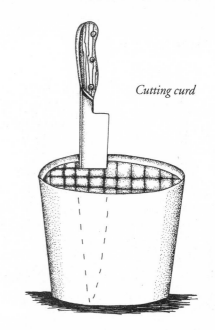

Cutting curd

perature to 100°F (38°C) as you do this. Cutting the curd creates more surface area on the curd exposed to the rennet. Each piece of curd will tighten and shrink. The curd is fragile and must be carefully sliced rather than broken apart. Try to cut curd into pieces of roughly uniform size, around 1-inch cubes, as curds varying much in size will also vary in texture. As you cut curds, keep them moving; gently agitate and stir to prevent them from sinking.

4. Keep it warm. For a soft cheese, maintain the just-above-body-heat temperature for about 10 minutes after cutting the curd. Keeping it warm longer, up to about 1 hour, will make the individual curds continue to tighten, resulting in a harder cheese. Increasing the temperature also hardens the cheese, but don't increase the temperature higher than 110°F (43°C) or you will kill the live cultures. If you increase the temperature fast, you will end up with a more crumbly, grainier cheese. If you increase the temperature gradually, at a rate of no more than 1 degree per minute, you will end up with a smoother, even-textured hardness. "Little wee nuances make a completely different product," explains Pinkie.

5. Strain and salt the cheese: Be gentle! The curds are still fragile. Line a colander with cheesecloth and place in the sink. Use a slotted spoon to carefully scoop out curds and place them in the colander. For cheese, we are primarily concerned with the curds, but whey has many uses, so you might want to save it. (See "Fermenting with Whey," page 88.) Layer curds with salt. Don't be afraid of using lots of salt. It draws water out of the curds and drains away. You can also add herbs or other flavorings at this juncture, if you wish. My friend Toad made an outrageously good cheese layering in toasted crushed sesame seeds. Collect the curds in the cheesecloth into a ball by lifting the corners of the cheesecloth out of the colander; then join the corners together and twist the cheesecloth to tighten the ball and force water out. Hang the ball from a hook and let it drip into a bowl.

6. You can serve the cheese young or age it. The cheese will hold its form once it hangs for a few hours. Eat it right away and it is sure to be delicious. But if you can wait, given some time, cheese develops intense flavors and miraculous textures. Just a week or two of aging can radically alter a cheese. One aging method is to form a dry protective skin. The day after you make the cheese, wrap it in fresh, dry cheesecloth. Do not allow flies to touch the cheese or you may encounter maggots later on. Rewrap the cheese again the next day and the next. The cheesecloth wicks moisture from the cheese. Repeat this daily until the cheesecloth is no longer wet from the moisture of the cheese. Then wrap the cheese in a clean towel and put it in a cool, dark place, or enclose it in wax for longer storage. Alternatively, you can simply submerge the cheese in brine, like sour pickles. This produces a salty, feta-like cheese. However you do it, cheesemaking is an exciting and rewarding adventure.

THE BATTLE OVER RAW CHEESE REGULATIONS

Traditionally, most cheeses have been prepared with methods like those just described, using raw milk and seeking to maintain the enzymes and live cultures present in the milk. Research on pasteurization in the cheesemaking process was first undertaken at the University of Wisconsin in 1907. By 1949, Congress passed a law requiring pasteurization of all milk and dairy products, including cheeses, unless the cheese is aged for at least 60 days.

This has been the status quo for half a century. It has meant that many of the world's finest soft cheeses are unavailable (legally, at least) in the United States. U.S. delegates to the Codex Alimentarius, an international food-standards commission, recently petitioned for an international cheese pasteurization standard and lost. Currently, the

U.S. Food and Drug Administration, the federal agency charged with regulating food safety, is studying possible health hazards related to aged raw-milk cheeses, with an eye toward even more stringent regulations. The possibility of more restrictive cheese pasteurization requirements has quickly galvanized a grassroots response. The FDA study is being branded "an attack on one of society's greatest, most traditional foods. . . . Tampering with fine aged raw-milk cheeses is like slashing an ancient painting by a master, or shredding the original score of a classic symphony." This from the American Society for Microbiology.[6]

A "Cheese of Choice Coalition" of producers and connoisseurs has come together to advocate for the continued availability of raw cheeses. "These cheeses have been with us for thousands of years— and the FDA is trying to turn us into a nation of Velveeta eaters," says coalition-member K. Dun Gifford of the Oldways Preservation and Exchange Trust. "Pasteurization results in increased consistency in the cheesemaking process and more uniform quality in the end product," explains Ruth Flore of the American Cheese Society. "This translates to a lowering of the flavor bar, eliminating the potential to produce a depth and complexity of flavor that can exist with unpasteurized milk cheese." The European Alliance for Artisan and Traditional Raw Milk Cheese (EAT) concurs: "We call on all food-loving citizens of the world to respond now to the defense of . . . a food that has for hundreds of years inspired, given pleasure, and provided sustenance, but is now being insidiously undermined by the sterile hand of global hygiene controls."[7]

Do unpasteurized cheeses really pose a health threat? The U.S. Centers for Disease Control (CDC) compiled a study entitled "Cheese-Associated Outbreaks of Human Illness in the United States, 1973–1992." The CDC analysis found 58 deaths from contaminated cheeses, 48 of them from *listeriosis* traced to a single California factory producing *queso fresco,* a Mexican-style cheese made from milk that had been pasteurized. Food writer Jeffrey Steingarten investigated the CDC findings and reported that not a single death could be attributed to raw-milk cheeses, only a single case of *salmonella.*[8]

If a single case of salmonella justified banning a food, we would have precious few foods to choose from. "If you can't stand a little risk . . . shoot the cow," quipped an anonymous microbiologist.[9] "There

(AND VEGAN ALTERNATIVES)

are no scientific reasons or health needs to compel the sacrifice of these cheeses on the altars of mass production and worldwide standardization," states Flore. Quirky local cheeses that cannot be easily reproduced do not hold much potential in the global marketplace. The homogenization of culture rears its ugly head in the regulatory arena.

Fermenting with Whey: Sweet Potato Fly

Whey is highly nutritious and has many uses. You can use it as a soup stock, in baking, and in the garden. Whey from cultured milk is full of *Lactobacilli,* and can be used as a starter to get all sorts of other things to ferment, from mashed potatoes to ketchup. Sally Fallon's cookbook *Nourishing Traditions* has lots of great ideas for fermenting with whey. Here's a recipe I adapted from that book for a soft drink called Sweet Potato Fly, from Guyana. It's sweet and light and fruity, with only a mild tartness. Eggshell is an ingredient that serves to neutralize the acidity of the lacto-fermentation. Sweet potato fly appeals even to kids and other folks who mostly don't like fermented flavors.

TIMEFRAME: 3 days

INGREDIENTS (for 1 gallon/4 liters):
1 teaspoon/5 milliliters powdered mace
2 large sweet potatoes
2 cups/500 milliliters sugar
½ cup/125 milliliters whey

2 lemons
Cinnamon
Nutmeg
1 eggshell

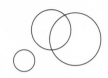

PROCESS:

1. Boil 1 cup (250 milliliters) of water with mace. Remove from heat and allow to cool.

2. Grate the sweet potatoes, and rinse well through a strainer to remove starch.

3. In a large bowl, combine the grated sweet potatoes, 1 gallon (4 liters) of water, sugar, whey, the juice and grated peel of the lemons, and a pinch each of nutmeg and cinnamon.

4. Crush the cleaned eggshell into the mixture. The recipe that inspired me called for folding in stiff beaten egg whites at this point; I don't eat raw eggs so I didn't try it, but it sounds intriguing, doesn't it?

5. Add the cooled boiled mace.

6. Stir, cover to keep flies and dust out, and leave in a warm spot to ferment for about 3 days.

7. Strain into a jug, bottles, or jars, refrigerate, and enjoy.

VEGAN ADAPTATIONS

As I've been working on this project, River, the lone vegan residing at Short Mountain at present, has been experimenting with fermenting a wide variety of non-dairy substances with *kefir*. His results have been excellent and delicious, and I will share them here. I hesitate a bit with the pronouns when I refer to River. Pronouns are so programmed into us and generally selected at a subconscious level. With River, I find that pronoun selection is not only conscious but consciousness-raising. He is biologically female, but male-identified. He is a tranny.

Trannies, or transgendered people, are folks who do not fit neatly into either of the two gender categories we are offered. One response is to create new categories to contain the variety, like drag kings and queens, and transsexuals. More power to them all. But there will always be people whose unique sense of themselves does not conform neatly to the parameters of any gender subcategory. We can take it a step further and treat gender as a fluid construct that can shift over time and through different cultural milieus. Microorganisms do this all the time, transmogrifying into different forms to adapt to shifting conditions. Why can't gender identity be a simple right of self-determination? Trannies are organizing and speaking out and gaining visibility, and I see them as a positive force for change in our world. I'm a bio-boy for gender freedom and self-determination, and I embrace gender-blenders of diverse description. People struggling in the margins need respect and support.

River has made *kefir* from a number of different milk alternatives, every single one of them delicious. My favorite was coconut milk *kefir*. It was a taste sensation, bubbly and rich and sweet and sour. All he did was add about 1 tablespoon (15 milligrams) of *tara/kefir* grains to a can's worth of coconut milk and leave it in a jar (not the can, since fermentation acids can react with metal) for a day or two at room temperature. Though *kefir* has traditionally been used to culture milk, the grains themselves are not animal products. They are communities of yeast and bacteria bound in a gelatinous mass chemically described as a polysaccharide. These grains can be rinsed and soaked in water, then switched to other nutritive liquids. You can *kefir* fruit or vegetable juice, or water with any sweetener you like, or rice milk, soymilk, or nut milk. Cranberry juice dyed the grains red, and Gatorade (!) left a neon blue stain. Whatever the medium, the grains seem to transform it, though they do not rapidly multiply as they do in milk. The process is exactly the same as *kefir*ing milk, described in detail earlier in this chapter.

Pepita Seed Milk and *Kefir*

River's favorite *kefir* is from pepita seed milk. Pepitas are pumpkin seeds, rich in flavor and nutrition; any edible seeds or nuts could be used. River's method is deceptively simple, much easier than soymilk, and tasty, too. The really great thing about finding an alternative to commercial soymilk is that most of the commercial soymilk has such wasteful packaging. Do-it-yourself seed milk just goes in a jar, no fancy multilayered disposable carcass required. Here's River's pepita milk process.

TIMEFRAME: 20 minutes for milk; 1 to 2 days for *kefir*

INGREDIENTS (for about 1 quart/1 liter):

1 cup/250 milliliters pepita seeds (or substitute any seed or nut)

Water

1 teaspoon/5 milliliters lecithin (optional—serves as a binder)

PROCESS:

1. Place pepita seeds in a blender and grind into a fine meal.

2. Add ½ cup (125 milliliters) water and blend into a paste.

3. Add 3 cups (750 milliliters) water and lecithin, if desired, and blend some more.

4. Strain through cheesecloth, pressing to squeeze moisture from the seed solids. I like to throw the solid remains into breads.

5. Add more water a little at a time and stir, until you reach your desired consistency. Store in the refrigerator and stir before use.

6. To *kefir* pepita milk, add 1 tablespoon (15 milliliters) of *kefir* grains to 1 quart (1 liter) of milk, and leave them together in a jar at room temperature for a day or two. Then strain out the curds, as detailed in the *kefir* section. The fermented pepita milk, like every medium transformed by *kefir*, tastes tangy and delicious. And it is full of healthful *Lactobacilli*.

Cultured Soymilk

Yogurt cultures are adaptable to soymilk, though I have not had success with rice or seed milks. Live-culture soy, to use as starter, is available in many health food stores. Use the same proportion of starter, 1 tablespoon (15 milliliters) per quart (liter) of milk, as dairy yogurt, and follow the same steps (see page 76). Cultured soymilk is often thicker than dairy yogurt, and very tasty, too.

Sunflower Sour Cream

Seeds are very versatile and can be transformed into many different textures and consistencies (much like milk). Our community is part of a local food buying club, which provides us with most of the bulk foods we eat. Barbara Joyner, our neighbor who runs this convenient and money-saving enterprise, puts out a newsletter every month and always includes a few recipes, including this one for sunflower cream from fellow buying-club member Lorraine. Orchid whipped up a batch, and I couldn't help myself from putting some of it aside with *kefir* grains. The delicious tart result was the most sour-creamy non-dairy concoction I've ever tried. It tasted great on baked potatoes.

TIMEFRAME: 2 days

INGREDIENTS (for about 2½ cups/ 625 milliliters):

1 cup/250 milliliters raw sunflower seeds

2 tablespoons/30 milliliters raw flaxseed

4 tablespoons/60 milliliters cooked leftover grains

3 tablespoons/45 milliliters olive oil

1 teaspoon/5 milliliters honey (or alternative vegan sweetener)

1 tablespoon/15 milliliters finely chopped onion, scallion, or chives

¼ teaspoon/1 milliliter celery seed

⅓ cup/80 milliliters lemon juice

1 tablespoon/15 milliliters *kefir* grains

PROCESS:

1. Soak sunflower seeds and flaxseed for about 8 hours in enough water to cover them.

2. Drain off and reserve excess water, then purée soaked seeds with other ingredients (except *kefir* grains) in a blender or food processor. Add reserved water, just a little at a time, until the mixture reaches a thick, creamy consistency.

3. Place the mixture in a jar or nonmetal bowl with *kefir* grains. Allow to ferment 1 to 3 days.

4. Remove the *kefir* grains, if you can find them. If not, don't worry; they are edible and nutritious. Enjoy sunflower sour cream on potatoes or as a spread or dip.

FURTHER READING

Carroll, Ricki. *Home Cheese-making.* North Adams, Mass.: Storey Books, 2002.

Carroll, Ricki, and Phyllis Hobson. *Making Cheese, Butter, and Yogurt.* Pownal, Vt.: Storey Books, 1997.

Ciletti, Barbara. *Making Great Cheese.* Asheville, N.C.: Lark Books, 2001.

Stepaniak, JoAnne. *The Uncheese Cookbook.* Summertown, Tenn.: Book Publishing Company, 1994.

8 BREAD (AND PANCAKES)

In Western culture, bread is synonymous with sustenance. This is reflected in our slang, where money can be called "dough" or "bread" and pretty butts are "buns," as well as in our prayers: "Give us this day our daily bread." Bread is more than mere food. The elaborate process of growing wheat and making bread "symbolized civilization's mastery over nature," writes Michael Pollan in *The Botany of Desire*.[1] Bread, or the lack thereof, has inspired revolutions. A rise in the price of bread was one of the sparks that ignited the French Revolution. Bread is a staple food in many parts of the world. It is made in an extraordinary variety of styles. Not all of them are formed into loaves and baked—fried breads and steamed breads, for instance.

Yeast is used in breadmaking to make dough rise. Yeast is a fungus. The predominant type used in breadmaking is classified as *Saccharomyces cerevisiae: saccharo* means sugar, *myces* means fungus, and *cerevisiae* might seem more familiar when you think about the Spanish word for beer, *cerveza*. The same yeast that makes beer makes bread. Both these processes developed simultaneously as grain agriculture developed in the "Fertile Crescent" region of the Middle East.

Beers can be used to start breads, and breads can be used to start beers. They are made from the same ingredients, just with different processes and in different proportions. In both, the yeast does the same thing; the primary thing yeast knows how to do: It consumes carbohydrates and transforms them into alcohol and carbon dioxide. In bread, the carbon dioxide is the more important product. Its bubbles are what rise the bread, giving it texture and lightness. The alcohol evaporates as the bread is cooked.

Though yeast organisms were not isolated or identified until the mid-nineteenth century, the word "yeast" comes from Middle English, with Indo-European roots. Prior to the science of microbiology, yeast referred to the visible action of fermentation, the rising of a dough, or the frothing of a batter or a beer, and to the various clever methods that people developed to perpetuate that transformative power.

"Pure" yeast as we know it was not commercially available until the 1870s. For the thousands of years that bread and beer were being made prior to that industrial development, people relied upon natural yeasts for their fermented pleasures. Yeast is probably already on the flour you make your bread from. It is in the air everywhere, always ready to stop and feast when it comes upon carbohydrate-rich food.

The difference between the yeast you can buy in a store and what you can find and interact with in the world around you is purity. The products available for sale are selected strains. They have been chosen as superior specimens, isolated, and bred. French historian Bruno Latour, in his provocative book *The Pasteurization of France,* observes: "For the first time—for them [microorganisms] as well as for us—they were to form homogenous aggregates . . . which none of their ancestors ever knew."[2] Specialty suppliers sell dozens of strains of yeast, each selected to confer different desired characteristics. They thrive at different temperatures, reproduce at different speeds, tolerate different levels of alcohol, and produce different enzymes and flavors. In laboratories, scientists are busy engineering yeast genes to produce even better breeds. Consumers have a lot of choices, as usual.

The yeasts you find in nature are never pure. They travel in motley company. They are always found with other microorganisms. They embody biodiversity. They have unique flavors. And they are everywhere.

Pure yeasts need to act quickly, before any wild microorganisms have a chance to establish themselves. Wild fermentation is slower. The dough is given a chance to really ferment, breaking down hard-to-digest gluten into more easily absorbed nutrients, and adding B-vitamins. The yeasts are accompanied by *Lactobacilli* and other bacteria, which produce acids and contribute complex sour flavors. I can smell that sour fragrance filling the kitchen as one of my breads bakes in the oven.

Prior to the widespread availability of commercial yeast, people used any one of a number of methods to propagate their yeasts. It can be as simple as using the same vessel repeatedly without washing it in between. Most often breadmakers reserve a bit of their yeasty batter or dough as a "starter." A starter can be maintained for a lifetime and passed on for generations. It often accompanied immigrants on their journey to new unknown lands. Starter is mostly referred to nowadays as "sourdough" or "natural leaven". In recipe books and on store and bakery shelves, sourdough is widely included as a gourmet novelty. But I like to remember that until 130 years ago, all bread was made this way. Any kind of bread you like, except perhaps the totally bland, squishy kinds that fill supermarket shelves, can be made with natural leavening.

People have devoted their lives to the fine art of breadmaking. All sorts of excellent books have been written on various nuanced techniques for making bread. Actually, many bakers I have known feel that breadmaking is a spiritual exercise that connects them to life forces. I quite agree: Like any ferment, bread requires the harnessing and gentle cultivation of life forces. Bread also requires the full-body involvement of kneading. Kneading develops gluten, the rubbery component of wheat (and some other grains, though in smaller quantity), which enables the dough to trap bubbles of gas released by the yeast as it reproduces, thus yielding a light and airy loaf of bread.

First let me walk you through the process of establishing and maintaining a sourdough starter; then I'll explain how that starter can be used in a variety of breads. Sourdough is quite versatile. Once you experience the magic of sourdough breadmaking you are likely to want to experiment. Use your sourdough to create the bread of your dreams.

Basic Sourdough Starter

Starting a sourdough is as easy as mixing flour and water in a bowl and leaving it on the kitchen counter for a few days, stirring as often as you think of it. The yeast is there and will reveal itself. The work is in maintaining the sourdough and keeping it alive and fresh. A sourdough starter requires regular feeding and attention, not unlike a small pet. Potentially you could pass it on to your grandchildren. I have never kept one going for more than a year at a time, fickle lover of travel adventure that I am. But luckily, sourdoughs are easy to start, so I keep starting new ones. Here is the process I use.

TIMEFRAME: About 1 week

INGREDIENTS:
Flour (any kind)
Water
Organic plums, grapes, or berries (optional)

PROCESS:

1. In a jar or bowl, mix 2 cups (500 milliliters) each of water and flour. Do not use water that smells or tastes heavily chlorinated. Starchy water from cooking potatoes or pasta is rich in nutrients that yeasts like, and can be used (cooled to body temperature) instead of plain water. I generally use rye flour because I love all-rye bread, but the flour of any grain will do.

2. Stir the mixture vigorously. One effective technique for speeding up the introduction of wild yeasts into your sourdough starter is to drop a little unwashed whole fruit into it. Often on grapes, plums, and berries you can actually see the

chalky film of yeast ("the bloom") that is drawn to their sweetness. These and other fruits with edible skins (not bananas or citrus) are great for getting sourdoughs bubbling. Use organic fruit for this. Who knows what antimicrobial compounds could lurk on the skins of the fruits of chemical agriculture?

3. Cover the jar with cheesecloth or any other porous material that will keep out flies but allow the free circulation of air.

4. Store your batter in a warm place (70° to 80°F/21° to 27°C is ideal, but work with what you have) with good air circulation. Visit your batter as often as you think of it, at least daily, and stir it vigorously. Agitation distributes yeast activity and stimulates the process.

5. After some number of days you will notice tiny bubbles releasing at the surface of the batter. That is how you can tell the yeast is active. Note that the action of stirring the batter may create some bubbles. Do not confuse these with the bubbles the batter produces when you are not actively introducing air into the mixture. The number of days it will take for yeast to become active in your batter will depend upon environmental factors. Every ecosystem has its own unique microorganism populations. This is why sourdoughs from specific locations can be so distinctive. Can you guess where *Lactobacillus sanfranciscensis* is found?

6. Many cookbooks recommend starting a sourdough with a pinch of packaged yeast to get the process going more quickly. I myself prefer the gratifying magic of the wild yeasts finding their way to the dough. If you do not find bubbles forming after 3 or 4 days, try to find a

(AND PANCAKES)

warmer spot. Or add a commercially available sourdough starter or a pinch of packaged yeast.

7. Once yeast activity is evident, strain out the fruit. Then add 1 or 2 tablespoons (15 to 30 milliliters) more flour to the mixture each day for 3 or 4 days, and continue stirring. You can add any kind of flour, leftover cooked grains, rolled oats, or whole grains. You are now feeding the sourdough. The batter will get thicker, and start to rise, or hold some of the gas the yeast releases, but you want it to remain essentially liquid in form. Add more water if the sourdough gets so thick that it starts to cross over into solidity.

8. Once you have a thick, bubbly batter, your starter is ready to use. When you use it, pour out what you need and be sure to save some of the starter in the jar to keep the sourdough going. All you need is a little; what remains on the edges of the jar will suffice. To replenish the starter, add water roughly equal to the volume you removed for bread (2 cups/500 milliliters for most of the recipes in this book) and the same volume of flour. Stir well and leave it in a warm place to bubble. Keep it going by feeding it a little flour every day or two if you are baking at least weekly. If you use it less frequently you can refrigerate it (thus slowing the yeast's activity). It is best to refrigerate sourdough after the replenished starter has had at least 4 to 8 hours of active bubbly fermentation. A refrigerated starter still needs to be fed once a week or so. A day or two before you plan to bake, move the starter from the fridge to a warm location and feed it, to warm it up and get the yeast active again.

Maintaining a Sourdough Starter

Your sourdough starter can live forever, given regular attention. Replenish it with water and flour every time you use it. Feed it a little fresh flour every day or two. If you go away, feed your sourdough, let it ferment for a few hours, then cover and refrigerate. Sourdough can be stored in the refrigerator for several weeks, or frozen for longer periods. If you neglect your sourdough, it may get very acidic, then eventually putrid. Up to a point, sourdoughs can be easily revived by feeding them fresh flour. Other organisms dominate after the yeast has consumed all its nutrients. But the yeasts remain present and can usually return to dominance when nourished.

Recycled Grain Bread

My fanaticism about recycling food and not letting it go to waste leads me to make most of my breads out of leftover grains. Bread can incorporate a great variety of leftovers, not only grains but vegetables, soups, dairy products, and more. My friend Amy, a champion dumpster diver, is guided by a goddess she calls Refusa. Refusa says: Be creative and daring in your food recycling.

As we embark upon breadmaking together, let me confess that I never ever measure anything when I make bread. I find appropriate proportions through texture. I have tried to offer measurements to guide the novice. Take them with a grain (or is that two?) of salt. Consider the descriptions of consistency and texture more closely than my quantifications. Proper proportions of flour and water can vary quite a bit, depending on humidity.

TIMEFRAME: About 2 days (Exactly how long will depend upon temperature. Be patient. It takes time for food to ferment. Enjoy the smells that the sourdough creates, and the anticipation of how good the bread will taste.)

SPECIAL EQUIPMENT:

Large mixing bowl
Towel
Loaf pans

INGREDIENTS (FOR 2 LOAVES):

2 cups/500 milliliters leftover cooked rice (or oatmeal, millet, buckwheat, or any grain)

2 cups/500 milliliters bubbly sourdough starter

2 cups/500 milliliters water (half can be another leftover liquid: soup stock, beer, sour milk, *kefir*, whey, or pasta or potato cooking water)

8 cups/2 liters flour (at least half of it wheat or spelt)

1 teaspoon/5 milliliters sea salt

PROCESS:

1. Mix a "sponge": Place leftover grains into a large bowl. Pour sourdough starter over it. (Don't forget to replenish your starter.) Add lukewarm water and 4 cups (1 liter) of flour, enough to make it a thick batter. Use at least half wheat flour (whole or white or some of each, or spelt, which is very wheat-like but easier for some people to digest), but augment that with some of whatever other flours you have: buckwheat, rye, and cornmeal are all good. Stir the batter well. This glutenous mass is called a "sponge". Let the sponge sit in a warm place, covered with a moist towel or cloth, for 8 to 24 hours (it can be somewhat flexible around your schedule), stirring occasionally, until it is good and bubbly.

2. When it is good and bubbly, add salt. Salt inhibits the yeast, which is why we keep it out of the starter at the beginning of the process. But salt contributes to the development of the dough and prevents the yeast from acting too quickly; bread without salt tastes flat and lacking. Were the grains you added cooked with salt? If so, add a little less salt.

3. Add flour, about 4 cups (1 liter), gradually. Keep adding flour and stirring it in, until the dough becomes so thick that you cannot effectively stir it with a spoon.

4. Knead the dough well on a floured surface. If you have never kneaded, this involves pushing the heel of your palm into the dough, stretching and flattening it, then folding an edge into the center, pushing and stretching with the heel of your hand, then rotating the dough, folding another edge into the center, and so on. As

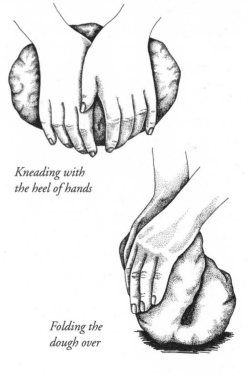

Kneading with the heel of hands

Folding the dough over

(AND PANCAKES)

BREAD **97**

wild

you knead, you will probably need to sprinkle additional flour onto the dough and the kneading surface as the dough starts to feel sticky, which it will do as the flour absorbs the moisture of the dough. You need to knead long enough to "work the gluten" so the dough develops elasticity. Give it at least 10 minutes. A good way to tell if you've kneaded enough is to poke a finger into the dough and remove it. Well-kneaded elastic dough should resist the indentation and push back toward its original form.

5. Place the kneaded ball of dough into a clean, lightly oiled bowl. Cover with a moist, warm towel and set the bowl in a warm place for the dough to rise.

6. Rise the dough until its bulk increases roughly 50 percent, which may take several hours, and is quite variable depending on the temperature and the character of the dough and the yeast that has developed. In a cool space, such as an unheated kitchen at temperatures around 50° to 60°F (10° to 16°C), rising can take as long as a couple of days. But it will happen.

7. Once the dough has risen, form it into loaves. First, lightly oil 2 loaf pans. Then knead each loaf for a moment, sprinkling a little more flour if the dough is sticky. I generally flatten dough into a small oval or rectangular form and roll it into loaves, which I then lay into the oiled loaf pans.

8. Rise for another hour or two, until the loaves have risen substantially.

9. Preheat oven to 400°F (205°C), and bake. (Note that ovens vary; at high temperatures, some ovens burn bread on the outside before it fully cooks inside. If that should happen to you, try baking at 350°F (175°C) for about 10 minutes longer.)

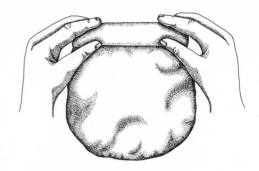

Forming loaves

10. Check loaves after 40 minutes. Most likely they will require a little more time than this—maybe 45 or 50 minutes, maybe even longer. The way to test doneness of bread is to remove it, upside down, from the loaf pan. Tap the bottom of the loaf. When it is done it will sound hollow, like a drum. If it's not done, return it to the oven quickly and continue baking.

11. When the bread is done, remove it from the hot pan and cool it on a rack or cool surface. The bread continues to cook and set as it cools. It's hard to be patient when it smells so good, but try to wait 15 minutes before cutting and it'll taste that much better.

This is the basic process. From here, using your sourdough starter, the possibilities are endless.

Onion-Caraway Rye Bread

My favorite kind of bread to eat is rye bread. The flavor of rye is very rich. Most cookbooks offer rye bread recipes using half wheat flour, which is a fine variation, but I love bread that is all rye. Historically, this was the bread of the northern regions of Europe, where the weather is cold and damp. Rye bread is hearty sustenance for people in harsh climates. After wheat was introduced in these regions (mostly spread by the Catholic Church as its influence moved north), wheat became the grain of the elite while rye remained the staple of ordinary people working the land.

Rye is different from wheat in a number of ways. In rye bread, gluten is not the primary component that traps the carbon dioxide produced by fermentation. Rye contains polysaccharide compounds called "pentosans," which are extremely viscous and enable the dough to hold gas.[3] Pentosans do not require kneading, so 100 percent rye breads do not need to be kneaded.

TIMEFRAME: About 2 days

INGREDIENTS (for 2 loaves):
4 onions
2 tablespoons/30 milliliters vegetable oil
2 cups/500 milliliters sourdough starter

3 cups/750 milliliters water
1 tablespoon/15 milliliters caraway seeds, whole or crushed
8 cups/2 liters rye flour (for best results, coarsely grind whole rye berries, though using pre-milled rye flour is fine)
1 teaspoon/5 milliliters salt

PROCESS:

1. Chop onions, and sauté in vegetable oil until browned. Cool.

2. Mix a sponge: Combine the browned onion, sourdough starter, water, caraway seeds, and half the rye flour in a bowl and stir well. Cover and leave to ferment in a warm place, stirring occasionally, for 8 to 24 hours, until it is good and bubbly. (Don't forget to replenish your starter.)

3. Add more flour and salt. Keep adding rye flour, a little at a time, until the dough becomes so thick that you cannot effectively stir it with a spoon. Cover with a moist towel and leave to ferment and rise, for 8 to 12 hours, until its bulk has increased noticeably.

4. Form into loaves: Rye dough is sticky, nowhere as cohesive and self-contained as wheat dough. Wetting your hands will make rye dough easier to handle and form. Form loaves with your wet hands and place them in lightly oiled loaf pans; alternatively spoon dough into loaf pans, then smooth the top with your wet hands. Leave loaves for another hour or two, until they rise noticeably.

5. Preheat oven to 300°F (150°C) and bake.

6. Check loaves after 1½ hours. It will probably take 2 hours, or even longer, but check earlier. Test doneness by removing a loaf from its pan and tapping the bottom.

When it is done it will sound hollow. If it's not done, return it to the oven quickly and continue baking.

7. Cool bread on racks. Most yeasted breads you are used to are best eaten fresh and dry out quickly. A major advantage of sourdough rye bread is that it retains its moisture and gets better with age, for several *weeks* (no kidding). The crust can become hard and dry, but slice through it with a sharp serrated knife to find soft, moist, delicious, sour bread. Dense breads like this are best in thin slices.

Pumpernickel

Pumpernickel is a dark rye bread, traditionally made from coarsely ground rye and often darkened with molasses, espresso, carob powder, and even cocoa powder. You can add one or all of these ingredients to the above rye bread recipe (and omit the onions and caraway seeds, or not) to yield dark pumpernickel bread. Use espresso, cooled until comfortable to the touch, in place of 1 cup (250 milliliters) of water, and carob and/or cocoa powder in place of 1 cup (250 milliliters) of flour in the sponge. Add a couple of tablespoons (30 milliliters) of molasses also at the sponge stage, then proceed as for rye bread.

Sonnenblumenkernbrot (German Sunflower Seed Bread)

France and Italy are the European nations most acclaimed for their breadmaking traditions, perhaps because their loaves are so light and airy. But the European country whose bread most excites me is Germany.

I particularly love the dense moist *sonnenblumenkernbrot.*

TIMEFRAME: About 2 days

INGREDIENTS (for 2 loaves):
2 cups/500 milliliters bubbly sourdough starter
2 cups/500 milliliters lukewarm water
4 cups/1 liter sunflower seeds (hulled)
6 cups/1.5 liters wheat flour (white and/or whole-wheat, as you prefer)
2 cups/500 milliliters rye flour
1 teaspoon/5 milliliters salt

PROCESS:
1. Mix a sponge: Stir together in a bowl the sourdough starter, lukewarm water, sunflower seeds, and half of the wheat and rye flour. (Don't forget to replenish your starter.)
2. Ferment in a warm place 8 to 24 hours, until it is good and bubbly.
3. Add the salt and remaining flour. Mix into a stiff dough, and knead. Then proceed as for "Recycled Grain Bread," from step 4, page 97.

Challah

Sourdough breadmaking is most definitely not limited to dense whole grain loaves like the ones covered so far. The traditional bread of the Jewish Shabbat (Sabbath) ritual is *challah,* a light, eggy, braided loaf. In my family, we didn't observe much religious tradition, but we sure loved *challah.*

My Uncle Len's mother Tobye Hollander was famous for the *challah* she made for her Shabbat observance every Friday. She was born in the nineteenth century, and when I was a child, she and her husband Herman were the most ancient people in my universe. Tobye's *challah*-making was acclaimed enough that her recipe was deemed "fit to print" in *The New York Times*. Tobye's recipe (like every *challah* recipe I've seen) calls for commercial yeast, but I've adapted it to illustrate the versatility of wild yeast sourdough.

TIMEFRAME: 12 to 24 hours

INGREDIENTS (for 1 large loaf):
1 cup/250 milliliters bubbly sourdough starter
1¼ cup/310 milliliters water, divided
7 cups/1.75 liters white flour
1 tablespoon/15 milliliters sugar
2 teaspoons/10 milliliters sea salt
3 tablespoons/45 milliliters vegetable oil
3 eggs, beaten

PROCESS:

1. Make a sponge by mixing active, bubbly sourdough starter with 1 cup (250 milliliters) of lukewarm water and 2 cups (500 milliliters) of sifted white flour. (Don't forget to replenish your starter.) Stir the sponge well, cover it, and leave it in a warm spot for a few hours, until the whole thing is good and bubbly. You can leave the sponge for as long as about 24 hours. It can be flexible to your schedule.

2. Combine the sugar, salt, oil, and ¼ cup (60 milliliters) of water in a heat-resistant measuring cup or small metal bowl. Heat it by setting the cup or bowl in a saucepan of warm water over a low flame. When the mixture is lukewarm, add the beaten eggs, reserving about 1 tablespoon (15 milliliters) of the eggs for brushing on the finished loaf. Continue to gently heat

the pan of water while whisking or stirring the mixture, until it is smooth and custard-like. Do not allow this mixture to heat to the point where it stings your finger; keep it under 115°F (46°C).

3. Blend the warm egg mixture into the bubbly sponge.

4. Sift the remaining 5 cups (1.25 liters) of flour into a large bowl, and form a well in the center. Pour the sponge-egg mixture into the well and mix into a dough. The dough may not absorb all the flour, or it may require a little more; let texture guide you. Once it forms a soft, cohesive ball, Tobye told *The New York Times*, "then comes the revolution."

5. Tobye recommends kneading directly in the bowl, which is much easier to clean up than using a countertop. Knead for at least 10 minutes. "Knead away for dear life," instructs Tobye, "up and around, down and outwards. Pat it gently and say a prayer." This part is very important: Put clear intentions into your loaf.

6. Lightly oil the surface of the ball of kneaded dough and place it in the bowl. Wet a towel with warm water, wring excess water out, and cover the bowl with the damp towel. Set the bowl in a warm place and leave it to rise for about 3 hours, until the dough has doubled in bulk.

7. Punch down the risen dough, knead for a few moments, and then divide it into three equal parts. Shape the braided loaf by rolling and squeezing each ball into a rope about 18 inches (45 centimeters) long. Line the three ropes up side by side, join them together at one end, and braid them, lifting a rope from one side into the middle, then from the other, and so on. (See illustration on the next page.) When

wild

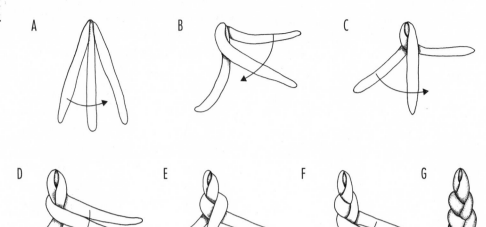

Braiding challah

you reach the end of your ropes (as it were), join them together and tuck them under the end of the braid.

8. Lightly oil a cookie sheet, and gently lift the braided loaf onto it. Leave the loaf in a warm spot to rise for 1 or 2 hours, until it has roughly doubled.

9. Preheat oven to 400°F (250°C).

10. Brush the top of the loaf *gently* with the reserved egg.

11. Bake 40 to 45 minutes, until lightly browned. Cool on a rack near an open window to increase crustiness.

12. Enjoy *challah* fresh. If it dries out, it makes outstanding French toast.

Afghani Bread

I worked on this book through the tragic events of September 11, 2001, and felt powerless as the repercussions of that day unfolded. When the United States retaliated with massive attacks against Afghanistan, I decided to honor the culture of that country by learning something about Afghani cuisine. Of course, like every cui-

sine, it contains fermentation traditions. Once I read about Afghani bread, I remembered eating it as a kid in New York, one of the many exotic ethnic foods my adventurous mother discovered and brought home.

Afghani bread is a delicious flatbread, spiced with black cumin seeds *(Nigella sativa)*, a Middle Eastern spice quite distinct from the larger cumin seeds more commonly found in the United States and used in Mexican and Indian cuisines.

TIMEFRAME: About 4 to 8 hours

INGREDIENTS (for 1 large flatbread, enough for 6 to 8 servings):

1 cup (250 milliliters) bubbly sourdough starter

2 cups (500 milliliters) whole-wheat flour

2 cups (500 milliliters) unbleached white flour

1 teaspoon (5 milliliters) sea salt

¼ cup (60 milliliters) vegetable oil

½ cup (125 milliliters) lukewarm water

1 egg yolk

1 tablespoon (15 milliliters) black cumin seeds

PROCESS:

1. Check to see if the sourdough starter is actively bubbling. If not, add some flour, mix well, and leave it in a warm spot for 1 hour or so until it is visibly active.

2. Mix the flours and salt in a mixing bowl and create a well in the center.

3. Pour sourdough starter and oil into the well in the flour and mix into a dough. Add additional lukewarm water just a little at a time until all the flour blends into a cohesive ball. (Don't forget to replenish your starter.)

4. Knead the dough on a lightly floured surface for 5 to 10 minutes.

5. Return the dough to the bowl and cover the bowl with a moist towel. Leave the dough in a warm spot to rise.

6. Allow the dough to rise until it has roughly doubled in volume. This time can be highly variable, depending upon tem-perature and how active your starter is. It could take just 2 to 3 hours, or possibly 8 hours or even longer.

7. Preheat the oven to 350°F (175°C).

8. On a floured surface, roll the dough into a sheet less than 1 inch (2.5 centimeters) thick. Roll from the center out toward the sides, trying to maintain uniform thickness. Flip the sheet of dough over and work on the other side. You could aim for a rectangle or an oval, or let it assume an amorphous amoeba-like form. Place the sheet of dough onto an ungreased cookie sheet.

9. Mix the egg yolk with 1 tablespoon (15 milliliters) of water. Brush (or otherwise spread) the egg and water mixture onto the surface of the dough, then sprinkle black cumin seeds over it.

10. Bake for 20 to 25 minutes, until the top is golden. Do not be alarmed if it puffs up like a giant pita bread.

SPROUTING GRAINS AND ESSENE BREAD

Essene bread is a very unusual, moist, sweet style of bread. It is made by sprouting whole grains, then grinding them into dough and drying, rather than baking the loaves, at very low temperatures. Sprouting grains makes them much sweeter. Germination creates an enzyme, diastase, that transforms the starch of the grain into sugars. Sprouting is a method commonly used in beer-making, which we will get to in chapter 11. Sprouted grains are always used in Essene bread, but they make a delicious addition to any kind of bread.

The Essenes were a Jewish ascetic sect in existence from about the second century B.C. to the second century A.D. They were pacifists who shared property communally, did not engage in commerce, and followed very specific dietary strictures. Traditionally, Essene bread is made without any fermentation. However, adding sourdough to the ground grains and letting them ferment for a day or two adds a delicious sour flavor to the sweet bread, and makes the loaves a bit less dense.

Sprouting Grains

A number of other fermentation processes in the remaining chapters also involve sprouting and refer to these directions. Each recipe specifies the type and amount of grain to use. For a hearty loaf of Essene bread, start with 3 cups (750 milliliters) of any whole grain: wheat berries and/or rye berries and/or spelt berries and/or oat groats and/or others.

TIMEFRAME: 2 to 3 days

SPECIAL EQUIPMENT:

Sprouting setup: If you have something specifically designed for sprouting, use what you've got. I sprout in a wide-mouth gallon (4-liter) jar with a piece of mesh or cheesecloth stretched over the mouth, secured with a rubber band.

PROCESS:

1. Soak whole grains in water, in a jar as described above, for about 12 to 24 hours at room temperature.

2. Drain the water (drink it as Rejuvelac, described on page 121). Set the jar

Sprouting jar with mesh, draining

upside down in a quart-size (liter) measuring cup or a small bowl. The important thing is that the jar rests safely above wherever the water drains. If the grains sit in water they will rot rather than germinate.

3. Rinse the sprouts with fresh water at least twice a day, morning and evening, more often if you think of it. In hot weather especially, rinse often. The aim is to keep the sprouts from drying out or molding.

4. You'll know the grains have germinated when you see little tails emerging from them. Use them (or dry them) within 2 or 3 days of germination for maximum sweetness. Be sure to keep rinsing the sprouts at least twice a day.

Essene Bread

TIMEFRAME (including sprouting time):
4 to 5 days

INGREDIENTS (for 1 hearty loaf):
3 cups/750 milliliters whole grains, sprouted
¼ cup/60 milliliters sourdough starter
½ teaspoon/2 milliliters sea salt

PROCESS:

1. Sprout grains, as described above.

2. Grind the sprouted grains. I've always done this with a food processor, but I imagine the Essenes used some stone grinding implement. Use the tools available to you. Leave some of the sprouted grains whole, if you wish.

3. Add the sourdough and salt, and stir the mixture thoroughly. (Don't forget to replenish your starter.) You could also add sunflower seeds and herbs, or raisins and grated carrots. As always, add whatever additional ingredients you like.

4. Lightly oil a loaf pan and pour the sprouts-sourdough-salt mixture into the pan.

5. Ferment in the pan, covered to keep out flies, at room temperature for a day or two.

6. Dry loaf: The Essenes dried their bread in the sun. You can too, if it's a hot sunny day in summer when the days are long. Dry it in the loaf pan for half the day, then flip it over and remove the pan to dry the bottom. I've often dried mine in an oven set at 200°F (95°C) for about 4 hours. You can tell it's ready when the bread shrinks away from the sides of the pan. A solar oven that intensifies the Sun's heat or an air-dryer would be other effective tools for drying Essene loaves.

Injera (Ethiopian Sponge Bread)

One special sourdough bread I love is *injera,* the spongy bread that is a staple in Ethiopian cuisine. In Ethiopian restaurants, food is served on trays lined with *injera,* and you eat by ripping off pieces of *injera* and scooping food into it. *Injera* is generally cooked in advance and served at room temperature. A recipe for Groundnut Sweet Potato Stew follows this one. However, any saucy dish would be good with *injera,* and an Internet search will yield many other yummy Ethiopian recipes.

TIMEFRAME: About 24 hours

INGREDIENTS (for 18 to 24 *injera*):
2 cups/500 milliliters bubbly sourdough starter
5 cups/1.25 liters lukewarm water
2 cups/500 milliliters whole-wheat flour
2 cups/500 milliliters *teff* flour (*Teff* is a grain grown and used in Ethiopia. If you can't find it, use millet flour or all wheat.)
1 teaspoon/5 milliliters salt
1 teaspoon/5 milliliters baking soda or baking powder (optional)
Vegetable oil

PROCESS:

1. Mix the batter in a large jar or bowl: Start with bubbly sourdough starter (don't forget to replenish the starter), then add water and flour, and stir. The mixture should have the consistency of thin pancake batter. Add more water if necessary. Cover to keep flies out.

2. Leave to ferment in a warm place, stirring as often as you think of it. Leave it for about 24 hours.

3. When you are ready to cook *injera,* add salt.

4. For the next step you have a few options. If you really like sour flavors and you can be content with moderately bubbly bread, make the *injera* as a natural leaven. Stir 1 tablespoon (15 milliliters) of fresh flour into the batter to invigorate the yeast. For a more bubbly bread, add 1 teaspoon (5 milliliters) of baking soda to the batter and stir well. Baking soda leavens because it's alkaline and reacts with the acid in the sourdough, thereby neutralizing some of the sour flavor. Alternatively, you can leaven with 1 teaspoon (5 milliliters) of baking powder. Baking powder contains baking soda as well as acid compounds that react with the soda when wet, so it produces comparable bubbling with less of a neutralizing effect on the acid flavor.

5. Whichever leavener you add, stir well and let the mixture sit for a few moments before cooking.

6. Heat a well-seasoned cast-iron skillet (or anything you would make pancakes on) over medium heat. Lightly coat pan with oil using a brush or paper towel.

7. Pour the batter onto the hot skillet, taking care to spread it as thinly as possible. If the batter won't spread thinly, thin it with a little more water. Cook over medium heat, hot enough to sizzle when you pour batter on, but not so hot that the *injera* browns quickly.

8. Cover the pan as the injera cooks. Cook until holes appear all over and the top is dry. Cook on one side only; do not flip. Remove from pan onto towel to cool.

9. Cooled *injera* may be stacked and wrapped in a towel.

Groundnut Sweet Potato Stew

MaxZine, who lives down the road at IDA, another queer community 10 miles away, has encouraged my fermentation fetish for years, mostly by organizing major feasts around fermented goodies. One year it was tempeh Reuben sandwiches for two hundred people. Ethiopian nights have become an annual event. I make *injera* and *t'ej*, Ethiopian-style honey wine (see page 129), and he makes the rest. This dish is one he adapted from the cookbook *Sundays at Moosewood Restaurant*. "Groundnut" is what the peanut (*Arachis hypogaea*) is called in English-speaking regions of Africa. In Africa, yams would probably be used rather than sweet potatoes, but MaxZine grows amazing sweet potatoes, and they are what is gener-

ally found (and often confused with yams) in this country. This recipe is augmented by Jerusalem artichokes, which are not an African vegetable at all, but a beloved winter tradition among many American gardeners. The Jerusalem artichokes add a lovely varied texture to this dish. If you don't have Jerusalem artichokes available, just proceed without them.

TIMEFRAME: 30 to 40 minutes

INGREDIENTS (for 6 to 8 servings):
2 cups/500 milliliters chopped onions
2 tablespoons/30 milliliters vegetable oil
3 cups/750 milliliters cubed sweet potatoes
3 cloves garlic, chopped
½ teaspoon/2 milliliters cayenne
2 teaspoons/10 milliliters ginger
1 teaspoon/5 milliliters cumin
1 tablespoon/15 milliliters paprika
1 tablespoon/15 milliliters fenugreek
1 teaspoon/5 milliliters salt
Dash each cinnamon and clove
4 cups/1 liter fresh or canned tomatoes
1 cup/250 milliliters apple juice, or 1 cup/250 milliliters water plus 1 tablespoon/15 milliliters honey
¾ cup/185 milliliters peanut butter
2 cups/500 milliliters sliced Jerusalem artichokes
3 cups/750 milliliters cabbage or other dark leafy greens, chopped

PROCESS:

1. In a good-sized, deep cooking pot, sauté the onions in oil until translucent, about 5 minutes.

2. Add sweet potatoes, garlic, and cayenne; sauté, covered, for 5 minutes.

3. Add all the other ingredients except the peanut butter, Jerusalem artichokes, and greens. Bring to a boil, reduce heat, and simmer about 10 minutes.

4. Remove ½ to 1 cup (125 to 250 milliliters) of the hot liquid from the pot, and combine it with the peanut butter into a creamy paste. Add the thinned peanut butter, Jerusalem artichokes, and greens to the pot, and simmer about 5 more minutes, until the vegetables are tender. Add more liquid if the stew is too thick, and adjust seasonings to taste.

5. Serve with *injera* and/or over millet.

Alaskan Frontier Sourdough Hotcakes

Sourdough was an important and mythological food along the American frontier. Pioneers valued sourdough for its rich nutrition, its hardiness and reliability, and the ease of replenishing it in places where groceries were hard to come by. San Francisco's signature sourdough is a memento of the California gold rush. In Alaska, the frontiersmen themselves were known as "sourdoughs," so dearly did they cherish this staple provision. "A real Alaskan Sourdough would as soon spend a year in the hills without his rifle, as to tough it through without his bubbling sourdough pot."

This quote is from Ruth Allman's longhand volume *Alaska Sourdough: The Real Stuff by a Real Alaskan.*[4] Allman recounts fantastic stories about the popularity of sourdough. "Somehow, word got around that baking powder, like saltpeter, was an anaphrodisiac. The he-man of the North was justly proud of his virility, as attested by the size of some of Alaska's half-breed families. He took no chances of his libido being impaired. The old-time Alaskan would not include baking powder biscuits in his regular diet. Thus was born the fame and popularity of sourdough."

The Arctic cold presented challenges to sourdough. "There is a serious problem when the thermometer skids down to –50 degrees," Allman writes. "Many a winter traveler has wrapped his sourdough pot in a canvas tarp and taken it to bed to keep it from freezing—to make sure he would have his sourdough for food tomorrow. While mushing on the trail with the temperature flirting below zero, Jack [her husband] would put some sourdough in an old Prince Albert tobacco can. This he tucked inside the pocket of his wool shirt to make certain it would not freeze. It takes very little sourdough to start the old sourdough pot a-bubbling again."

Allman recommends using baking soda in sourdough pancakes to neutralize sourness. "Sourdoughs never need to have the strong sour taste—only a fresh yeasty flavor . . . Remember *soda sweetens*."

TIMEFRAME: 8 to 12 hours (Mix batter the night before for breakfast pancakes.)

INGREDIENTS (for about 16 pancakes):
1 cup/250 milliliters bubbly sourdough starter
2 cups/500 milliliters lukewarm water
2½ cups/625 milliliters whole-wheat pastry flour (and/or white flour)
2 tablespoons/30 milliliters sugar (or other sweetener)
1 egg
2 tablespoons/30 milliliters vegetable oil
½ teaspoon/2 milliliters salt
1 teaspoon/5 milliliters baking soda

PROCESS:

1. In a large bowl, mix the sourdough starter, lukewarm water, flour, and sugar. Stir until smooth. Cover and leave to ferment in a warm spot, 8 to 12 hours. (Don't forget to replenish your starter.)

2. When you are ready to make pancakes, beat the egg and add it to the batter, along with the oil and salt. Stir until the texture is smooth and even.

3. Mix the baking soda with 1 tablespoon/15 milliliters of warm water and fold it gently into the sourdough mixture.

4. Heat a cast-iron pan or other griddle, and brush with oil.

5. Ladle the batter into pancakes of whatever size you like. When many bubbles have formed on the surface, flip and cook the other side. Cook well, to a medium brown.

6. Serve the pancakes as they are cooked, or place in a warm oven until they are all cooked. Serve with yogurt and maple syrup.

Savory Rosemary-Garlic Sourdough Potato Pancakes

These excellent and unusual potato pancakes are another creation of Short Mountain's culinary wonder, Orchid.

TIMEFRAME: 8 to 12 hours (or longer if desired)

INGREDIENTS (for about 30 3-inch/ 8-centimeter pancakes):

2 to 3 potatoes or sweet potatoes (enough for 2 cups/500 milliliters grated)
1 cup/250 milliliters sourdough starter
2 cups/500 milliliters lukewarm water
1 cup/250 milliliters whole-wheat pastry flour
1 cup/250 milliliters rye flour
½ cup/125 milliliters white flour
1 tablespoon/15 milliliters rosemary, crushed
1 egg
2 tablespoons/30 milliliters vegetable oil
½ teaspoon/2 milliliters salt
5 tablespoons/75 milliliters (or more) minced garlic

PROCESS:

1. Parboil the potatoes in water for about 15 minutes, until they are easy to penetrate with a fork. Cool and grate potatoes.

2. In a large jar or bowl, mix the active, bubbly sourdough starter with the lukewarm water, the grated potatoes, flours, and rosemary. Stir well, cover, and leave to ferment at least 8 to 12 hours. Be sure to replenish your starter with additional water and flour.

3. When you are ready to make pancakes, add a beaten egg, oil, and salt to the bubbly sourdough batter.

4. Heat a skillet and brush with oil. Using a measuring cup, pour the batter into small 3-inch (8-centimeter) pancakes. Sprinkle some minced garlic on each pancake. When many bubbles have formed, flip and cook the other side. Cook well, to a medium brown.

5. Serve the pancakes as they are cooked, or place in a warm oven until they are all cooked.

6. Serve with yogurt, *kefir*, or sour cream.

Sesame Rice Sourdough Crackers

Crackers are easy to make, especially delicious from sourdough, and gorgeously irregular when handmade. One of my fellow communards described mine as "organically shaped fractals." This recipe was inspired by a recipe in *The Tassajara Bread Book* by Edward Espe Brown.

TIMEFRAME: 16 to 24 hours (or more)

INGREDIENTS (for about 50 crackers):
1 cup/250 milliliters leftover cooked rice
½ cup/125 milliliters sourdough starter
½ cup/125 milliliters water
2 tablespoons/30 milliliters vegetable oil
2 tablespoons/30 milliliters sesame oil
1 cup/250 milliliters whole-wheat pastry flour
1 tablespoon/15 milliliters salt
4 cloves garlic, crushed or finely chopped
1 cup/250 milliliters rice flour
3 tablespoons/45 milliliters sesame seeds

PROCESS:

1. Mix a sponge of the leftover cooked rice, sourdough starter, water, oils, and whole-wheat pastry flour. Stir into a thick batter and leave it to ferment about 8 to 12 hours.

2. Once it is good and bubbly, add the salt, garlic, and rice flour. Knead into dough, adding a little more flour if the dough seems sticky. There is no need to knead for a long time. Leave the dough to ferment about 8 to 12 more hours.

3. Preheat the oven to 325°F (160°C). Brush a cookie sheet with oil. On a floured surface, roll out baseball-sized balls of dough one at a time, getting each as thin as you can roll it. Break rolled-out dough by hand or with a cutting tool into individual crackers and place on the cookie sheet. Prick crackers with a fork to increase surface area and help them crisp during baking.

4. Brush crackers with oil, sprinkle sesame seeds on the surface, and bake 20 to 25 minutes, until dry and crispy.

OTHER BREAD AND PANCAKE RECIPES

See "*Dosas* and *Idlis*" in chapter 6, "*Drawoe Kura*" (Tibetan *Tara*-Buckwheat Pancakes)" in chapter 7, and "Sour Corn Bread" in chapter 9.

FURTHER READING

Brown, Edward Espe. *The Tassajara Bread Book* (25th Anniversary Edition). Boston: Shambhala Publications, 1995.

Leader, Daniel, and Judith Blahnik. *Bread Alone: Bold Fresh Loaves from Your Own Hands*. New York: William Morrow & Co., 1993.

Reinhart, Peter. *Brother Juniper's Breadbook: Slow Rise as Method and Metaphor*. Reading, Mass.: Aris Books, 1991.

Robertson, Laurel, Carol Fliners, and Bronwen Godfrey. *Laurel's Kitchen Bread Book: A Guide to Whole-Grain Breadmaking*. New York: Random House, 1985.

Wing, Daniel, and Alan Scott. *The Bread Builders: Hearth Loaves and Masonry Ovens*. White River Junction, Vt.: Chelsea Green Publishing Co., 1999.

Wood, Ed. *World Sourdoughs from Antiquity*. Berkeley, Calif.: Ten Speed Press, 1996.

9 FERMENTED-GRAIN PORRIDGES AND BEVERAGES

BREAD IS a very refined grain product. The leavening works best with only a few specific grains like wheat and rye. You almost never hear of bread made primarily from oats or millet, for example. Also, it takes quite a bit of time and energy to mill grain, knead it, and heat an oven. Ovens themselves are a relatively advanced technology, not accessible to many people surviving (or not) with scarce resources. Bread as we know it is not found at all in some cultures, and even in cultures with long histories of breadmaking, bread has often been available only to the elite. Fermentation, on the other hand, has always been accessible to people of all social strata.

There are many traditions of grain fermentation that cannot be described as bread, or even as pancakes. Just as flour and water left to their own devices become sourdough that can be made into bread, so millet and water will ferment, and that ferment is used in West Africa to make a porridge called *ogi*. Grain ferments can appear in solid forms, like *ogi*, sweet Japanese *amazaké*, and countless other porridge-like ferments.

Grains can also be fermented into liquid forms, not only alcoholic brews like beer (covered in chapter 11), but into a huge variety of nutritious acidic beverages. Where I live in Tennessee, the earlier Cherokee inhabitants of the land drank a sour corn drink called *Gv-no-he-nv*. In Russia, people drink *kvass,* made by refermenting old bread. And raw foods enthusiasts enjoy a fermented tonic drink called *rejuvelac.*

Corn and Nixtamalization

Corn was the main agricultural staple of the Americas, North and South, prior to the arrival of Europeans. Life revolved around corn, and still does for many people. Traditional usage of corn differed from how Europeans adapted it in one important respect: a process called "nixtamalization". This is the anglicized version of an Aztec word. In the middle of the word you can find the word *tamale.* Tamales and most other Mexican corn products are prepared using this process. Nixtamalized cornmeal in Mexican markets is called *masa,* and the whole kernels are called *posole.* The corn so treated is known in North America as *hominy.*

The process of nixtamalization is simple. The corn is soaked, and then cooked with lime (the alkaline substance, not the citrus fruit) or wood ash, then rinsed. This alkalinizing process greatly enhances the nutritional quality of corn. Specifically, it alters the ratio of available amino acids, rendering nixtamalized corn a complete

protein, and making niacin in the corn more available to humans.[1] "So superior is nixtamalized maize to the unprocessed kind that it is tempting to see the rise of Mesoamerican civilization as a consequence of this invention," writes historian Sophie D. Coe.[2] Europeans imported maize, but not the nixtamalization process, and maize-dependent cultures that developed outside the Americas consistently developed widespread pellagra, a niacin deficiency disease, and kwashiorkor, a protein deficiency disease, which are rare where nixtamalization is practiced.

Nixtamalization is not itself a fermentation process. But the traditional corn fermentation processes use nixtamalized corn as the point of departure, so I will briefly describe the process.

TIMEFRAME: About 12 to 24 hours

INGREDIENTS (for about 4 cups/1 liter posole):

2 cups/500 milliliters whole-grain corn

Water

½ cup/125 milliliters wood ash or 2 tablespoons/30 milliliters hydrated lime (also called calcium hydroxide; available from canning/pickling suppliers as well as agricultural suppliers. Make sure it's food grade, as the same compound, less pure, is used as a building material.)

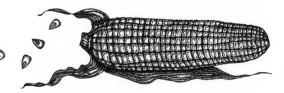

PROCESS:

1. Soak the corn in water for 12 to 24 hours.

2. Strain and transfer the soaked corn to a pressure cooker or other large cooking pot.

3. Add about 8 cups/2 liters of water to the pot; add hydrated lime or sifted wood ash, if you have access to a fireplace, woodstove, or fire pit. Be sure to use only the ash of untreated real wood—not plywood, particleboard, or other glued-together products, or pressure-treated lumber. It is important to sift the ash as large chunks are difficult to rinse out.

4. Bring the mixture to a boil. Pressure cook for about an hour, or boil for about 3 hours, stirring periodically.

5. To test for doneness, rub a kernel of corn between your fingers to see if the skin is loose. If so, remove from heat; if not, continue cooking.

6. Rinse the corn, kneading and rubbing it to loosen and remove skins. Rinse until the water is clear.

7. Cook with the whole posole: it's great in chili, polenta, soups, and stews; grind it into a dough for tortillas or tamales; or ferment it as follows, or as *chicha,* an Andean chewed-corn beer featured in chapter 11.

Gv-No-He-Nv (Cherokee Sour Corn Drink)

Cherokee people inhabited the lush region of Tennessee where I live until they were forcibly removed to reservations in Okla-homa in 1838. Many Cherokees actually adopted the ways of the European settlers and built an elaborate assimilated society in the Southeast in the late eighteenth and early nineteenth centuries. The strategy did not save them, though; the Cherokee people were forced to migrate westward with other eastern tribes in the Trail of Tears.

Loving this land and receiving powerful nurturance from it, I feel acutely aware of the absence of the native people here. As I researched this book, I became determined to find a Cherokee fermentation tradition. On the Internet, I found the Web site of the southeast Kituwa Nation (a name for the Cherokee land), which contains recipes, including this one for *gv-no-he-nv* (the *v* is pronounced like the *u* in "but").[3] In the first week or so of fermentation, this thick, milky drink has the sweet flavor of corn accented by mild hints of sourness. Once it ages a couple of weeks, *gv-no-he-nv* develops a strong, almost cheesy flavor; Buffy, a fellow Short Mountain steward, described the taste as "a *quesadilla* puréed in the blender with water." Only there's no cheese, just corn transformed. These are complex and ancient flavors with stories and wisdom to impart. And if *gv-no-he-nv* gets stronger than appeals to you as a beverage, it also makes a great ingredient in cooking, as in the cornbread and polenta recipes that follow, as well as in chili, stews, soups, casseroles, and breads.

TIMEFRAME: 1 week or more

INGREDIENTS (for about 2 quarts/2 liters):
2 cups/500 milliliters nixtamalized corn (see page 111)

Water

PROCESS:

1. Follow nixtamalization process, as described on page 111. Though *nixtamal* is an Aztec word, the process of cooking corn with wood ash was widespread in the Americas, practiced by the Cherokee and many other North American tribes.

2. Crush the kernels with a mortar and pestle or in a food processor.

3. Cook the corn in 10 cups/2.5 milliliters of water for about 1 hour, stirring frequently to prevent burning, until the corn chunks are soft and the liquid is thick.

4. To sour, leave the liquid in a jar in a warm spot, stirring periodically. It starts out sweet and slowly develops its sourness. According to the recipe I found: "The drink may be kept for quite a while unless the weather is very hot. This was a customary drink to serve to friends who dropped by for a visit." You can drink it chunky or strain it. If you strain it, use the fermented corn chunks in sour cornbread or polenta, below, or in other cooking.

Sour Cornbread

This cornbread, using *gv-no-he-nv* (above) and the corn chunks strained from it, is a transhistorical fusion. It is a cultural reintroduction, incorporating a corn tradition of the Cherokee people into a corn tradition of the white settlers who took over their land. It is fitting that the *gv-no-he-nv* lends a delicious sour edge to this Southern staple.

TIMEFRAME: About 40 minutes

INGREDIENTS (for 1 skillet cornbread, 9 to 10 inches/23 to 25 centimeters in diameter):

1¼ cups/310 milliliters cornmeal

¾ cup/185 milliliters whole-wheat pastry flour

2 teaspoons/10 milliliters baking powder

1 teaspoon/5 milliliters salt

1 egg (optional)

3 tablespoons/45 milliliters vegetable oil or melted butter

2 tablespoons/30 milliliters honey

¾ cup/185 milliliters *gv-no-he-nv* (liquid)

½ cup/125 milliliters *kefir* or buttermilk (or omit this and use more *gv-no-he-nv*)

1 cup/250 milliliters strained corn chunks from *gv-no-he-nv*

3 to 4 spring onions, chopped

PROCESS:

1. Preheat the oven to 425°F (220°C). Place a cast iron skillet in the oven to heat up.

2. Sift the cornmeal, flour, baking powder, and salt into a bowl and mix thoroughly.

3. In a separate bowl, beat the egg (if using) and add oil or butter, honey, *gv-no-he-nv*, and *kefir* or buttermilk (if using), and mix the liquid ingredients until well blended.

4. Add the liquids to the dry ingredients and mix together to form a thick batter. Add the strained corn chunks and spring onions, and mix until well combined.

5. Remove the heated skillet from the oven, grease the pan with oil or butter, pour the batter into pan, and return it to the oven.

6. Bake 25 to 30 minutes. Test doneness by sticking a fork into the center; if it comes out clean, the cornbread is ready.

Multicultural Polenta

This interpretation of the rich Italian corn pudding incorporates nixtamalized *posole* of Central American tradition, *gv-no-he-nv* of the Cherokees, *kefir* from the Caucasus, and Italian aged Parmesan cheese.

TIMEFRAME: 1½ hours

INGREDIENTS (FOR 6 TO 8 SERVINGS):
1 cup/250 milliliters nixtamalized whole *posole* (see page 111)
1 cup/250 milliliters strained corn chunks from *gv-no-he-nv* (see page 112)
1 cup/250 milliliters polenta (dry coarsely ground corn)
1 cup/250 milliliters *gv-no-he-nv* (see page 112)
½ cup/125 milliliters white wine
1 to 2 teaspoons/5 to 10 milliliters salt
6 to 8 cloves garlic, peeled and coarsely chopped
1 cup/250 milliliters kefir or yogurt (see chapter 7)
1 cup/250 milliliters ricotta cheese
¼ cup/60 milliliters grated Parmesan cheese

3 to 4 cups/0.75 to 1 liter tomato sauce (best if homemade with fresh herbs, garlic, and wine)

PROCESS:

1. Bring 2 cups/500 milliliters of water to a boil.

2. Add nixtamalized whole-grain corn. (If some time has passed since the nixtamalization process and the corn soaking in water has started to bubble, all the better.)

3. After the corn has boiled about 15 minutes, add the chunks of corn strained from fermented *gv-no-he-nv*. Lower the heat and stir well until the mixture returns to a boil.

4. Mix the polenta with unheated *gv-no-he-nv* liquid and wine, stir into a paste, and add to boiling pot. Add salt, and stir mixture constantly, about 10 to 15 minutes, until it thickens. Meanwhile, preheat oven to 350°F (175°C).

5. Turn off the heat under the pot and stir in the garlic, yogurt or *kefir*, ricotta cheese, and half the Parmesan cheese.

6. Pour the polenta into a baking pan (approximately 9 by 16 inches/24 by 40 centimeters), pour tomato sauce over it, and sprinkle the remaining Parmesan cheese over the top.

7. Bake 20 to 30 minutes and serve.

GENETIC ENGINEERING OF CORN

This ancient grain, around which the civilizations of the Americas developed, is one of the major crops being genetically engineered these days. Corn has been engineered for resistance to a chemical pesticide (Monsanto's Roundup), so growers can spray easily to kill weeds without harming the "Roundup-ready" corn. Lots of other staple crops are also being engineered by profit-driven global corporations, notably soybeans. GE wheat is about to hit the market. Genetically engineered seeds insert the corporation into a role previously fulfilled by farmers themselves—saving seed as a natural, self-generated part of the growing process—thus ensuring dependence and opening new avenues for increased global corporate control and cultural homogenization.

Genetic engineers assert that what they are doing is just an improved form of selective breeding. But where selective breeding involves taking certain desirable traits that nature has created and favoring them over multiple generations, genetic engineering creates something brand new, intermingling the genes of entirely different species, with unpredictable results.

Corn itself is the result of selective breeding over countless generations, of the wild progenitor grain *teosinte*. Now "genetic pollution" threatens the survival of the ancient native corn varieties growing in the region of Mexico considered the world's center of biodiversity for corn. The naturalized heirloom corn has been contaminated with DNA from genetically engineered corn. The potential repercussions are enormous. "If any of the foreign genes are very advantageous, plants carrying those genes could begin to dominate the population," reports *The New York Times*. "In such cases genetic variation will be lost as the diversity of plants not carrying the foreign genes decreases or disappears."[4] The biodiverse legacy of millennia of evolution is sacrificed to laboratory-created, patented life forms. And still the genetic engineers and the agrochemical conglomerates and the government regulators proceed with their ambitious biotech fantasies. "What we are seeing is the emergence of food totalitarianism," writes Vandana Shiva in *Stolen Harvest: The Hijacking of the Global Food Supply,* "in which a handful of corporations control the entire food chain and destroy alternatives so that people do not have access to diverse, safe foods produced ecologically."[5]

The source of this particular genetic contamination is unknown. Genetically modified corn is not even approved for planting in Mexico, but it is imported from the United States as food. And once these engineered genes are out there, they cannot be controlled or called back. A couple of years ago in the United States, genetically modified StarLink corn, approved only for animal feed, turned up in corn chips, prompting a major product recall. A catalogue that I order seeds from states, "Fedco does not knowingly carry genetically engineered seeds," followed by this disclaimer: "Please note the word *knowingly.* Because of the issue of contamination, over which we have no control, our pledge necessarily stops short of being an absolute guarantee. . . . We apologize for having to split legal hairs, but we all share the reality of genetic drift."[6]

Face the reality: Get informed. Get involved, if not for your own health, for the future of biodiversity. Greenpeace maintains a Web site including information on genetically engineered ingredients in specific products and brands, as well as activist links, at www.truefood now.org. Other groups with good information and action resources are Genetically Engineered Food Alert (www.gefoodalert.org) and the Organic Consumers Association (www.organicconsumers.org).

PORRIDGE

Nothing is better for gently waking up your digestive tract and energizing you for the day ahead than porridge. In its many guises, it is the ultimate breakfast food. Crazy Owl, my miso-making mentor, makes porridge that he calls *congee,* in the Chinese tradition. He places whole grains in a stainless steel thermos at night (with various healing herbs), pours boiled water over them, and leaves them to steep in the insulated environment overnight. The *congee* is deeply restorative. Lately, one of my fellow communards, Buffy, has been on a porridge-for-breakfast kick, and I've been a happy beneficiary of his mush-mania. Most mornings you can hear him cranking our hand grain-grinder, coarsely grinding whole grains, preparing for breakfast. He mixes different grains, toasts the ground grains in a dry cast-iron skillet, and cooks them in water, at a ratio of 1 part grain to 5 parts water. After about 20 minutes of cooking, they are creamy and delicious.

Fermentation can add new dimensions to grain porridges. A 12- to 24-hour soak will increase digestibility and creaminess without altering flavor. Sally Fallon, author of the pro-fermentation cookbook *Nourishing Traditions,* is emphatic about soaking grains to make them digestible. "The well-meaning advice of many nutritionists, to consume whole grains as our ancestors did and not refined flours and polished rice, is misleading and often harmful in its consequences; for while our ancestors ate whole grains, they did not consume them as presented in our modern cookbooks in the form of quick-rise breads, granolas, and other hastily prepared casseroles and concoctions. Our ancestors, and virtually all preindustrialized peoples, soaked or fermented their grains before making them into porridge, breads, cakes,

Millet

and casseroles."[7] Her scientific rationale, confirmed by Paul Pitchford in *Healing with Whole Foods,* is that the outer layer of most grains contains a compound called phytic acid, which can block mineral absorption during digestion.[8] Fermenting grains by soaking them before cooking neutralizes phytic acid and renders the grain far more nutritious. A short soak—24 hours in cool weather, 8 to 12 hours in hot weather—accomplishes this without affecting the flavor.

Then again, sometimes you want to affect the flavor. Not everyone likes their food mild and bland. Some of us crave intense sour flavors. The longer you allow grain fermentation to proceed, the more acidic flavors will develop, thanks to the presence everywhere of lactic acid-producing *Lactobacilli.*

Ogi (African Millet Porridge)

Thick, starchy porridges are a staple food in Africa. Everywhere there you see and hear women pounding on grains and cassava roots, and most meals feature the resulting porridges as a central element. According to the United Nations Food and Agriculture Organization, "Cereals account for as much as 77% of total caloric consumption in African countries, and contribute substantially to dietary protein intake. . . . A majority of traditional cereal-based foods consumed in Africa are processed by natural fermentation. Fermented cereals are particularly important as weaning foods for infants and as dietary staples for adults."[9]

Millet porridge is called *ogi* in parts of West Africa and *uji* in East Africa. In Africa, porridges are generally served thick, with a solid consistency that you can shape and eat with your fingers, and are often accompanied by saucy stews. I

have adopted *ogi* as a quick and hearty breakfast food that I enjoy savory, with butter, garlic, *kefir,* salt, and pepper.

TIMEFRAME: Extremely flexible, from 1 day to more than 1 week

INGREDIENTS (for about 8 servings):
2 cups/500 milliliters millet
Water
Sea salt

PROCESS:

1. Coarsely grind millet using a grain mill or other grinding technology.

2. Soak the millet in about 4 cups/ 1 liter of water. Soaking time can range from about 24 hours to 1 week, and the taste will become progressively more sour as the days pass. I mix up a batch, let it ferment, and cook it a little at a time over the course of a week or so.

3. When you are ready to make porridge, boil about ½ cup/125 milliliters of water per serving, with a dash of salt.

PORRIDGES AND BEVERAGES

4. Mix the fermented millet blend to a uniform consistency and add about ⅔ cup/160 milliliters per serving to the boiling water. Lower heat and stir constantly to prevent burning, until the porridge cooks and thickens, just a few minutes. Add more water as needed to reach the desired consistency. You can enjoy this porridge thick or thin, as you prefer.

Oat Porridge

Oatmeal (or "oytmeal," as my father always calls it, in imitation of his immigrant grandmother) is the quintessential comfort food. It is soft and mushy, harkening back to that long ago time of infancy, when all our food was of such a consistency and lovingly spoon-fed to us. In early modern Europe, according to an article by Elizabeth Meyer-Renschhausen in the anthropology journal *Food and Foodways,* porridges were generally fermented and eaten as a "sour soup."[10] Fermenting oats before cooking them not only makes them more nutritious and digestible, it makes the resulting oatmeal much creamier as well.

For the freshest, most nutritious oatmeal, coarsely grind whole oats yourself when you are ready to use them, though steel-cut oats or rolled oats will work fine, too.

TIMEFRAME: 24 hours

INGREDIENTS (for 3 to 4 servings):
1 cup/250 milliliters oats, coarsely ground, steel-cut, or rolled
5 cups/1.25 liters water
Sea salt

PROCESS:

1. Coarsely grind whole oat groats (or measure out rolled or steel-cut oats).

2. Soak oats for 24 hours (longer is okay, too) in 2 cups (500 milliliters) of water in a bowl or jar, covered to keep dust and flies out. The oats will absorb most of the water.

3. When you are ready to cook oatmeal, bring an additional 3 cups (750 milliliters) of water, with a pinch of salt, to a boil. Lower the heat, add the soaked oats with any remaining water, and stir until the oats are hot and have absorbed all the water, about 10 minutes. Stir constantly, as the thick, sticky oatmeal can burn easily.

4. Serve. However you like to eat your oatmeal, sweet or savory, you'll love the creaminess of this fermented version.

Amazaké

Amazaké is a rich, sweet Japanese pudding or drink that is one of the most dramatic fermentations I've seen. Plain rice (or any other grain) is made intensely sweet in a matter of hours by the action of a mold. It astounds me that a grain could be so sweet without any added sugar or other sweetener. The rapid digestion of the complex carbohydrates into simple sugars is the work of *Aspergillus oryzae,* the same mold used to make miso.

Aspergillus is most readily available in the form of *koji,* grain inoculated with spores of *Aspergillus.* For sources, see the Cultural Resources section.

Traditionally, *amazaké* is made with sweet rice, a variety of rice that is not actually sweet, but high in gluten and therefore sticky when cooked. *Amazaké* can be made from any grain, though. I especially enjoy *amazaké* made from millet.

TIMEFRAME: Less than 24 hours

SPECIAL EQUIPMENT:
1 gallon (4-liter) wide-mouth jar
Insulated cooler big enough for jar to fit inside

INGREDIENTS (for about 1 gallon/4 liters):
2 cups/500 milliliters sweet rice (or any other grain)
2 cups/500 milliliters *koji*
Water

PROCESS:

1. Cook the grain in about 6 cups (1.5 liters) of water. Use a pressure cooker if you have one. This high proportion of water (3:1) will result in somewhat softer than usual grain.

2. Meanwhile, preheat the insulated cooler and the gallon jar by filling both with hot water.

3. When the grain is cooked, remove from the heat, uncover the pot, and allow the grain to cool for a few minutes, stirring from the bottom to release heat. Don't let it get too cool. *Koji* can tolerate heat as high as 140°F (60°C). Cool to this temperature or, if you are without a thermometer, until you can hold a finger to it for a moment but it is still steaming hot.

4. Add the *koji* to the cooked grain and stir well.

5. Transfer the cooked grain and *koji* mix to the preheated gallon jar. Screw the lid on the jar and place it in the preheated insulated cooler. If the cooler is much larger than the jar, add additional jars of hot water (not too hot to touch), to help maintain the heat. Shut the cooler and place it in a warm place.

6. Check the *amazaké* after 8 to 12 hours. *Amazaké* takes about 8 to 12 hours at 140°F (60°C), or 20 to 24 hours at 90°F (32°C). If the *amazaké* is very sweet, it's ready. If not, heat it up with gentle heat: If your cooler is big and you added extra bottles of water, replace these with fresh hot water; if your cooler is small, add hot water directly to the cooler to surround the jar of *amazaké*. Leave it to ferment for a few more hours.

7. Once your *amazaké* is sweet, gently bring it to a boil to stop fermentation. *Amazaké* left to ferment after it becomes sweet becomes an alcoholic grog (the first step in the process of making saké, the strong Japanese rice wine). Be careful not to burn the *amazaké* when you boil (pasteurize) it. The way I do this is to first boil about 2 cups (500 milliliters) of water in a pot, then slowly add the *amazaké*, stirring constantly to avoid burning the bottom.

8. You can serve *amazaké* as a pudding at this point, thick and with the grains intact, or you can thin it with more water and run it through a food processor to break down the grains into a liquid consistency. *Amazaké* is delicious either hot or cold.

9. Plain *amazaké* has a very distinctive sweetness, or you can season it. *Amazaké* seasoned with a little nutmeg (and perhaps even rum) makes a nice eggnog alternative. Vanilla extract, grated ginger, slivered toasted almonds, and espresso are other flavorings I've enjoyed in *amazaké*. *Amazaké* can also be used as a sweetener in baking.

Amazaké can be stored for a few weeks in a refrigerator.

Amazaké Coconut-Milk Pudding

This is a delicious pudding using *amazaké*. It is sweetened by *amazaké* and coconut milk, with no other added sweeteners.

TIMEFRAME: 3 hours

INGREDIENTS (for 6 to 8 servings):

1 can coconut milk

1 cup/250 milliliters rice milk (or cow or soy milk)

2 tablespoons/30 milliliters arrowroot powder

1 teaspoon/5 milliliters powdered cardamom

1 quart/1 liter *amazaké*

1 cup/250 milliliters dried shredded coconut

1 teaspoon/5 milliliters vanilla extract

Salt

PROCESS:

1. Pour the coconut milk and ½ cup (125 milliliters) of the rice milk into a pot and bring to a boil.

2. Reserve ½ cup (125 milliliters) of the rice milk and stir arrowroot powder and cardamom into it. Once the arrowroot powder is fully dissolved, add it to the pot on the stove.

3. When the liquid comes to a boil, add *amazaké*; lower the flame and stir often, until the pudding boils for about 10 minutes and starts to thicken.

4. Meanwhile, in a heavy cast-iron skillet, toast the shredded coconut. Use low heat and stir constantly, until the coconut starts to darken.

5. Add the vanilla extract and half of the toasted coconut to the pudding and stir in.

6. Once the pudding has boiled for about 10 minutes, remove from heat and pour into a bowl, pie form, or loaf pan.

7. Sprinkle the remaining toasted coconut on top of the pudding. Allow to set at room temperature, then chill in refrigerator before serving.

Kvass

Kvass results from a great recycling process. It is made from stale bread, refermented. Tolstoy's Anna Karenina drank fine wine in her palace, but when she looked out at the fields of her estate, the peasant laborers she watched were drinking *kvass*. It is still popular in Russia, in cities as well as the countryside, and can be found in Russian neighborhoods of New York.

Kvass is nutritious and energizing. This recipe is for fairly sour *kvass*, as I imagine it was traditionally enjoyed by peasants in rural Russia, with little access to sweeteners. It is ever so mildly alcoholic, full of healthful *Lactobacilli*, thick and milky, almost viscous. I think it is delicious but some people wince at its sour flavor. The bottled *kvass* I found in the Brighton Beach neighborhood of Brooklyn was much sweeter, and heavily carbonated, like molasses-flavored soda.

TIMEFRAME: 3 to 5 days

INGREDIENTS (for ½ gallon/2 liters):

1½ pounds/750 grams stale bread (traditionally hearty Russian black bread, made of coarsely ground whole-grain rye and/or barley, but any bread will do, and it doesn't have to be stale)

3 tablespoons/45 milliliters crushed dried mint

1 lemon, juiced

¼ cup/60 milliliters sugar or honey

¼ teaspoon/1 milliliter sea salt

¼ cup/60 milliliters sourdough (or 1 package yeast)

A few raisins

PROCESS:

1. Cut bread into cubes, and toast in an oven preheated to 300°F (150°C) for about 20 minutes, until dry.

2. Place the bread cubes in a crock or wide-mouth gallon jar, with the mint, lemon juice, and 12 cups (3 liters) boiling water. Stir, cover, and leave for 8 hours (or longer).

3. Strain out the solids, pressing out as much liquid as possible. The soggy bread will retain some water, so you will end up with less volume of liquid than you started with.

4. Add the sugar or honey, salt, and sourdough or yeast to the strained liquid. Mix well, cover, and leave to ferment 2 to 3 days.

5. Transfer *kvass* to quart (liter) bottles, filling bottles only about three-quarters full. Add a few raisins to each bottle and seal. Leave the bottles at room temperature for a day or two, until the raisins float to the top. *Kvass* is then ready to drink, and may be stored in the refrigerator for a few weeks.

Okroshka (*Kvass*-based Soup)

This is a refreshing Russian summer soup, served chilled. It uses not only *kvass* but pickle brine or sauerkraut juice, and it doesn't cook them, so it's a live culture soup! I adapted this recipe from *The Food and Cookery of Russia* by Lesley Chamberlain.

TIMEFRAME: 2 hours

INGREDIENTS (for 4 to 6 servings):
2 potatoes
1 carrot
1 turnip
½ pound/250 grams mushrooms
3 eggs (optional)
4 spring onions
1 apple
1 cucumber
1 quart/1 liter *kvass*
½ cup/125 milliliters pickle brine or sauerkraut juice
2 teaspoons/10 milliliters ground mustard
1 tablespoon/15 milliliters fresh or dried dill
1 tablespoon/15 milliliters fresh parsley
Salt and pepper to taste

PROCESS:

1. Cut the potatoes, carrot, turnip, mushrooms, and other seasonal vegetables, if desired, into spoon-sized pieces, and steam or boil for about 10 minutes, until soft.

2. If you wish to include eggs, hardboil them in a separate pot for about 10 minutes.

3. Chop the spring onions, apple, and cucumber into spoon-sized pieces.

4. Mix *kvass,* pickle brine or sauerkraut juice, mustard, dill, parsley, and vegetables. Stir well and refrigerate for at least 1 hour.

5. Peel and chop eggs.

6. When you are ready to serve, add the eggs, salt, and pepper to the soup. Serve in a bowl with an ice cube, accompanied by kefir, yogurt, or sour cream.

Rejuvelac

My friend Mat Defiler, who lives at IDA, turned me on to rejuvelac, a nutritious, energizing, and refreshing fermented tonic that is a byproduct of the grain-sprouting process. Mat has become a fellow fermentation freak, compelled by *Candida* yeast infections. Live fermented foods can help restore balance when *Candida* yeasts, always present in your body, overly proliferate. Rejuvelac, popularized by raw-foods guru Ann Wigmore, is extremely simple to make.

TIMEFRAME: 3 days

INGREDIENTS (for about 2 quarts/2 liters of rejuvelac):
4 cups/1 liter of any whole grain
Water

PROCESS:

1. Soak the grain in about 12 cups (3 liters) of water in a gallon (4-liter) jar.

2. After 12 to 24 hours, drain the water off the swollen grains. The soaking water is rejuvelac. (Sprout the grains, as detailed on page 104.)

3. Ferment rejuvelac in a jar, loosely covered to keep flies and dust out, for about 2 days at room temperature.

4. Store rejuvelac in the refrigerator, and drink as desired.

Kombucha

Kombucha is not actually a grain ferment, so it's a bit out of place in this chapter, but it doesn't quite fit into any of my other chapter categories either. Kombucha is a sour tonic beverage, like rejuvelac and *kvass,* and in Russia, where it has enjoyed long popularity, it is often referred to as "tea *kvass.*" Kombucha is sweetened black tea, cultured with a "mother," also known as "the tea beast," a gelatinous colony of bacteria and yeast. The mother ferments the sweet tea and reproduces itself, like kefir grains.

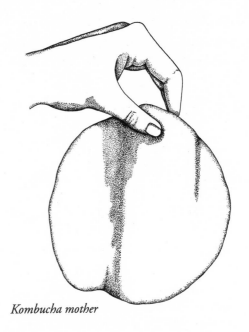

Kombucha mother

Kombucha is thought to have originated in China, and has been popular at different times in many different lands. It is beneficial to health, like other live fermented foods, and for a few years in the mid-1990s it was a big American health fad. Any potential cure is appealing to people living with chronic disease. My friend and fellow AIDS survivor Spree got caught up in the kombucha craze. Soon he had more "mother" than he knew what to do with, and started getting everyone to try it. Almost everyone enjoyed the sweet-sour flavor of kombucha. People got really creative with alternative sweet substances for the mother to ferment. I remember our friend Brett Love made kombucha from his favorite soft drink, Mountain Dew. Fermentation processes are very versatile.

The trickiest part of making kombucha is finding a mother. Ask at local health food stores. On the Web, kombucha enthusiasts maintain a Worldwide Kombucha Exchange at www.kombu.de, where mothers are widely available for just shipping costs. Kombucha mothers are also available from G.E.M. Cultures. (See the Cultural Resources section.)

TIMEFRAME: About 7 to 10 days

INGREDIENTS (for 1 quart/1 liter):
1 quart/1 liter water
¼ cup/60 milliliters sugar
1 tablespoon/15 milliliters loose black tea or 2 teabags
½ cup/125 milliliters mature acidic kombucha
Kombucha mother

PROCESS:

1. Mix water and sugar and bring to a boil in a small cooking pot.

2. Turn off the heat; add tea, cover, and steep about 15 minutes.

3. Strain the tea into a glass container. It's best to use something wide; kombucha needs adequate surface area and works best if the diameter of the container is greater than the depth of the liquid. Allow the tea to cool to body temperature.

4. Add the mature acidic kombucha. When you obtain a culture, it will be stored in this liquid. Save a portion of subsequent batches for this purpose.

5. Place the kombucha mother in the liquid, with the firm, opaque side up.

6. Cover with a cloth and store in a warm spot, ideally 70° to 85°F (21° to 29°C).

7. After a few days to 1 week, depending on temperature, you will notice a skin forming on the surface of the kombucha. Taste the liquid. It will probably still be sweet. The longer it sits, the more acidic it will become.

8. Once it reaches the acidity you like, start a new batch and store your mature kombucha in the refrigerator. You now have two mothers, the original one you started with, and a new one, the skin that formed on your first batch. Use either the new or the old mother in your new batch, and pass the other one on to a friend (or the compost). Each generation will give birth to a new mother, and the old mother will thicken.

10 WINES (INCLUDING MEAD, CIDER, AND GINGER BEER)

CERTAINLY ALCOHOL is the oldest, most widespread, and most well-known product of fermentation. Fermented alcoholic beverages are perhaps very nearly universal, though there is some confusion about this. Into the twentieth century, many ethnographers propagated the idea that fermented beverages were not found among "uncivilized" peoples.[1] This is simply not true.

It is still commonly accepted that Native Americans did not know alcoholic beverages until the arrival of the European conquerors. Though practices varied among different tribes in different regions, many native peoples of the Americas most definitely enjoyed fermented beverages. The alcohol that natives of the Americas had not experienced prior to the European arrival was distilled liquor, many times more potent and dangerous than fermented alcohol.

Historical reality is further obscured by rules imposed by colonizing invaders in many places, forbidding natives from fermenting their traditional drinks. Such hypocritical laws, along with the wholesale slaughter and displacement of entire cultures, caused many traditional practices, fermentation among them, to be lost and forgotten.

Enough of these ancient fermented alcohol traditions survive, however, to suggest that they were widespread, if not universal.

The context for making and consuming fermented alcohol drinks in traditional cultures was, as a general rule, communal and ritualistic. Some cultures created noisy rituals, with the idea that "excited, sometimes even angry, strong energy helped the yeast to work more effectively."[2] Other cultures, with the notion that the ferment needed peace and quiet and could be startled or scared by sounds and movement, approached fermentation processes with quiet reverence. Either way, the context was ritualistic and sacred. Making your own wines, beers, meads, and ciders is a powerful way of reclaiming the ritual sacredness of alcohol fermentation.

When I first tried fermenting wine and beer, I learned from books. But I found the complex methods most of the books detailed discouraging. I especially dislike the emphasis on chemical sterilization, and the predominant practice of killing the wild yeast present on the skins of fruit to assure the success of a particular proven commercial strain of yeast. This practice offends my wild fermentation sensibilities.

I knew that simple, quick, and delicious alcohol ferments were possible, having sampled many different indigenous local brews when I traveled in Africa (long before my interest in fermentation developed). Almost every rural village we passed through had some ferment to share, among them palm wines and cassava and millet beers. These local ferments were never poured from bottles or stored for long. They were drunk young (not aged) and generally served from gourds or other large fermenting vessels.

Why was there such a chasm between these low-tech indigenous fermentation traditions I had sampled, and all the information I could find about making beer and wine at home? The European traditions of beer and wine evolved into traditions of refinement, emphasizing pure strains of yeast, uncontaminated by wild organisms, highly clarified products free of cloudy yeast residue, and bottling for long-term aging. I do not dispute that these practices can yield sublime and wonderful products. But I knew from my African travels that far more accessible methods existed.

The recipes that follow include both low-tech wild fermentations and more conventional methods. This chapter covers wines, broadly defined to include any non-grain-based fermented beverages (grain-based beers are the subject of chapter 11). My own alcohol fermentation methods are extremely simple. Experts may scoff at them. To supplement my primitive approach, I also describe the techniques used by some of my friends. Though the methods vary, along with some of the assumptions behind them, they all produce delicious ferments. Jump in, experiment, and find the process that works best for you.

HOOCH

To illustrate how little is required in the way of specialized equipment or ingredients to ferment alcohol, I'll start with hooch, slang for surreptitiously brewed alcohol. This recipe comes from Ron Campbell, veteran of eighteen years in the Illinois prison system. While doing his time, Ron earned the affectionate nickname "Bartles & Jaymes" (a brand name of wine coolers) for his prolific winemaking behind bars. Here's how he did it, in his own words:

> First, we sent two to three people to the chow hall to score some fruit cocktail or peaches. This would be used for the "kicker." The kicker sits out one to two days in the open air to collect all the yeast that is abundant in it. [It is not possible to eradicate culture! Wild fermentation is everywhere.] We mixed this with six 6-packs of Donald Duck orange juice, along with 1 pound of sugar for each 6-pack, dissolved thoroughly in 1 quart of hot water. Some said I used too much sugar, but nobody ever complained when the finished product was drank.
>
> We poured all of this into a 55-gallon garbage bag, double-bagged it to keep the smell down, and let it sit in a warm place for three days, letting the pressure off whenever needed. We couldn't have an explosion, could we? The rest was waiting, and staying up nights to let the air out. We took shifts to do that. Our homebrew was much too important to have wasted. When three days passed, or the brew was no longer cooking off, we took it and strained the fruit out. We could usually tell when it was done, because we would have to burp the bag only once every two to three hours, instead of every thirty minutes or so. We also tasted it for potency, by sipping a small amount and letting it sit in the front of the mouth while inhaling through the lips. We could taste the alcohol this way.

The whole process was risky, because it was obviously against the rules, and punishable by isolation time if caught. Years ago, if you stayed under five gallons you didn't have to worry about a major case if caught, but they're now taking people to court for any amount. I only got caught once, and that was only a few weeks before my release in 1997. I sat in solitary for a month, and went home. My last batch was shared with a group of guys *in* solitary. We saved our breakfast juices, sugar, jelly, and fruit for days, and made about 3 gallons. Other people in prison use ketchup, or tomato purée, but I always preferred the fruit. It's an acquired taste, but it sure does the job!

Spontaneous Cider

The simplest alcohol ferment I know how to make, or rather let happen, is hard cider. For a more elaborate, harder cider, see "Cider Take Two," page 137.

TIMEFRAME: About 1 week

INGREDIENTS (for 1 gallon/4 liters):
1 gallon/4 liters fresh apple cider or apple juice (Make sure it does not contain preservatives, because preservatives are used to prevent microorganisms from growing, and you want the yeast to come and feast upon the sweet juice.)

PROCESS:

1. Leave the cider out at room temperature, with the cap removed. Cover the top with cheesecloth or mesh to keep flies out but give yeast access.

2. After a few days, taste it, then continue to taste at frequent intervals. When I took notes on the process, after 3 days it was "bubbly, mildly alcoholic, sweet"; after 5 days it had "lost its sweetness, still bubbly, not at all sour"; after a week "hard and dry"; and a day later "starts to have a sour edge." Homebrewing can be as simple as this.

CARBOYS AND AIRLOCKS

A bit of simple technology enables fermentation to proceed with minimum exposure to the organisms that transform alcohol into vinegar. This technology is a vessel called a carboy and a plastic device called an airlock. A carboy is a large bottle with a narrow neck, shaped like the large bottles of water used in office water coolers. The narrow neck is the important feature, as it permits the easy blockage of airflow into the vessel, preventing exposure to airborne vinegar organisms. If you ferment in one-gallon batches, simple glass juice jugs confer the same

wild

advantage. If you want to ferment in larger quantities, carboys are invaluable.

Carboy and juice jug

An airlock is a device that prevents air from entering the vessel while permitting the carbon-dioxide gas produced by alcohol fermentation to escape. There are various designs, but they all use water to block the free flow of air, while still allowing pressure to release. In long-term ferments using airlocks, be sure to check them periodically, as the water can evaporate out of them and break the air lock; just add a little water as necessary. Airlocks are available from wine- and beer-making supply shops and mail-order sources for around a dollar.

For airlocks, carboys, and other alcohol fermentation supplies, look in the yellow pages under "Beer Homebrewing Equipment and Supplies" or "Winemaking Supplies." An Internet search will yield countless mail-order suppliers, and the Home Wine and Beer Trade Association maintains a searchable listing of local suppliers at www.hwbta.org.

If you don't have an airlock, a balloon or condom stretched over the mouth of the fermenting vessel is a good alternative. It prevents air from entering the vessel and absorbs the pressure of the carbon dioxide released in fermentation by inflating. Just be sure to manually release the pressure as needed or the balloon/condom may fly off or burst.

Airlock and balloon alternative

Often alcohol ferments are started as "open ferments" not sealed off from the air. In the early stages of fermentation, when bubbling is most vigorous, the alcohol yeasts are dominant and other organisms cannot compete. It is when the bubbling subsides that other types of organisms, notably the vinegar-producing ones, can easily become established. Alcoholic beverages produced using exclusively open fermentation vessels can be excellent, though they must be consumed quickly, as it is only a matter of time before they become vinegar. Alcoholic beverages intended for aging are generally completed as "closed ferments" in an airlocked vessel.

T'ej (Ethiopian Honey Wine): Flavor Variations

I introduced the how-to portion of this book with a recipe for *t'ej* on page 29. That is the basic process I generally use when I make wine, only I almost always give it some additional flavor, ferment it to dryness in an airlocked vessel, and age it. I first learned how to make *t'ej* in a cookbook called *Exotic Ethiopian Cooking* by Daniel Jote Mesfin. Following these basic proportions and steps, I have made many excellent Ethiopian-style honey wines. *T'ej* is a variant of mead, the most ancient fermented pleasure. Though *t'ej* is usually consumed young, ready to drink in a matter of weeks, meads in the European tradition generally age for years, and *t'ej* likewise can be fermented longer, bottled, and aged. See the "Aging Wine: Siphoning and Bottling" section below.

Traditionally, *t'ej* calls for a plant called *gesho,* or woody hops. I have never found this herb in the United States, and have had fine results without any bittering agent.

Plum or Berry **T'ej:** Add at least 1 quart (liter) of organic whole plums or berries (any kind) to 1 gallon of honey water at the beginning of the process. They'll get it bubbling fast. Leave the fruit in for about 5 days to 1 week, then strain it out, transfer wine to a clean gallon (4-liter) jug, and proceed as for plain *t'ej.* You could substitute any fruit you like.

Lemon Herb **T'ej (Metheglin):** Take a handful each of fresh or dried lemon balm, lemon verbena, lemon thyme, lemongrass, and lemon basil, and add them to the gallon (4 liters) of honey water at the beginning of the process. Leave the herbs in the crock for about a week, stirring periodically, then strain them out, transfer the wine to a clean gallon (4 liter) jug, and proceed as for plain *t'ej.* Use any other herbs you like for flavoring.

Coffee-Banana **T'ej:** This is a really unusual flavor for a wine. Once the honey-water in the crock starts to bubble, add ½ cup (125 milliliters) coarsely ground roasted coffee beans and 4 peeled and sliced bananas. Stir as often as you think of it. After about 5 days, strain out the solid ingredients and transfer the wine into a clean gallon (4-liter) jug. Then proceed as for plain *t'ej.*

AGING WINE: SIPHONING AND BOTTLING

T'ej is alcoholic and delicious after a few weeks; however, like any wine, it is far better after a few years. Wines to be aged or stored for any length of time need to be bottled. Even before bottling, once vigorous fermentation slows, wines are often siphoned from the initial fermentation vessel into a clean one, leaving the sediment, or "lees", behind. This process is called "racking". The siphoning agitates and aerates the wine to help complete fermentation, and the removal of the sediment prevents it from imparting any undesirable flavor to the wine.

The contemporary wine aesthetic values a clear product. Commercial wines are full of strange clarifying agents, including egg whites, milk caseins, gelatin, and isinglass, an extract from the bladder of sturgeon (you don't read about these because alcoholic beverages are not required to be labeled with ingredients like other food and drinks).[3] I personally have come to love yeasty sediment and appreciate the lees' vitamin-richness (especially B vitamins). But don't let me discourage you from racking your wine; it is much more beautiful that way, and its flavors more delicate. (Try using some of the nutritious yeasty sediment in salad dressings or wine dregs soup, featured later in this chapter.)

Winemaking supply shops sell siphoning tools, which consist of flexible plastic tubing attached to a few feet of hard plastic tubing. This hard tube goes into the carboy, to a point above the sediment, and is much easier to control than flexible tubing. In the absence of this specific tool, any flexible plastic tubing will do.

Before siphoning, set your carboy on a table or counter, and let it sit undisturbed for a few hours so any sediment that dispersed when you moved it has a chance to settle. Place another clean fermentation vessel on the floor or a lower surface. For this to work, gravitationally, the vessel you are filling needs to stay lower than the point you are siphoning from. Be sure to have a glass nearby, so you can enjoy a taste of your wine. When you are ready, remove the airlock from the carboy, and place the hard tube end of the siphon into the carboy, with the end in the wine but higher than the level of the sediment.

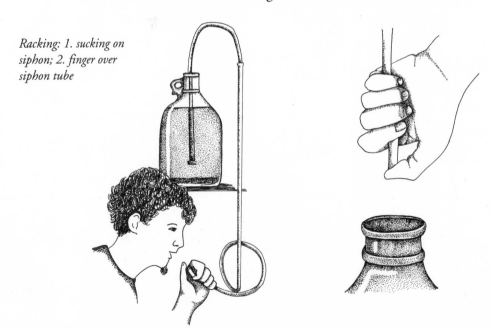

Racking: 1. sucking on siphon; 2. finger over siphon tube

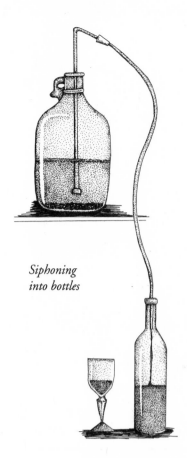

Siphoning into bottles

Hold it (or better yet, have a second person hold it) at that level as you siphon. Place your mouth on the exposed end of the hose, and suck until you taste your wine. Then place a clean finger over the end of the hose to hold the liquid in the siphon, bring it to the mouth of the clean carboy or jug, release your finger, and fill.

Place an airlock in the new carboy and leave it to continue to ferment. In general, ferment wines for at least six months to a year before bottling. If you bottle them before fermentation is complete, you run the risk of having corks pop out. Even if there is no visible bubbling or release of air after a few weeks, slow fermentation continues for months.

Meanwhile, save bottles from (corked, not screw-top) commercial wines for your bottling, or collect them at a local recycling center. When you are ready to bottle, clean them thoroughly with soap and hot water, using a flexible bottle brush, if necessary, to remove crud from the upper part of the bottle where the glass narrows. Rinse the bottles thoroughly; you don't want soap residue in your wine. Thorough cleaning is generally sufficient, but some meticulous winemakers sterilize by steaming the bottles standing upside down in a big pot, covered, for about 10 minutes.

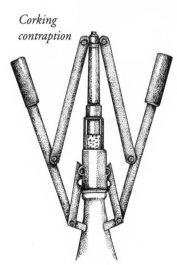

Corking contraption

Set your carboy on a table or counter, arrange clean bottles nearby, on the floor or a lower surface, and siphon into the first bottle. As each bottle fills (not to the rim, but to about 2 inches/5 centimeters below it), use your finger, or fold the tube on itself, to create a vacuum as you move the siphon to the next bottle. Somewhere in there, fill up a glass to enjoy. Fill bottles until you are about to reach the yeasty sediment.

Once your wine is in bottles, you need to cork them. Traditional corks come from trees native to the Mediterranean; some winemakers prefer synthetic corks. Both are available at winemaking

(INCLUDING MEAD, CIDER, AND GINGER BEER)

suppliers. Corks are fatter than the necks of the bottles, so you will need a corking tool to force them into the bottles. There are a number of cleverly designed contraptions for this, some as cheap as five dollars. Steam corks for a few minutes to sterilize and soften them.

Aging mellows the harshness of wines. Store wine in a cool dark place (such as a cellar). With traditional corks, leave bottles upright for a week or so until the corks fully expand and seal, then store bottles on their sides, so the wine keeps the corks moist and expanded. (This is not necessary with synthetic corks.) Mark your wines clearly so you can distinguish different vintages.

COUNTRY WINES

Though the word "wine" comes from the word "vine," and wine classically is made from grapes, wine can be made by fermenting any sweet substance, and wines from sweetened teas of all kinds of fruits, vegetables, and flowers are known as country wines.

Living in a rural community where many different people have experimented with the simple techniques of making wine, I have had the great privilege of sampling an awesome array of far-out country wines. My friends Stephen and Shana made tomato wine, which was terrific, though not particularly tomatoey, and jalapeño wine, which was hot and delicious. The only limit on what can be made into wine is your imagination. To give you a sense of the variety that is possible, I took an inventory of the wines in our root cellar. The Short Mountain vintners have kept busy the past several years. The fruit wines I found were blueberry, "black and blueberry," mulberry, cherry, strawberry, apple, plum, muscadine (a variety of grape), persimmon, elderberry, sumac, "mystery fruit wine," hibiscus-strawberry, peach, wild grape, prickly pear, and banana. Then there were the flower and herb wines: daylily, dandelion, phacelia, trillium, morning glory petal mead, lilac petal mead, echinacea, stinging nettle, mugwort, wild cherry bark, "hops-chamomile-valerian-catnip-sorghum honey wine," and garlic-anise-ginger. Then there were vegetable wines and a couple that cross categories: potato wine, beet-honey wine, sweet onion wine (an exceptional cooking wine), redbud with orange and plum, and watermelon-chamomile. To expand the horizon just a bit more, I checked the IDA root cellar, where I found still more weird varieties: carrot wine, sour cherry wine, pear champagne, apple-pear champagne, almond wine, elderflower, nectarine, cantaloupe, mint mead, and corn wine. Anything you have an abundance of can be made into wine.

The basic process for country winemaking is to ferment a sweet infusion of the fruit or flower or vegetable or whatever you are using to flavor it. Methods vary: Some people cook the fruit or flavoring in water. Some folks steep it in boiled water, like tea, preserving volatile aromatic oils that would evaporate if boiled. My friend Hector Black, who has been making wine for more than thirty years, uses an ingenious three-tiered "steam juicer" from Finland to steam blueberries and then condense the steam into sterile juice for winemaking.

One major variable in winemaking is the amount of sweetener added to the unfermented mixture (known as the "must"). To my palate, dry wines taste better than sweet wines. Less can be more. Up to a point, additional sweetener can yield higher alcohol content. After that point, adding more sugar just makes the wine sweeter. One of the ironic twists of alcohol fermentation is that as yeasts produce alcohol and the alcohol level rises, the environment becomes less hospitable to yeasts, and they die off. The alcohol level that yeast can survive varies somewhat with different strains; champagne yeast, for example, is selected for its relatively high alcohol tolerance.

Another major variable is the type of sweetener used. You can ferment any sweetener. I generally prefer to use honey rather than cane sugar, mostly because it does not require importation or mechanical refinement, and it seems more natural. For a beautiful and informative ode to honey, check out Stephen Harrod Buhner's *Sacred and Herbal Healing Beers*. He points out that ancient honey ferments included not only honey but the other related substances and beings found in the hive (bee pollen, propolis, royal jelly, and even angry bees, full of venom), and he catalogues the great health benefits of every one of these whole-hive components. The one great advantage of sugar in winemaking (other than its price, which no other sweetener can approach) is that its flavor and color are neutral, allowing the flavors and colors of flowers and berries to shine without rivalry. Honey exerts more of its own flavor and color influence over wines. Maple syrup, sorghum, rice syrup, and molasses can be used, as well; each sweetener imparts its own unique flavor and qualities to alcohol ferments.

wild

Elderberry

Elderberry Wine

My friend Sylvan, a resident of our community for ten years and now a neighbor, is a prolific winemaker. Every year, he makes consistently excellent wine from the most abundant and easily available fruit in our area, elderberries, which grow like a weed around here and bear ripe fruit in August. You could adapt his process to any fruit you are lucky enough to have in great abundance.

TIMEFRAME: 1 year or more

INGREDIENTS (for 5 gallons/20 liters):
1 heaping bushel elderberries (at least 3 gallons
   after destemming)
Water
1 packet commercial wine or champagne yeast
10 to 12 pounds/5 to 6 kilograms sugar

PROCESS:

1. Destem and clean berries. This is a good job to do with helpers. Collect a bowlful of destemmed berries at a time, cover with water, and stir. Ripe berries sink while leaves, insects, and overripe berries float to the top. Skim off what floats with a strainer, pour off water, and place clean berries in a 5-gallon (20-liter) bucket or crock. Repeat until all the berries are clean. You should end up with at least 3 gallons (12 liters) of berries. "The more berries, the richer the flavor," says Sylvan.

2. Boil 3 gallons (12 liters) water and pour enough of it (probably only about 2 gallons/8 liters) over the berries to submerge them under water. Cover the bucket with a towel and leave it overnight to steep and cool.

3. In the morning, remove 1 cup of the liquid, dissolve a packet of yeast in it, and leave for a few minutes, until it appears bubbly and active. Then add it to the berries and water, stir using a wooden spoon, and cover.

4. Ferment 2 to 3 days, stirring often, at least three to five times a day. No additional sugar has been added yet. "The yeast should feed on the sugar in the fruit before you give it something else to feed on," explains Sylvan. During this time, the wine gets somewhat frothy, but not nearly as active as it will get when sugar is added.

5. After 2 or 3 days, add sugar. Pour 10 pounds/5 kilograms (20 cups/5 liters) of sugar into a cooking pot, then add just enough water to liquefy and heat slowly, stirring constantly, until the sugar dissolves into a clear syrup. Cover the syrup until it cools, then add it to the elderberry mash.

6. Ferment 3 to 5 days, covered, stirring often.

7. Once vigorous bubbling begins to slow, strain wine into a 5-gallon (20-liter) carboy. It will only fill the carboy part way. Place the berry solids in a second container, and cover with water. Mash the berries in the water, then strain this water into the carboy. You want to have a full carboy, but not too full. Leave a few inches of headroom for foam. Insert the airlock.

8. Store the carboy at room temperature for the first month. At first, place it in a large pan to contain the mess in case it gets so frothy that it overflows. If this should occur, temporarily remove the airlock and clean it and the mouth of the carboy. Fermentation will slow gradually.

9. Test the sugar content: Sylvan has an unusual method for testing the sugar content once fermentation has slowed. Remove the airlock and sprinkle 2 tablespoons (30 milliliters) of sugar onto the surface of the wine. As it sinks, it may or may not stimulate a dramatic yeast reaction. If it does not react dramatically, the sugar content is right. If it does, add 1 cup (250 milliliters) more sugar and ferment another few days (or more), then repeat the test. Add just 1 cup (250 milliliters) of sugar at a time, and no more than an additional 4 cups (1 liter) total.

10. After 2 months in a warm spot, siphon the wine into a clean carboy, leaving the sediment behind. Insert an airlock and relocate the carboy to a cool, dark location. Ferment there for at least 9 months. Periodically check to make sure the water hasn't evaporated out of the airlock, and refill and clean the airlock, as necessary.

11. After 9 months (or more), bottle and enjoy.

Flower Wines

"Wine made from flowers preserves the exquisite flavors and benevolent properties of the blossoms from which it is made. It also preserves the memories of fine, clear, sunshiny days—alone or with Someone Else—in woods, meadows, and hills, picking millions of tiny flowers for hours until they become etched on the insides of the eyelids." These wise words were written by my friend and neighbor Merril Harris, in an article, "Nipping in the Bud: How to Make Wine from Flowers," published in *Ms. Magazine* nearly thirty years ago.

Dandelion wine is the classic flower wine, made with the bright yellow flowers of the plentiful and easy-to-find weed. Don't believe the hype of the manicured lawn lobby; dandelion is not only beautiful and tasty, but potent liver-cleansing medicine. Many other flowers can transfer their delicate bouquets and distinctive essences into wines, as well, including (but certainly not limited to) rose petals, elderflowers, violets, red clover blossoms, and daylilies.

"Begin by gathering your flowers," writes Merril, "perhaps the most pleasurable part of the winemaking process." As a general guideline, pick about a gallon of flowers per gallon of wine you intend to make. If you cannot gather this many in a single outing, freeze what you gather until you accumulate enough. Be sure to pick flowers from places that have not been sprayed, which usually means not roadsides.

TIMEFRAME: 1 year or more

INGREDIENTS (for 1 gallon/4 liters):
1 gallon/4 liters flowers in full bloom
2 pounds/1 kilogram (4 cups/1 liter) sugar
2 lemons (organic, because you will use the peel)
2 oranges (organic, because you will use the peel)

(INCLUDING MEAD, CIDER, AND GINGER BEER)

1 pound/500 grams raisins (golden raisins will preserve the dandelion's light hue better than dark raisins)

Water

½ cup/125 milliliters berries (for wild yeast) or 1 packet wine yeast

PROCESS:

1. As much as possible, separate flower petals from the base of the blossoms, which can impart bitter flavors. With dandelions this can be a tedious project.

2. Reserving about ½ cup/125 milliliters to add later in the process, place the flower petals in a crock with the sugar, the juice and thinly peeled rinds of the lemons and oranges (to add acidity), and the raisins (to introduce astringent tannins). Then pour 1 gallon (4 liters) of boiling water over these ingredients, and stir until sugar is dissolved. Cover the crock to keep flies away, and leave to cool to body temperature.

3. Once the mixture cools, add the reserved flower petals and berries to introduce wild yeasts. (Or to use commercial yeast, remove 1 cup of the cooled mixture, dissolve a packet of yeast into it, and once it starts to bubble vigorously add it to the crock.) Cover the crock, and stir as often as you think of it, for 3 to 4 days.

4. Strain out the solids through a clean cheesecloth and squeeze moisture out of the flowers. Then transfer liquid to a carboy or jug with an airlock, and ferment about 3 months, until fermentation slows.

5. Siphon into a clean vessel and ferment at least 6 months more before bottling.

6. Age bottles at least 3 months to mellow wine; even longer is better.

Ginger Champagne

Any variety of country wine can be produced as a sparkling wine. In 1998, more than a year before Y2K, Nettles, with whom I built and share my home, started 5 gallons (20 liters) of this ginger champagne. With all the hype about computers crashing, and civilization with them, we ended up with over a hundred people at our sanctuary, figuring this would be a good remote place to survive a doomsday scenario. We were prepared, at least for the New Year's celebration, with endless bottles of this amazing "why tu qué" champagne: dry, bubbly, and with plenty of the desired kick. Lucky for us, Nettles recorded his ingredients and steps in our beloved kitchen journal, and he helped me recreate the recipe to pass on to you.

Sparkling wines use a specific variety of yeast—champagne yeast—that can tolerate higher levels of alcohol. After all the sugar is converted to alcohol and it is ready to be bottled, a little extra sugar is added so that fermentation continues in the bottle, trapping carbon dioxide and creating the sparkle. Since significant pressure builds in the bottle, champagne is bottled in heavy bottles. Special corks that you can grasp are available from winemaking suppliers, called "champagne stoppers," and you have to secure the stoppers with "champagne wires" (or you can improvise with any available wire).

TIMEFRAME: 1 year

INGREDIENTS (for 5 gallons/20 liters):
½ to 2 pounds/.25 to 1 kilogram fresh gingerroot
12 pounds/6 kilograms (24 cups/6 liters) sugar
Juice of 5 lemons

1 tablespoon/15 milliliters vanilla extract
1 package champagne yeast

PROCESS:

1. Finely chop or grate ginger (the amount used will determine the intensity of ginger flavor). Place it in a large pot with the sugar and 5 gallons/20 liters of water. Cover, bring to a boil, and simmer for 1 hour, stirring occasionally.

2. After 1 hour, turn off heat. Add the lemon juice and vanilla. Cover to keep flies away, and leave to cool to body temperature.

3. Once it reaches body temperature, strain 1 cup (250 milliliters) of the cooled mixture into a measuring cup and dissolve a packet of yeast into it. Strain the rest of the mixture into the carboy. Once the cup with the yeast starts to bubble vigorously, add it to the carboy and insert airlock. Ferment 2 to 3 months at room temperature.

4. After 2 to 3 months, once fermentation slows, siphon the wine into a clean carboy, leaving the yeasty sediment behind. Since you are losing some volume, top off with boiled and cooled water. Replace airlock and ferment about 6 more months.

5. At the end of 9 months of fermentation, it is time to bottle the champagne. Champagne requires heavy-duty bottles to contain the pressure. (Try recycling centers after the New Year for lots of champagne bottles.) Before the champagne is bottled, it must be primed. Priming creates the conditions for a final fermentation in the bottle, by adding additional sugar to reactivate the yeast, now dormant since it has consumed all the available sugar and

converted it into alcohol and (escaped) carbon dioxide. Add about 1 teaspoon (5 milliliters) of sugar per quart (liter) [just under ½ cup (125 milliliters) for a 5-gallon (20-liter) batch], directly into the bottles. Nettles also likes to sprinkle a few grains of yeast (3 to 5) into each bottle, just in case the dormant yeast is dead.

6. Siphon wine into the primed bottles. Cork bottles with champagne stoppers, secure stoppers with champagne wires, and wait at least a month before opening. Champagne can store for years, ready to make any occasion a celebration.

7. Chill bottles before opening; otherwise they will spew champagne all over.

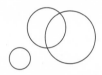

Cider Take Two

As it turns out, my editor, Ben Watson, is the author of the book *Cider, Hard and Sweet*. Ben felt that my earlier recipe for Spontaneous Cider doesn't do cider justice. "Hard cider that is truly fermented to dryness can require up to six months to make and mature before bottling," he wrote on a post-it note attached to my manuscript. I sure do enjoy good hard, dry cider, so I am including what Ben calls in his book "Cider 101."[4]

Hard cider was the favorite drink of colonial New England. Apple orchards provided the primary source of fruit to ferment into alcohol for the settlers. In Massachusetts in 1767, cider consumption was greater than 35 gallons (140 liters) per person.[5] Cider faded in popularity as

(INCLUDING MEAD, CIDER, AND GINGER BEER)

wild

America's agrarian society urbanized, and only now is it seeing a resurgence.

This process produces a dry, still (uncarbonated), traditional farmhouse cider.

TIMEFRAME: 6 months or more

INGREDIENTS (for 1 gallon/4 liters):

1 gallon/4 liters fresh apple cider (without chemical preservatives)

PROCESS:

1. Fill a fermentation vessel (jug or carboy) nine-tenths full of sweet cider. That would mean leaving out a little less than a pint from a gallon jug. Cover the container loosely with plastic wrap and place it in a cool location out of direct sunlight.

2. In a few days, the cider should begin to froth up vigorously and "boil over." Remove the plastic wrap and let the cider continue to ferment. Wipe off the sides of the container every day to remove any scummy residue.

3. Once this vigorous fermentation subsides (which may take several weeks, depending on the temperature), clean off the sides and neck of the container as much as possible. Fill up the vessel with fresh cider, leaving about 2 inches (5 centimeters) of head space at the top. Fit the jug or carboy with an airlock filled with water.

4. Let the cider continue to ferment slowly for 1 or 2 months, until the steady *glub-glub* of escaping carbon dioxide slows down considerably and the cider begins to clear. There will be a lot of sediment on the bottom of the container.

5. Insert a siphon hose and rack the cider off into another clean container, leaving the lees, or sediment, behind.

Place a fermentation lock filled with fresh water on the top. Let the cider continue to age and mellow for 1 or 2 months.

6. Approximately 4 to 5 months after you've started, the cider should be completely fermented to dryness, or nearly so, and ready for bottling. The cider's flavor will improve if it is aged in the bottle for another 1 or 2 months before drinking.

Persimmon Cider Mead

Cider fermented with honey is traditionally called "cyser". This cyser is a wild fermentation I made with my very favorite fruit, persimmons. I have long been acquainted with the large Asian varieties of persimmon, but since moving to Tennessee I have fallen in love with the smaller American persimmon (*Diospyros virginiana*) that is indigenous to this region. Every day from September through December I search the ground underneath the persimmon trees for these luscious fruits. I experience their sweet, sticky flesh as a healing ambrosia, nourishing my body and soul with all the rich goodness of the Earth. This seasonal pursuit has become an elaborate ritual of self-care, something I do for myself because it makes me feel so good, in the same category as, say, yoga—another practice that never fails me. The sweet persimmon taste triggers a powerful visualization in my mind, in which I see the persimmon's concentrated vital energy permeating my being. One thing that I've learned about healing is that clearly visualizing it helps enable it to happen. Not too many other people seem interested in these persimmons; mostly just me, the deer, and the goats.

Sometimes there are so many persimmons on the ground that I can't stuff them all in my mouth. One autumn day I collected a bowlful and made this cyser. Unripe persimmons have an awful astringent aftertaste, and already fermenting ones can be nasty, too, so I recommend tasting each persimmon (!) before using it. I offer this not so much as a recipe to be replicated, but to illustrate how you can hybridize techniques.

TIMEFRAME: Weeks to months

INGREDIENTS (for 1 gallon/4 liters):
2 cups/500 milliliters honey
½ gallon/2 liters water
½ gallon/2 liters fresh apple cider (without chemical preservatives)
4 cups/1 liter (or more) ripe persimmons

PROCESS:

1. Mix honey, water, and cider in a crock. Stir well to dissolve honey. Add persimmons. Cover to keep flies and dust out. The persimmons (like many fruits) are covered with wild yeast, so active fermentation begins very quickly.

2. Ferment about 5 days with the fruit, stirring often. Then strain out the fruit and transfer the wine to a glass jug with an airlock. (With any luck you'll have a little more than will fit in the jug, so taste some now.)

3. Ferment for a few weeks, until the bubbling slows, which will be sooner in hot weather (or a warm room) and longer in cold. Enjoy this cyser young, or rack and bottle to age it.

Wine Dregs Soup

When you rack and bottle wines, you are left with yeasty sediment at the bottom of the fermenting vessel. This sediment is not pretty, so generally it is not bottled or served. But all the deceased yeast is full of B vitamins. If you've ever used nutritional yeast, it is essentially the same thing as this.

Wine dregs make a rich and flavorful soup base. Try following a recipe for French onion soup, substituting wine dregs for one-quarter of the liquid. Be sure to boil it for awhile to cook off the alcohol. Inhale the fumes for an intense sensory experience!

Ginger Beer

This Caribbean-style soft drink uses a "ginger bug" to start the fermentation. I got this idea from Sally Fallon's *Nourishing Traditions*. The ginger bug is simply water, sugar, and grated ginger, which starts actively fermenting within a couple of days. This easy starter can be used as yeast in any alcohol ferment, or to start a sourdough.

This ginger beer is a soft drink, fermented just enough to create carbonation but not enough to contribute any appreciable level of alcohol. If the ginger is mild, kids love it.

TIMEFRAME: 2 to 3 weeks

INGREDIENTS (for 1 gallon/4 liters):
3 inches/8 centimeters or more fresh gingerroot
2 cups/500 milliliters sugar
2 lemons
Water

PROCESS:

1. Start the "ginger bug": Add 2 teaspoons (10 milliliters) grated ginger (skin and all) and 2 teaspoons (10 milliliters) sugar to 1 cup (250 milliliters) of water. Stir well and leave in a warm spot, covered with cheesecloth to allow free circulation of air while keeping flies out. Add this amount of ginger and sugar every day or two and stir, until the bug starts bubbling, in 2 days to about a week.

2. Make the ginger beer any time after the bug becomes active. (If you wait more than a couple of days, keep feeding the bug fresh ginger and sugar every 2 days.) Boil 2 quarts (2 liters) of water. Add about 2 inches (5 centimeters) of gingerroot, grated, for a mild ginger flavor (up to 6 inches/15 centimeters for an intense ginger flavor) and 1½ cups (375 milliliters) sugar. Boil this mixture for about 15 minutes. Cool.

3. Once the ginger-sugar-water mixture has cooled, strain the ginger out and add the juice of the lemons and the strained ginger bug. (If you intend to make this process an ongoing rhythm, reserve a few tablespoons of the active bug as a starter and replenish it with additional water, grated ginger, and sugar.) Add enough water to make 1 gallon (4 liters).

4. Bottle in sealable bottles: Recycle plastic soda bottles with screw tops; rubber gasket "bail-top" bottles that Grolsch and some other premium beers use; sealable juice jugs; or capped beer bottles, as described in chapter 11. Leave bottles to ferment in a warm spot for about 2 weeks.

5. Cool before opening. When you open ginger beer, be prepared with a glass, since carbonation can be strong and force liquid rushing out of the bottle.

OTHER SOFT DRINK RECIPES

See "Fermenting with Whey: Sweet Potato Fly" in chapter 7 and "Shrub" and "Switchel" in chapter 12.

FURTHER READING

Cresswell, Stephen. *Homemade Root Beer, Soda, and Pop*. Pownal, Vt.: Storey Books, 1998.

Garey, Terry A. *The Joy of Home Winemaking*. New York: Avon, 1996.

Spence, Pamela. *Mad about Mead! Nectar of the Gods*. St. Paul: Llewellyn Publications, 1997.

Vargas, Pattie, and Rich Gulling. *Making Wild Wines and Meads: 125 Unusual Recipes Using Herbs, Fruits, Flowers, and More*. Pownal, Vt.: Storey Books, 1999.

Watson, Ben. *Cider, Hard and Sweet*. Woodstock, Vt.: Countryman Press, 1999.

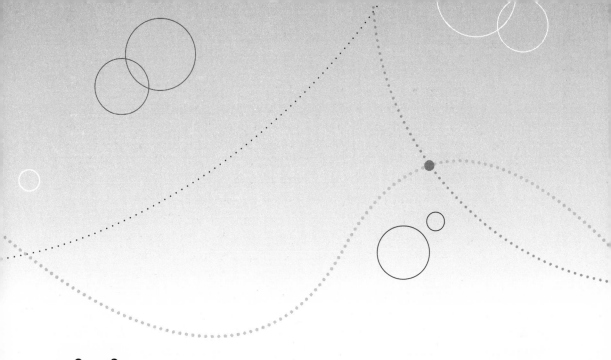

11 BEERS

THE *Reinheitsgebot,* the Bavarian beer purity law of 1516 to which German beermakers still boast of their adherence, permits only four ingredients in beer: water, barley, hops, and yeast. I love the beer this recipe produces, but the world is full of diverse beers incorporating many other ingredients. What distinguishes beers from the other alcohol ferments is that they are made primarily from grains. People brew beer not just from barley but also from wheat, corn, rice, millet, and others. Every grain that is cultivated and eaten has some beer tradition.

Grains do not spontaneously ferment to alcohol, the way honeywater or fruit juices do. For this reason, beermaking is more complex than winemaking. For grains to produce any significant amount of alcohol during fermentation (as opposed to primarily acidic beverages such as we encountered in chapter 9), their starch (complex carbohydrates) must first be converted to sugars (simple carbohydrates).

The standard way to accomplish this is called malting, which means actually germinating, or sprouting, the grain. The germination releases an enzyme, diastase, that breaks down starch into sugars, which would nourish the baby plant but, as fate would have it, end up nourishing yeast instead to produce alcohol. Directions for sprouting grains are on page 104. I'll walk you through a couple of beers that are started from whole grains. I learned them because I'm obsessed with transformative processes starting with the rawest resources possible. Most home brewers I know do not actually malt their own grain. Commercially available malted grains and malt extracts are much easier to use, and still produce flavorful, distinctive brews.

There are two other ways that starch can be converted to sugar. One is through the action of molds. Recall (from chapter 9) *amazaké*, the Japanese sweet rice ferment, made from rice incubated with the mold *Aspergillus oryzae*. Saké, Japanese rice wine, is made by fermenting *amazaké* with yeast. *Chang*, Nepalese beer, uses a mold cake called *marcha* to convert the starch in rice. Across Asia, people ferment grains with cakes containing various fungi that convert starch to sugar.

The other way to convert starch to sugar is with saliva, which contains the enzyme ptyalin. Perhaps you have noticed that if you chew long enough on a morsel of starchy food it starts to taste sweet. Digestion begins in the mouth, and your body wastes no time breaking down food into simpler nutrients. Chewing on grains and spitting them out is a low-tech and ancient means of starch conversion for beer-making. This is exactly how we'll make our next ferment, *chicha*.

Chicha (Andean Chewed-Corn Beer)

Chicha is an ancient tradition in the Andes, and still popular in Peru, Bolivia, and Ecuador. It has a light, delicious, corny flavor. *Chicha* was beloved by the Incas, who considered it "the vehicle that linked man to his gods through the fecundity of the earth."[1] According to a recent report in *National Geographic*, *chicha* even predates the Inca civilization, and it played an important ceremonial role in the Wari empire, which flourished in what is now Peru nearly a thousand years before the Incas. Wari lords threw grand feasts, in which copious quantities of *chicha* were served from elaborately decorated ceramic jugs, which were then smashed by the drunken revelers. Entire villages are believed to have been relocated by the Wari and put to work growing corn. "The Wari needed huge quantities of corn for their state-sponsored ceremonies since those held the empire together."[2]

Chewed corn gobs

An integral part of the *chicha*-making process is chewing the corn to saturate it with enzyme-rich saliva. (Later in the process the brew is boiled, killing any germs in the saliva.) The salivated corn gobs are called *muko*. Traditionally, *muko* has been produced communally, by old people and children sitting in a circle and telling stories.

Recruiting people to chew corn with me was very interesting. To me it seems adventurous and weirdly intimate to chew food, spit it out, and intermingle it. Some of my friends were excited to try this simple process, and join a circle of chewers. But the squeamish ones were utterly repulsed by the thought of it. We intrepid chewers derived much pleasure from the emphatic refusals of the saliva-phobes. If you embark upon a *chicha*-making adventure, the sensational accounts of it are likely to persist long after you've exhausted your supply of delicious corn beer.

The two descriptions of the *chicha* process that I had to guide me both called for starting with cornmeal, mixed with enough water to make a thick dough that can be formed into balls. This mixture immediately dried out the mouth of whoever chewed it, and proved to be impractical. What works much better, and I'd venture to guess was the more traditional process, is to chew a spoonful of moist whole-grain

posole, nixtamalized kernels of corn. The nixtamalization process is simple, and is described on page 111.

This recipe uses berries to start the fermentation, yielding a variation of chicha called *frutillada.* I used black raspberries, which gave the pale yellow corn brew a salmon hue.

TIMEFRAME: About 2 weeks

INGREDIENTS (for 1 gallon/4 liters):
4 cups/1 liter nixtamalized corn (see page 111)
1 cup/250 milliliters polenta or grits
Water
½ cup/125 milliliters organic berries

PROCESS:

1. Make *muko*: Get several friends to help you with this process, which can only proceed one mouthful at a time. Take a good tablespoon of the moist nixtamalized corn kernels at a time into your mouth. Gently chew the corn, mixing it with saliva, as you hold it together in a mass and form it with your tongue against the roof of your mouth. Then spit out the formed ball. The biggest problem people seem to encounter is the corn becoming too liquid and dispersing in their mouths. This recipe calls for a bit more corn than you actually need, as some will inevitably be swallowed as you chew.

2. Dry the *muko* in the sun or in the oven with just the pilot light. Once dried, *muko* is stable and storable, so it is possible to chew just a little at a time and accumulate the quantity you need over time.

3. In a cooking pot, mix the *muko* with polenta or grits and 5 cups (1.25 liters) of water. The reason for adding the polenta or grits is that there is enough ptyalin in the *muko* to convert the starch of additional corn. Heat this mixture to 155°F (68°C), at which temperature ptyalin becomes highly active. Break up the chunks of *muko,* and hold the mixture at this temperature for 20 minutes.

4. Cover the pot, remove from heat, and leave it for a few hours until the corn mash cools.

5. Strain, discarding the solids. Boil the remaining liquid for 1 hour, then cool.

6. After the liquid cools to body temperature, transfer it to a crock, and add berries to start fermentation. Stir well and cover to keep flies out. Continue to stir periodically.

7. After 4 or 5 days, strain out the fruit and transfer the *chicha* to a carboy until fermentation slows, about a week to 10 days, then drink or bottle.

Bouza (Ancient Egyptian Beer)

Bouza has been consumed in Egypt continuously for 5,000 years. That tradition may be dying out, as increasingly fundamentalist authorities have outlawed alcohol and revoked the licenses of *bouza* shops. This recipe is 5,000 years old. I adapted it from an article in the anthropology journal *Food and Foodways.*[3] My friend Jai, who used to live in Kenya, drank *bouza* there, and he confirmed the authenticity of the *bouza* this recipe produced.

Bouza requires only two ingredients, wheat and water, manipulated in incredibly clever ways. The process for *bouza* vividly illustrates the bread-beer connection. Wheat formed into loaves of bread is part of the process, and traditionally the

way yeast was stored for *bouza*-making was in partially cooked loaves, where the center remained raw and alive. "In essence, making bread was a convenient way to store the raw materials for brewing beer," reports *Archaeology* magazine.[4]

TIMEFRAME: About 1 week

INGREDIENTS (for 1 gallon/4 liters):
4 cups/1 liter wheat berries
1 cup/250 milliliters bubbly sourdough starter (see page 95)
Water

PROCESS:

The process for making *bouza* consists of three distinct steps: malting, or sprouting, one-quarter of the wheat berries; making loaves of the remaining wheat berries; and finally brewing the *bouza* out of these ingredients. The products of the first two processes are stable and storable, so there is no need to do it all at once.

MALTING

1. Follow the sprouting instructions on page 104, using 1 cup (250 milliliters) of wheat berries.

2. Dry the sprouted wheat by spreading it on a cookie sheet and baking at the lowest setting of your oven for 20 to 30 minutes, until it is good and dry. Store in a jar until you are ready to make *bouza*.

FORMING LOAVES

1. Coarsely grind the remaining 3 cups (750 milliliters) of wheat berries. In the absence of a grinder, use whole-wheat flour instead.

2. Add 1 cup (250 milliliters) of bubbly sourdough starter.

3. Mix into a stiff dough, adding additional water, just a little at a time, if needed.

4. Form into a round loaf, and leave for 1 to 2 days to ferment.

5. Bake the loaf at 300°F (150°C) for about 15 minutes, so the outside is cooked but the center is still raw, with live yeast.

BREWING *BOUZA*

1. Fill a crock or bucket with 1 gallon (4 liters) of water.

2. Coarsely grind the dried malted wheat and add it to the water.

3. Break the partially baked loaf into the water.

4. Add a little fresh sourdough starter for good luck, stir, and cover the crock with a cloth to keep out dust and flies.

5. Ferment for about 2 days, then strain out the solids and drink. *Bouza* will keep for a week or two in the refrigerator.

Chang (Nepalese Rice Beer)

This is a warm, milky beer, very different from what we generally think of as beer. Chang plays an important symbolic role in Nepalese life, both as a show of hospitality and as an offering to deities. Anthropologist Kathryn S. March studied the Tamang and Sherpa peoples of the Nepal highlands, and observed: "The aspiration underlying offerings of beer is that the natural propensity of yeast and beer to multiply, heat up, froth, and bubble will spill over into an analogous growth and prosperity for those placing the offerings."[5]

Chang traditionally calls for yeast cakes called *marcha* (in Nepal) or *pap* (in Tibet), which are not widely available in the United States. My friend Justin Bullard brought *marcha* back with him from Nepal and showed me how he had learned to make *chang*. This adaptation substitutes a mixture of *koji* and sourdough starter for the traditional yeast cake.

TIMEFRAME: 2 days

INGREDIENTS (for 8 cups/2 liters *chang*):
½ cup/125 milliliters *koji* (see page 60)
½ cup/125 milliliters bubbly sourdough starter (see page 95)
4 cups/1 liter cooked rice (cooked without salt)

PROCESS:

1. Mix the *koji* and sourdough starter; leave for 30 minutes or more to allow the dry *koji* to absorb moisture from the sourdough starter.

2. Mix the cooked rice, cooled to body temperature, with the koji-sourdough mixture. Combine well. Place in a jar, seal, and leave in a warm spot for 24 to 48 hours. Smell periodically. It is ready when it is fragrant, smelling sweet and alcoholic. At this stage it is called the *lum*; the longer the *lum* ferments, the more sour the fragrance and taste become.

3. When the *lum* is sweet and fragrant, transfer it to a bowl or larger jar. Pour 4 cups (1 liter) of boiling water over the *lum* and cover. Leave for 10 to 15 minutes and then strain. The white milky liquid is *chang*. Pour 4 more cups (1 liter) of boiling water over the *lum* for a second pressing, which will be a little weaker.

Beer from Malt Extracts

Tom Foolery, a friend who lives at IDA, is an avid beer brewer. This beer that he made to guide us through his process was his first beer in more than six months. He gave up drinking after a bout of hepatitis, and now he's prudently limiting himself to a single glass on occasion. To make a liver-tonifying beer, we started with dandelions. Though hops has become the standard beer-bittering herb, beers have been made with a wide variety of herbs, and any herbs you especially like can be incorporated into beer.

This beer is dark and mildly bitter. Many different types of malt extracts are available from home-brew suppliers; the type of extract, along with temperature of fermentation and amount of bittering herbs, will determine the character of the resulting beer. Some homebrewers are determined to recreate a favorite style of beer and get compulsive about controlling the many variables. Much of the literature reinforces this compulsiveness. "There is a lot of talk about the necessity for the use of chemicals to keep everything sterile, the need for other chemicals to make the beer work well, the crucial necessity for Teutonic authoritarian temperature controls, and the importance of complex understandings of miniscule differences in grains, malts, hops, and yeasts," writes Stephen Harrod Buhner in *Sacred and Herbal Healing Beers*. "Generally, this frightens off a lot of people and takes all the fun out of brewing."[6]

Tom Foolery, a professional juggler and clown, is more free-form and flexible about the product of his beer-making. His brewing motto is "cleanliness, not sterility." His primary brewing reference book is Charlie Papazian's *The New Complete Joy of Home Brewing*, from which he read me passages like this as we brewed: "Relax. Don't worry. Have a homebrew. Because worrying is like paying interest on a debt you may never have owed."[7] Profound advice.

TIMEFRAME: 3 to 4 Weeks

INGREDIENTS (for 5 gallons/20 liters):

4 cups/1 liter whole dandelion plants (roots, leaves, and flowers, if in flower)

4 cups/1 liter (about 2 ounces/55 grams) dried hops

3.3 pounds/1.5 kilograms roasted malt extract syrup

2 cups/500 milliliters extra-dark malt extract powder

PROCESS:

1. Dig dandelions. Dandelions are everywhere, especially where the soil has been disturbed, near roads, construction, and fires. It is a meditation to stare at the ground in search of these prolific plant allies. Use a fork or shovel about 6 inches (15 centimeters) from the plant to loosen the soil, then reach down to the root, grasp it, and pull it out. Where roots break, notice the white sap bleeding from them. This sap is dandelion's potent medicine.

2. Boil 2½ gallons (10 liters) of water in a pot big enough to add another gallon's worth of ingredients. Tom says the fresh and delicious IDA spring water is the secret ingredient that makes his beers so good. Indeed, water is the major ingredient in beer, and many commercial beers similarly boast about their unique water sources. If you've got access to a spring, lucky you; if not, bear in mind that brewing has also been used historically to make poor-quality water potable.

3. Clean the dandelions, scrubbing their roots and discarding any dead leaves. Chop finely.

4. When the water boils, add the dandelions, hops, and malt extracts. This soup is the "wort." The only reason we used two different forms of malt extract is simply that, after a 6-month brewing hiatus, that's what Tom had around. You could use all malt syrup or all malt powder or a combination. Cultivate flexibility. Loosely cover the wort and return it to a boil. It will be foamy, with the hops floating on top. After it boils, reduce the heat so it doesn't boil over. Simmer about 1 hour.

5. Strain the wort into a clean fermentation vessel. Top off with water to make about 5 gallons (20 liters). Don't fill a carboy all the way up to the neck with beer. Leave at least 3 inches (7.5 centimeters) of head space to allow for foaming during the active initial period of fermentation—otherwise pressure could force foam through the airlock and make a big mess.

6. Allow the wort to cool to blood temperature, then add the yeast. Ferment 1 week to 10 days at room temperature. Many brewers are fastidious about maintaining a constant temperature, but in our homesteading situation that simply is not possible, and Tom's beers never seem to suffer from the inevitable temperature fluctuations.

BOTTLING BEER

Once fermentation stops, beer needs to be primed and bottled. The easiest bottles, if you can find them, are rubber-gasket "bail-top" bottles that Grolsch and some other premium beers use. Save these when you come across them, and collect them from recycling centers. Also collect beer bottles with lips that hold "crown caps," the kind of beer caps you need to open with a bottle opener. Brewing suppliers sell caps and capping devices, so you can reuse these bottles indefinitely. Friends have also had success bottling beer in 2- and 3-liter plastic soda bottles with screw tops—an unorthodox and perhaps inelegant method, but effective and labor-saving. Here's the process for priming and bottling beer:

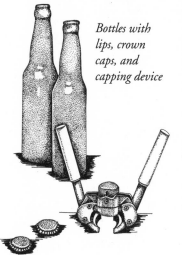

Bottles with lips, crown caps, and capping device

Bail-top bottles

1. Clean bottles: 5 gallons (20 liters) of beer will fill approximately 53 12-ounce bottles (60 33-milliliter bottles). Many books recommend sterilizing with bleach or other chemicals, but the brewers I know rely on thorough washing with a bottle brush, soap, and hot water. Tom Foolery swears by a high-pressure bottle-washing gizmo that attaches to a water spigot that he picked up at a brewing supply shop for about ten dollars.

2. Prime beer: "priming" means adding sugar to the beer at the bottling stage to initiate a final fermentation in which the carbon dioxide produced is trapped inside the bottle and thereby carbonates the beer. The best way to do this involves using a second 5-gallon (20-liter) vessel, a carboy, a crock, or a plastic bucket. Siphon the beer into the clean vessel, leaving the yeasty sediment behind. Remove about 1 cup (250 milliliters) of the beer, and dissolve in it 1¼ cups (310 milliliters) of malt syrup or ¾ cup (185 milliliters) of corn sugar or malt powder. Then stir this mixture into the rest of the beer to distribute the priming sugar evenly. Be sure to thoroughly clean all the implements that you use.

3. Siphon the beer into bottles and cap.

4. Leave the bottles to ferment and age at least 2 weeks before drinking.

Mashing:
Beer from Malted Grains

My friend Patrick Ironwood brews amazing beers in vast quantities. Patrick lives at Moonshadow, a homestead he shares with four generations of his family, including his two grandmothers, his parents, his wife, his brother and sister-in-law, and his newborn baby Sage Indigo Ironwood (three plant names!), as well as friends, interns, and visitors. The Kimmons-Ironwood clan's woodland homestead is also home to an environmental education center, the Sequatchie Valley Institute (see page 66). Patrick has been brewing since age fifteen, when his parents gave their budding do-it-yourselfer a homebrew kit and he made his first batch of beer for them.

Twenty years later, Patrick generally brews in 30-gallon (120-liter) batches and stores his beer in kegs, which involves much less work than bottling. After years of enjoying Patrick's beer, I recently assisted him as he brewed a batch. I'll describe his process adapted to a 5-gallon (20-liter) quantity first, then describe his setup for doing it in 30-gallon batches.

For the mashing process, an accurate thermometer is essential. The mash is heated and held at successively higher temperatures. The malted grains contain enzymes that behave differently at different temperatures. Mashing for periods of time at different temperatures gives the enzymes the opportunity to convert starches into sugars in several different modes, producing a wort that will ferment into a complex-flavored beer.

TIMEFRAME: 3 to 4 weeks

INGREDIENTS (for 5 gallons/20 liters):
2 pounds/1 kilogram pale malted barley
1 pound/500 grams Cara Munich malted barley
3 pounds/1.5 kilograms amber barley malt syrup
2 pounds/1 kilogram amber barley malt powder
3 ounces/85 grams Chinook pelletized hops
¾ teaspoon/4 milliliters Irish moss
1 packet beer yeast

PROCESS:

1. Coarsely grind the malted barley. Just crack each grain into a few chunky pieces to increase surface area; do not grind it into flour, which would make the mash pasty and cause problems.

2. Heat 2 gallons (8 liters) water in a large pot to around 160°F (71°C). Add the barley and stir well. Room-temperature barley will cool the mash. Check the temperature; we are aiming to hold the mash at 128°F (53°C). Either add cold water or continue heating until the mash reaches 128°F (53°C). Then cover, turn off the heat, and leave at this temperature for 20 minutes.

3. After 20 minutes, heat the mash to 140°F (60°C). As you heat, stir constantly so grain at the bottom won't burn. Once you reach 140°F (60°C), cover, turn off the heat, and leave at this temperature for 40 minutes. After 20 minutes, check the

temperature and reheat if it has dropped more than a couple of degrees.

4. After 40 minutes at 140°F (60°C), heat the mash to 160°F (71°C), where it will remain for 1 hour. Check the temperature every 20 minutes and reheat as needed to maintain temperature.

5. After 1 hour at 160°F (71°C), heat the mash to 170°F (77°C), stirring constantly.

6. Meanwhile, boil about 1 gallon of water.

7. After mash reaches 170°F (77°C), strain it. Set a colander in a large pot or crock and scoop the mash—grains and liquid—into the colander. As the colander fills with grain, press it with a potato masher or other kitchen implement to release liquid. Once the liquid is pressed out, pour a few cups of boiled water over the grains to rinse off additional sweet residue. This procedure is called "sparging". Press the grains and repeat the process. After sparging, spent grains can be fed to chickens or composted. Repeat this process until all the mash has been strained and you are left with just sweet, fragrant liquid, now called "wort".

8. Return the wort to the cooking pot and heat to a boil. Add the malt extracts and stir. This thick, concentrated wort could burn, so keep stirring. Once it returns to a boil, add half the hops. Boil with the hops for 45 minutes; keep stirring.

9. After 45 minutes, add the Irish moss, which helps clarify the beer. Five minutes later, add half the remaining hops; eight minutes after that, add the rest of the hops. Boiling hops extracts bitterness but cooks off some of volatile aromatic qualities. Adding hops toward the end of the process (these are known as "finishing hops") releases these volatile aromatics into the beer.

10. Once the wort has boiled for 1 hour, turn off the heat. Strain the wort into a carboy or other fermenting vessel. Patrick uses a 3 percent hydrogen peroxide solution to sterilize his fermentation vessels. If you are working with a glass carboy, add the hot wort slowly to avoid shocking and shattering the glass. Top off with additional water to make 5 gallons (20 liters). Be sure to leave a few inches of head space for the beer to foam, and seal with an airlock until beer cools to body temperature.

11. Once the beer cools, sprinkle on the yeast and seal with the airlock. Ferment about 1 week to 10 days, until it stops bubbling. Prime and bottle as described above, or read on for a description of Patrick's kegging system.

BEER IN KEGS

Patrick actually does the mashing process described above at a scale six times as large, a 30-gallon (120-liter) batch at a time, or the equivalent of three hundred and twenty 12-ounce (three hundred and sixty 33-milliliter bottles). He's not such a big drinker, but he and his community do like to host big, lively parties. At this scale, Patrick estimates the cost of ingredients to be two dollars per gallon (4 liters), much cheaper than the cheapest beer you could buy, and so much better. He brews in a 15-gallon (60-liter) pot that is actually a "half-barrel"-sized keg with the top cut out, though any big cooking pot with a 15-gallon (60-liter) capacity would work.

Cornelius keg

Patrick strains the mash into a single huge crock he has, with a 20-gallon (80-liter) capacity, though you could just as well strain it into a number of smaller-capacity vessels. Then he returns it to the 15-gallon (60-liter) pot to brew. He ferments the batch in two 15.5-gallon (62-liter) half-barrel kegs that he has modified by welding onto them "Cornelius" keg tops, so he can reach inside them to clean. (Patrick is the rare generalist who is equipped to do his own welding.) He scrubs the insides of the stainless steel kegs with a scouring pad, then sprays them with 3 percent hydrogen peroxide solution. It is important to rinse all the peroxide off because it eats away at metal if left in contact with it. Patrick stores empty kegs filled with an iodine solution to discourage bacterial growth.

After fermentation, Patrick siphons the beer (leaving behind the sediment) into 5-gallon (20-liter) Cornelius kegs, which are the canisters that until recently were used to hold soda syrups for restaurants and bars. These durable canisters are being phased out and replaced by disposable mylar and cardboard wrappings similar to boxed wines. A glut of Cornelius kegs are out there available free or cheap to resourceful scavengers. I found them for sale for as low as twelve dollars apiece on the Web. Patrick serves the beer straight out of these light-enough-to-carry canisters, propelled sometimes by the pressure of carbon dioxide from fermentation, sometimes by hand-pumped air, and sometimes by tanks of carbon dioxide. The CO_2 tanks are especially useful if a whole keg is not consumed at one sitting, as it keeps air, with its inevitable souring organisms, away from the beer.

If you want to try to ferment beer on a scale like this, you can ferment in the 5-gallon Cornelius kegs, provided that you have an extra one; you siphon each fermented keg into a clean keg, then clean the one you just siphoned from, to siphon the next one into.

FURTHER READING

Buhner, Stephen Harrod. *Sacred and Healing Beers: The Secrets of Ancient Fermentation.* Boulder: Siris Books, 1998.

Miller, Dave. *Brewing the World's Great Beers.* Pownal, Vt.: Storey Books, 1992.

Papazian, Charlie. *The Home Brewer's Companion.* New York: Avon Books, 1994.

Papazian, Charlie. *The New Complete Joy of Home Brewing.* New York: Avon Books, 1991.

12 VINEGARS

MOST OF MY EXPERIENCE with vinegar-making has been from wine-making gone awry. I imagine that is how vinegar first came into being, for alcohol ferments left in contact with the air inevitably become home to bacteria of the genus *Acetobacter* and aerobic yeasts, called *Mycoderma aceti,* that consume alcohol and transform it into acetic acid. The word "vinegar" comes from the French *vinaigre: vin,* wine, and *aigre,* sour. Vinegar is an excellent consolation for your wine-making failure. It is a preservative in its own right, healthful, with many delicious uses in cooking.

There are different types of vinegar, generally distinguished by the source of the alcohol from which the vinegar is made. Wine vinegar is made from wine; apple cider vinegar from apple cider; rice vinegar from rice wine; malt vinegar from malted grain beverages such as beer. The cheapest and most commonly used vinegar, distilled white vinegar, is made from grain, though it lacks the flavor and color characteristic of malt vinegar, and indeed its chief virtues are colorlessness and flavorlessness.

Wine Vinegar

If one of your homemade wines turns out sour, call it vinegar and use it in cooking and salad dressings. If you want to encourage vinegar fermentation in either a homemade or a commercial wine, bear in mind that vinegar fermentation is an *aerobic* process. Do it in a wide open vessel, like a crock or plastic bucket, to maximize the surface area exposed to the air. Cover it with cheesecloth or mesh to keep out flies and particles, and store it out of direct light and away from alcohol fermentation projects. For best results, ferment the wine completely with an airlock before deliberately exposing it to aerobic vinegar organisms. Also, don't use vessels for vinegar-making and wine-making interchangeably.

My friend Hector Black, a Tennessee back-to-the-lander with a blueberry orchard and more blueberries than he knows what to do with, makes blueberry wine vinegar in a big oak barrel. His blueberry wine vinegar is thick and fruity, so delicious that I drank it from a glass—which I even refilled several times. The barrel lays on its side to maximize the surface area in contact with the air. The hole in the barrel (known as the "bunghole") is stuffed with cheesecloth. This year Hector tried something new that he says sped the process: He used a small electric air pump designed for an aquarium to pump air into the developing vinegar. Since the vinegar-making organisms are aerobic, this stimulates them and increases their action.

The acidity of finished vinegar correlates with the alcohol content of the wine from which it was made. The time it takes for wine to become vinegar will vary quite

Barrel on its side, with bunghole stuffed with cheesecloth

a bit, depending upon alcohol content, temperature, and aeration. Figure roughly two weeks in summer, about a month in winter—less if you stir it often or devise some way to introduce air circulation. Taste the vinegar periodically to monitor its progress, and don't worry about leaving it too long. Vinegar is a stable product that will not quickly turn into something else.

You may observe a film or disk collecting on the surface of the vinegar. This is called the "mother-of-vinegar," or "mother" for short. It is a mass of vinegar-making organisms that can be transferred to your next batch of vinegar as a starter. The mother is edible and nutritious, so there is no need to be afraid of it. Vinegar may also contain solid blobs below the surface, which is sunken, dead mother-of-vinegar. You can either strain it out, or consume it with your vinegar.

Apple Cider Vinegar

In chapter 10, I described the simplest alcohol fermentation process I know, simply leaving a jar of fresh apple cider to spontaneously ferment, producing hard cider in less than a week (see page 127). If you leave that same jar on your counter for a couple more weeks, exposed to air, it will become apple cider vinegar just as spontaneously. You can help it along by transferring it to a wide container where its surface area is maximized.

Folk medicine of many traditions calls for a spoonful each day of raw, unfiltered apple cider vinegar. According to *The Vinegar Book* by Emily Thacker, "Since the beginning of time mankind has sought the magic elixir which bubbles from the fabled 'Fountain of Youth.' For most of us, apple cider vinegar may be as close as we'll ever come to such a universal remedy."[1] Thacker reviewed scientific and medical journals and found reports of vinegar's effectiveness in preventing arthritis, osteoporosis, and cancer, killing infections, soothing itches, burns, and sunburns, aiding digestion, controlling weight, and preserving memory.[2] Even Hippocrates, the Greek physician whose oath every contemporary American doctor must swear, prescribed vinegar as a remedy.

Vinagre de Piña (Mexican Pineapple Vinegar)

Pineapple vinegar is delicious and super-acidic. Many Mexican recipes call for pineapple vinegar, though you could use this in place of any kind of vinegar. Since this uses only the skin of the pineapple, you get to eat the pineapple flesh. This recipe was inspired by a recipe in *The Cuisines of Mexico* by Diana Kennedy.

TIMEFRAME: 3 to 4 weeks

INGREDIENTS (for 1 quart/1 liter):

¼ cup/60 milliliters sugar

Peel of 1 pineapple (organic, because you use the skin; overripe fruits are fine)

Water

PROCESS:

1. In a jar or bowl, dissolve the sugar in 1 quart (1 liter) of water. Coarsely chop and add the pineapple peel. Cover with cheesecloth to keep flies out, and leave to ferment at room temperature.

2. When you notice the liquid darkening, after about 1 week, strain out the pineapple peels and discard.

3. Ferment the liquid 2 to 3 weeks more, stirring or agitating periodically, and your pineapple vinegar is ready.

Fruit Scrap Vinegar

Just as the peel of pineapple makes delicious vinegar, so can any fruit scraps: peels and cores from apple pie-making; fallen, bruised fruit; overripe bananas; or the dregs of a bunch of grapes or berries (what's left after the finer specimens have been eaten). Vinegar is a recycling opportunity. Just pour sugar water (¼ cup/60 milliliters sugar dissolved in 1 quart/liter of water) over the fruit, and proceed as for pineapple vinegar. You could use honey instead of sugar, if you prefer, but the process might take a little longer.

Shrub

Shrub is a refreshing soft drink that was popular in the United States prior to the availability of carbonated sodas. Traditionally, it was made by soaking fresh berries in vinegar for up to 2 weeks, then straining out the berries and adding sugar or honey. This concentrate was stored, and diluted with water as needed and served over ice. If you have fruity wine or cider vinegar, it's easier to just mix it with fruit juice. Try mixing 1 part vinegar to 3 parts fruit juice and 3 parts water. You can make it more soda-like by using seltzer in place of water. Adjust proportions to taste. Sweet and sour flavors combine well.

Switchel

Switchel is another vinegar-based soft drink, flavored with molasses and ginger. This recipe is adapted from Stephen Cresswell's *Homemade Root Beer, Soda, and Pop.*

TIMEFRAME: 2 hours

INGREDIENTS (for ½ gallon/2 liters):
½ cup/125 milliliters apple cider or other fruity vinegar
½ cup/125 milliliters sugar
½ cup/125 milliliters molasses
2 inches/5 centimeters of fresh gingerroot, grated
Water

PROCESS:

1. Combine vinegar, sugar, molasses, ginger, and 1 quart (1 liter) of water, and cook about 10 minutes. Strain out the ginger.

2. Add additional water (or carbonated water) to make 2 quarts (2 liters).

3. Serve chilled.

Variation: Switchel is very similar to a restorative tonic drink my friend Ha! prepares using vinegar, lemon juice, and molasses: mix 1 tablespoon (15 milliliters) molasses, 2 tablespoons (30 milliliters) cider vinegar, and 3 tablespoons (45 milliliters) lemon juice into 1 cup of hot water. Drink warm.

Horseradish Sauce

Horseradish is a potent root; when you eat it, its heat spreads from your the mouth into your sinus cavity. I learned to love it on matzo as a kid, since it is used in the Passover seder ritual to symbolize the bitterness of oppression. I still love it on matzo, but also on sandwiches and *nori* rolls, and in sauces, dressings, and kimchis.

Horseradish sauce is very simple to prepare: First, grate fresh horseradish root finely. Whether you do this by hand or by machine, be aware that the fumes released as horseradish is grated are intense. Breathing it directly can be overwhelming, particularly as you open a sealed food processor. Cover grated horseradish with just a little vinegar and salt and let it infuse for a few hours or a few weeks.

Alternatively, you can ferment horseradish with a little honey-water. Pour honey-water over grated horseradish. Stir well, cover with a cheesecloth or mesh, and ferment for 3 to 4 weeks. This involves the horseradish in both the fermentation that creates alcohol from honey, and the fermentation that creates vinegar from alcohol. I like to think that the fermenting microorganisms are getting as much of a charge from the horseradish as I do.

Infused Vinegars

Vinegar's acidity makes it an effective solvent and preservative for extracting flavors and phytochemicals from foods and herbs. The flavors and medicinal compounds melt into the vinegar. Depending on what you infuse, you'll have distinctive vinegar for salad dressings or potent plant medicine (or both). Place whatever it is you want to infuse into the vinegar in a jar, cover with vinegar, and put a top on the jar. Vinegar will make metal tops corrode, so use plastic, or place a layer of wax paper between the bottle and a metal lid. Leave the vinegar to infuse in a dark spot for a few weeks (or longer). Strain the vinegar and discard the spent plant material. If the vinegar is light and you can see through it, place a fresh bit of whatever you infused in the vinegar when you bottle it. Put it in a sleek bottle and give it as a gift. Food boutiques are full of gorgeous bottles of infused vinegars at premium prices.

Here are a few ideas of foods and herbs to extract in vinegar: garlic; rosemary; thyme; tarragon; hot peppers; berries; mints; basil; dandelion roots, leaves, and/or flowers. . . . Anything you like.

Vinegar Pickling: Dilly Beans

Pickling food in vinegar is not a fermentation process. In brine pickling, covered in chapter 5, vegetables are preserved by lactic acid, which is produced by the action of microorganisms on the vegetables. Vinegar pickling makes use of a fermented product, vinegar, but the acidity of the vinegar prevents microorganism action. Vinegar pickles contain no live cultures. According to *Keeping Food Fresh*, a book by Terre Vivante, a French eco-education center focused on organic gardening and preservation of Old World food-preservation techniques, "Pickles were always lacto-fermented in times past, and then trans-

Infused vinegar with herbs in a bottle

Jar of dilly beans

ferred to vinegar solely to stabilize them for commercial purposes."[3] Indeed, the great advantage that vinegar pickling has over lacto-fermentation pickling is that vinegar pickles will last forever (well, almost), while brined pickles will last for weeks or months, but rarely for years, and definitely not forever. Cookbooks are full of vinegar pickling recipes, so I will offer just one: the dilly beans my father makes from his garden every summer and serves to his family and friends all year long.

TIMEFRAME: 6 weeks

SPECIAL EQUIPMENT:

Sealable canning jars: 1 1/2 pint/750 milliliter size is best, as its height perfectly accommodates the length of string beans

INGREDIENTS:

String beans

Garlic

Salt (my dad swears by coarse kosher salt, but sea salt is fine, too)

Whole dried chili peppers

Celery seed

Fresh dill (flowering tops best, or leaves)

White distilled vinegar

Water

PROCESS:

1. Guesstimate how many jars you'll fill with the string beans you have. Thoroughly clean jars and line them up.

2. Into each jar, place 1 clove of garlic, 1 teaspoon (5 milliliters) of salt, 1 whole red chili pepper, ¼ teaspoon (1.5 milliliters) of celery seed, and a flowering dill top or small bunch of dill leaves. Then fill the jar with beans standing on end, stuffing them as tightly as you can into the jar.

3. For each jar you have filled, measure 1 cup (250 milliliters) of vinegar and 1 cup (250 milliliters) of water. Boil the vinegar-water mixture, then pour it into the jars over the beans and spices, to ½ inch (1 centimeter) from the top of the jar.

4. Seal the jars and place them in a large pot of boiling water for a 10-minute heat processing.

Leave the dilly beans for at least 6 weeks for the flavors to meld, then open jars as desired and enjoy. My father serves these dilly beans as an hors d'oeuvre. Heat-processed pickles can be stored for years without refrigeration.

Vinaigrette

This is my version of the classic salad dressing. It's the first thing my mother taught me to make, and my job as a child was to make it whenever we ate salad. My mother taught me to use more vinegar than oil, lots of mustard, and lots of garlic. Salad dressing is easy; it always surprises me that people buy it prepared.

TIMEFRAME: 10 minutes

INGREDIENTS (for 1 cup/250 milliliters):

½ cup/125 milliliters wine vinegar

¼ cup/60 milliliters extra-virgin olive oil

8 cloves garlic, crushed into a pulp

2 tablespoons/30 milliliters spicy mustard

1 teaspoon/5 milliliters mustard powder

1 teaspoon/5 milliliters fresh or dried thyme

1 teaspoon/5 milliliters fresh or dried parsley

½ teaspoon/3 milliliters fresh or dried tarragon

1 tablespoon/15 milliliters toasted sesame oil (optional—for a flavor variation)

1 tablespoon/15 milliliters honey (optional—makes it sweet)

2 tablespoons/30 milliliters yogurt or tahini sauce (optional—for a creamy vinaigrette)

Salt and pepper to taste

PROCESS:

Place ingredients in a jar, cover, and shake well. Often I make salad dressing in mustard jars, incorporating the hard-to-remove last bit of mustard. Add a little pickle brine or sauerkraut juice if you have them around. If salad dressing sits and infuses, it only gets better. I like to pre-dress salads, and even let them wilt a bit. If there's a pool of dressing when the salad is done, return it to the jar and reuse.

FURTHER READING

Thacker, Emily. *The Vinegar Book*. Canton, Ohio: Tresco Publishers, 1996.

13 CULTURAL REINCARNATION

Fermentation in the Cycles of Life,
Soil Fertility, and Social Change

FERMENTATION IS a lot bigger than its food-transforming aspect. Fermentation also describes the process by which microorganisms digest dead animal and plant tissue into elements that can nourish plants. As the early microbiologist Jacob Lippman eloquently stated it in his 1908 *Bacteria in Relation to Country Life,* microorganisms

> are the connecting link between the world of the living and the world of the dead. They are the great scavengers intrusted [sic] with restoring to circulation the carbon, nitrogen, hydrogen, sulphur, and other elements held fast in the dead bodies of plants and animals. Without them, dead bodies would accumulate, and the kingdom of the living would be replaced by the kingdom of the dead.[1]

This image helps me to accept death and decay. It is clear evidence on the physical plane that life is a cyclical process, with death as an indispensable part. It makes the harshest reality of life more understandable, more acceptable.

During this same past decade that I have developed my fascination with fermentation, I have spent a fair share of my fantasy life pondering my own decay and death. How could I not imagine it after receiving the HIV-antibody test death-prophecy? Nobody has said this more eloquently than the late poet Audre Lorde:

> Living a self-conscious life, under the pressure of time, I work with the consciousness of death at my shoulder, not constantly, but often enough to leave a mark upon all of my life's decisions and actions. And it does not matter whether this death comes next week or thirty years from now; this consciousness gives my life another breadth. It helps shape the words I speak, the ways I love, my politic of action, the strength of my vision and purpose, the depth of my appreciation of living.[2]

I wonder: Can thinking about illness and death make them manifest? Diagnostic medical testing, like the HIV-antibody test, is often promoted as unambiguously good information technology, assuming that more information will simply help you and your medical providers make better decisions. On the basis of my experience of the slow transition from HIV-positive "asymptomatic" to the onset of AIDS symptoms, I question whether it really is helpful for a seemingly healthy person to receive a diagnosis of inevitable illness. Ignorance can definitely be bliss.

As I wrote this book, I turned forty. My age-group peers talk about mid-life. It does not seem implausible to me that I could be at the mid-point of my life, and that I will celebrate my eightieth birthday in the year 2042. I love life and I believe in the infinity of possibility. But I am a student of observation and realism and probability, and frankly forty more years seems extremely unlikely. The medicines that supposedly keep me alive are probably not sustainable over decades; they are toxic and take a heavy toll over time. Though people with AIDS are living longer, friends keep dying of it. I have had ample opportunity to get used to the idea that my body is in its decline, that this is the latter period of my life. I wonder: Is this resignation? Is this the loss of will to survive?

I feel there is wisdom in making peace with death. It will come. All I can do is embrace life as best I can, and when I die, I know, I

REINCARNATION

believe, I have faith, that all that is me will continue to be part of the cycle of life, fermenting and nourishing and becoming myriad other life forms. My fermentation practice is a daily affirmation of this faith.

GETTING ACQUAINTED WITH DEATH

Our society distances us from death. We have created impersonal institutions to handle the transition. What are we so afraid of? I feel lucky to have been present with my mother, at home, when she died. She had been unconscious for about a week, at the end of a long struggle with cervical cancer; edema (fluid accumulation) bloated her legs and slowly rose higher on her body. Her breathing grew labored as her lungs filled with fluid. Our family gathered around her in a death watch. Her breaths became shallower and spasmodic, until one involuntary muscle contraction was the last. We sat with her for a while and cried, trying to grasp the enormity of the event. The men who came to our apartment for her body in the middle of the night were right out of central casting, pale and grim. They lifted my mother's bloated body into a bag on a stretcher and rolled it to the elevator. To get it into the elevator they had to stand it up, and my mother's body fell like a lead weight. Death was graphic and real.

Since then I have spent time with two other bodies post-mortem. One was Lynda Kubek, a friend who died of breast cancer. In the period before she died I was part of her caretaking team. What I remember most vividly about caretaking Lynda is applying clay compresses to a baseball-size tumor protruding from her armpit. Cancer is such an abstract concept, so internal and hidden and shrouded in euphemism, yet that tumor was so very concrete.

When Lynda died, her body was left on her bed for twenty-four hours before her home burial. By the time we arrived from Short Mountain the morning after her passing, friends and family had created a shrine around her, with flowers and incense and photos and fabrics. It was truly beautiful, and felt like an appropriate transition between life and burial. We sat with Lynda's body for a while. It was a very peaceful time. Afterward we went swimming in a nearby pond, and when I came up from diving in, there was a snake skin floating on the surface of the water. It was a powerful affirmation for me of the idea that death is part of the process of life, nothing to fear.

Tennessee is one of the few states that allow home burial, and Lynda's nephews spent the day digging her grave; a carpenter friend built a simple pine casket. Late that afternoon, her assembled friends and family processed with songs and drums and chants to her gravesite and laid her to rest. It felt so good that no commercial establishments—the cemetery, the funeral home, the crematorium—were involved. It was people taking care of their own.

The other dead body I spent time with was Russell Morgan. Russell is a friend who died at the age of twenty-eight of AIDS, actually Kaposi's sarcoma lesions in his lungs. I was visiting him at the time of his death. He had been in and out of the hospital. His breathing became uncomfortably difficult, and he decided to go back to the hospital. I helped carry him down the front steps and into the car. He never returned home. I was in the corridor outside his hospital room when he died. He was with his lover Leopard, and his family. I knew he had died because I heard Leopard wailing. Russell had been connected to oxygen, and still his breathing became more and more labored. As the scene was recounted to me, Russell removed the respirator mask, threw it to the floor, said "Fuck this!" and dived bravely into the unknown beyond. I admire his courage. The hospital staff let us spend some time in the room with Russell's body. I helped Leopard erect a shrine around Russell in the hospital bed, trying to create a ritual of transition in that denatured environment.

These experiences have given me a vision for how I would like my own death to be handled. I'll be happy to live a good long time; but I have given death plenty of thought. I would like my body to be given a transition period as Lynda's was. I want my friends and family to be able to be with me during this in-between period, to touch my clammy skin and say good-bye to my lifeless form and have death demystified a little bit. Then I want to be returned to the earth without resort to the impersonal industries of death. A huge funeral pyre would be lovely; if that's too much to bear, just place me in a hole in the ground, no casket please, and let me compost fast.

COMPOST HAPPENS

I love to watch the compost decompose. Recognizable forms with histories, such as onion skins from last night's soup, gradually melt back into the all-oneness of the Earth. I find the process itself so beautiful: poetry. Walt Whitman found inspiration in compost, too:

> The summer growth is innocent and disdainful above all
> those strata of sour dead.
> What chemistry!
> That the winds are really not infectious.
>
> . . . .
>
> That all is clean forever and forever,
> That the cool drink from the well tastes so good,
> That blackberries are so flavorous and juicy,
> That the fruits of the apple-orchard and the orange-orchard,
> that melons, grapes, peaches, plums, will none of them
> poison me,
> That when I recline on the grass I do not catch any disease,
> Though probably every spear of grass rises out of what was
> once catching disease.
> Now I am terrified at the Earth, it is that calm and patient,
> It grows such sweet things out of such corruptions,
> It turns harmless and stainless on its axis, with such endless
> succession of diseas'd corpses,
> It distills such exquisite winds out of such infused fetor,
> It renews with such unwitting looks its prodigal, annual,
> sumptuous crops,
> It gives such divine materials to men, and accepts such
> leavings from them at last.[3]

I use the term *compost* broadly, to describe the piles of kitchen scraps, the piles of weeds and prunings, the piles of goat "muck" (their excrement mixed with bedding straw), and the piles of our own human feces from our outhouse, mixed with toilet paper, sawdust, and ash. After a year or two, each of these piles looks the same. They are all broken down into simpler forms by microorganisms in the act of fermentation. Composting is a fermentation process.

There are many different ideas about the best composting methods. Gardeners are a passionate bunch, with strong opinions about the best ways to do things. Rodale's *Complete Book of Composting* describes gardeners who "spend years running from method to method, charting secret figures, constructing weird bins, boxes, ventilating pipes and watering systems, and carefully measuring each bit of material which is placed just right on the heap."[4] Certainly you can manipulate conditions to encourage compost fermentation to proceed faster, or hotter, or more odor-free. But even if you do nothing and let the food scraps just accumulate in your kitchen, compost happens. There is nothing you can do to stop it. Fermentation makes organic compounds decompose. It is this process, the breaking down of fallen leaves, animal feces and carcasses, dead trees and other plants, and any other organic matter, that regenerates the soil. Fermentation is the basis of soil fertility.

In chapter 2, I referred to a nineteenth-century German chemist named Justus von Liebig, who staunchly opposed the idea that fermentation is a biological process. This same misguided man pioneered the idea of fertilizing soil with manufactured chemicals. "We have now examined the action of the animal or natural manures upon plants but it is evident that if artificial manures contain the same constituents, they will exert a similar action upon the plants to which they are applied."[5] Von Liebig's 1845 monograph *Chemistry and Its Application to Agriculture and Physiology* laid the groundwork for the chemical agricultural methods that have become standard practice and that are rapidly depleting soils everywhere. Fermentation is a natural, biological, self-generating process of decomposition that builds soil fertility and nurtures plant life. Chemical fertilization may be effective in terms of short-term yields, but it impairs the function of the soil as a self-regulating, biodiverse ecological system.

Thinking about mass food production makes me sad and angry. Chemical mono-crop agriculture. Genetic engineering of the most basic food crops. Ugly, inhumane factory animal breeding. Ultra-processed foods full of preservative chemicals, industrial byproducts, and packaging. Food production is just one realm among many in which ever more concentrated corporate units extract profits from the Earth and the mass of humanity.

Historically, food has been our most direct and tangible ongoing connection to the Earth. Increasingly, though, food has become a collection of mass-produced and aggressively marketed commodities.

This is the song of progress: We have supposedly been freed, by technology and mass social organization, from the burdens of growing or procuring our own food. Just going to the supermarket and putting the food into the microwave is burden enough. Most people do not know or care where their food comes from.

SOCIAL CHANGE

The astute reader will have noticed by now that my outlook can be rather bleak. Many current trends, not only mass food production, but war, global warming, accelerating species extinctions, the growing class divide, the persistence of racism, the incredible number of people in prisons, high-tech militarization and social control, consumerism as patriotic duty, and ever more insipid television programming, contribute to my pessimism.

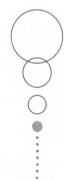

What gives me hope is the simple notion that current trends do not necessarily have to continue. It seems to me that they cannot possibly. The revolutionary spirit of liberation and hope always and everywhere remains, even dormant or confined to dreams, like a seed culture, ready anytime to multiply, thrive, and transform, given the right conditions.

Social change is another form of fermentation. Ideas ferment, as they spread and mutate and inspire movements for change. The *Oxford English Dictionary* offers as the second definition of ferment: "The state of being excited by emotion or passion, agitation, excitement . . . a state of agitation tending to bring about a purer, more wholesome, or more stable condition of things." The word "ferment" derives from the Latin *fervere,* "to boil." "Fervor" and "fervent" are other words from the same root. Fermenting liquids bubble just like boiling liquids. Excited people can channel the same intensity, and use it to create change.

Though fermentation is a phenomenon of transformation, the change it renders tends to be gentle, slow, and steady. Contrast fermentation with another transformative natural phenomenon: fire. As I wrote this book the awesome drama of fire seared itself into my consciousness in three separate events. The first was the one we all witnessed via images that we are destined to be reminded of frequently for the rest of our lives. I am referring to the great balls of fire that resulted from the impact of the jet planes hitting the World Trade Center, melting the steel structures and toppling the towers. Whatever other meanings we ascribe to the infamous events of September 11, 2001, we collectively witnessed the sudden collapse of one of the great feats of modern engineering, by the sheer indomitable force of fire.

Two months later, I found myself in the middle of a forest fire, when I visited my friends at Moonshadow. Approaching their place from miles away, I could see and smell smoke. The fires had been started by kids as Halloween pranks or possibly arson. They had burned along the forest floor for more than a week, reached Moonshadow's land, and threatened to burn their buildings and gardens. The fire itself was a line of flame hundreds of feet long, moving slowly downhill (uphill, I'm told, it would have traveled faster), leaving in its wake an eerie landscape of ash and burning tree trunks. My Moonshadow friends had been days without sleep, raking and digging to create firebreaks to contain the fire. The breaks were in place by the time we got there, but wind could easily blow embers across them and continue the spread of the fire. The imperative was to monitor the firebreaks so any stray embers could be put out or at least contained.

Living trees were surviving the fire, but many pine trees, dead from infestations of the southern pine beetle, were falling. We wore helmets near the fire, but as trees fell at frequent intervals, I wondered what good the helmet would do if fate dropped an eighty-foot tree on me. We slept near the firebreak that night, on call in case the fire jumped and hands were needed to contain it. I woke up a lot during the night, hearing falling trees, observing the flames move downhill, relieved that it was following the predicted course and not jumping the firebreak. By morning, the fire had reached the creek and died out, leaving a forest full of smoking ash and embers, and a grateful group of people, humbled by the fire's uncontrollable, transformative power.

Then, another two months later, during a January cold snap, our nearest neighbors on Short Mountain had a fire in the middle of the night. Embers fell from their woodstove undetected, and built into a sizeable fire before the sound of bottles bursting in the kitchen woke the guests sleeping in the next room. By the time they awoke, the smoke was thick. Their water line was frozen, so there was no quantity of water at hand. Luckily, with a fire extinguisher, blankets, rugs, and buckets of snow, they were able to put out the fire. Had they awakened a few moments later, or panicked in the confusion, their house would have been ashes. The fire was another humbling reminder, and a fire safety wake-up call for the rest of us heating with wood and reading by candlelight. Fire can change everything, in an instant.

In the realm of social change, fire is the revolutionary moment of upheaval; romantic and longed for, or dreaded and guarded against, depending upon your perspective. Fire spreads, destroying whatever lies in its path, and its path is unpredictable. Fermentation is not so dramatic. It bubbles rather than burns, and its transformative mode is gentle and slow. Steady, too. Fermentation is a force that cannot be stopped. It recycles life, renews hope, and goes on and on.

Your life and my life and everyone's lives and deaths are part of the endless biological cycle of life and death and fermentation. Wild fermentation is going on everywhere, always. Embrace it. Work with the material resources and life processes that are close at hand. As microorganisms work their transformative magic and you witness the miracles of fermentation, envision yourself as an agent for change, creating agitation, releasing bubbles of transformation into the social order. Use your fermented goodies to nourish your family and friends and allies. The life-affirming power of these basic foods contrasts sharply with the lifeless, industrially processed foods that fill supermarket shelves. Draw inspiration from the action of bacteria and yeast, and make your life a transformative process.

APPENDIX
Cultural Resources

SOURCES FOR STARTER CULTURES

G.E.M. Cultures
30301 Sherwood Road
Fort Bragg, CA 95437
(707) 964-2922
www.gemcultures.com
Kefir grains, koji, kombucha mothers, sourdough starters, tempeh starter, and many others. This family-run business is the best all-around source for fermentation cultures in the United States.

Kefir-Making E-Group
www.egroups.com/group/kefir_making
Kefir enthusiasts eager to share grains.

New England Cheesemaking Supply Company
85 Main Street
Ashfield, MA 01330
(413) 628-3808
www.cheesemaking.com
Cheese cultures, rennet, and other cheesemaking supplies.

South River Miso Company
Conway, MA 01341
(413) 369-4057
www.southrivermiso.com
Koji.

The Tempeh Lab
P.O. Box 208
Summertown, TN 38483
(931) 964-3574
e-mail: thfarm@usit.net
Tempeh starter.

Worldwide Kombucha Exchange
    www.kombu.de
Kombucha mothers.

SOURCES FOR EQUIPMENT

Home Wine and Beer Trade Association
    (813) 685-4261
    www.hwbta.org
Searchable listing of local wine- and beer-making supply retailers.

Home Canning Supply
    (800) 354-4070
    www.homecanningsupply.com
Crocks, Mason jars, and other canning supplies.

Lehman's Hardware
    (877) 438-5346
    www.lehmans.com
Crocks, grinders, and many other low-tech kitchenware and hardware items.

SOURCES FOR FRESH VEGETABLES AND SEAWEED

Robin Van En Center for CSA Resources
    (717) 264-4141 x3352
    www.csacenter.org
Online national directory of Community Supported Agriculture farms.

Ironbound Island Seaweed
    P.O. Box 23
    Winter Harbor, ME 04693
    (207) 963-7016
    e-mail: ironbound@acadia.net
Seaweed.

Larch Hanson
    P.O. Box 57
    Steuben, ME 04680
    (207) 546-2875
Seaweed.

Ryan Drum
    P.O. Box 25
    Waldron Island, WA 98297
    www.partnereartheducationcenter
    .com/islandherbs.html

SOURCES FOR FOOD INFORMATION AND ACTION

Genetically Engineered Food Alert
    (800) 390-3373
    www.gefoodalert.org

Greenpeace True Food Now Project
    (800) 326-0950
    www.truefoodnow.org

Organic Consumers Association
    (218) 226-4164
    www.organicconsumers.org

Sequatchie Valley Institute
    Route 1, Box 304
    Whitwell, TN 37397
    (423) 949-5922
    www.svionline.org
"Food For Life" food skills, information, and politics gathering held every summer.

FERMENTATION TROUBLESHOOTING
E-mail your questions to the author at sandorkraut@wildfermentation.com. Check out his website at www.wildfermentation.com to see questions, answers, links and other fermentation-related information.

NOTES

CHAPTER 1. CULTURAL REHABILITATION (pages 5 to 12)

1. Sue Shephard, *Pickled, Potted, and Canned: How the Art and Science of Food Preserving Changed the World* (New York: Simon & Schuster, 2000), 210.

2. Claude Aubert, *Les Aliments Fermentés Traditionnels* (Mens, France: Association Terre Vivante, 1985), cited in Sally Fallon, *Nourishing Traditions* (Washington, D.C.: New Trends Publishing, 1999), 95.

3. Shephard, *Pickled, Potted, and Canned,* 129.

4. R. Binita and N. Khetarpaul, "Probiotic Fermentation: Effect on Antinutrients and Digestibility of Starch and Protein of Indigenously Developed Food Mixture," *Nutritional Health* 11, no. 3 (1997).

5. Chavan et al., United Nations Food and Agriculture Organization, *Fermented Foods: A Global Perspective,* Agriculture Services Bulletin, 1999.

6. Bill Mollison, *The Permaculture Book of Ferment and Human Nutrition* (Tyalgum, Australia: Tagari Publications, 1993), 20.

7. Victor Herbert, "Vitamin B-12: Plant Sources, Requirements, and Assay," *American Journal of Clinical Nutrition* 48 (1988), 852–58.

8. L. A. Santiago, M. Hiramatsu, and A. Mori, "Japanese Soybean Paste Miso Scavenges Free Radicals and Inhibits

Lipid Peroxidation," *Journal of Nutrition Science and Vitaminology* 38, no. 3 (June 1992).

9. S. Bengmark, "Immunonutrition: Role of Biosurfactants, Fiber, and Probiotic Bacteria," *Nutrition* 14, nos. 7–8 (1998).

10. "New Chapter Health Report," 2000.

11. Sally Fallon goes on at some length about phytic acid in *Nourishing Traditions*, 452. This idea is confirmed in Paul Pitchford's *Healing with Whole Foods* (Berkeley: North Atlantic Books, 1993), 184.

12. Mollison, *The Permaculture Book of Ferment and Human Nutrition*, 20.

13. Cited in D. Gareth Jones, ed., *Exploitation of Microorganisms* (London: Chapman & Hall, 1993).

14. R. Binita and N. Khetarpaul, "Probiotic Fermented Food Mixtures: Possible Applications in Clinical Anti-Diarrhea Usage," *Nutritional Health* 12, no. 2 (1998).

15. Bengmark, "Immunonutrition."

16. Cited by BBC News Online, 16 June 2000.

17. Cited by Jane Brody, "Germ Paranoia May Harm Health," *The London Free Press*, 24 June, 2000.

18. Cited by Siri Carpenter, "Modern Hygiene's Dirty Tricks: The Clean Life May Throw Off a Delicate Balance in the Immune System," *Science News Online*, 14 August 1999.

19. Cited by MSNBC, 23 May 2001.

20. Melanie Marchie, "A New Attitude: Soap Gets Serious," *Household and Personal Products on the Internet* (www.happi.com), 13 December 2001.

21. Stephen Harrod Buhner, *The Lost Language of Plants* (White River Junction, Vt.: Chelsea Green Publishing Co., 2002), 134.

22. Mary Ellen Sanders, "Considerations for Use of Probiotic Bacteria to Modulate Human Health," paper delivered at Experimental Biology 99 Symposium.

23. Terence McKenna, *Food of the Gods* (New York: Bantam, 1992), 41.

24. Lynn Margulis and Karlene V. Schwartz, *Five Kingdoms* (New York: W. H. Freeman and Co., 1999), 14. See also Lynn Margulis and René Fester, eds., *Symbiogenesis as a Source of Evolutionary Innovation* (Cambridge: MIT Press, 1991).

25. Elie Metchnikoff, *The Prolongation of Life: Optimistic Studies*, translated by P. Chalmers Mitchell (New York & London: G.P. Putnam's Sons, 1908), 182.

CHAPTER 2. CULTURAL THEORY (pages 13 to 19)

1. Maguelonne Toussaint-Samat, *A History of Food,* translated by Anthea Bell (Cambridge: Blackwell Publishers, 1992), 34.

2. Claude Levi-Strauss, *From Honey to Ashes,* I translated by John and Doreen Weightman (New York: Harper & Row, 1973), 473.

3. Stephen Harrod Buhner, *Sacred and Herbal Healing Beers* (Boulder: Siris Books, 1998), 141.

4. Ibid., 81–82.

5. Friedrich Nietzche, *The Birth of Tragedy,* translated by W. A. Haussmann (New York: MacMillan, 1923), 26.

6. Solomon H. Katz and Fritz Maytag, "Brewing an Ancient Beer," *Archaeology* (July/August 1991), 30.

7. *The Egyptian Book of the Dead,* translated by E. A. Wallis Budge (New York: Dover Publications, 1967), 23.

8. Sophie D. Coe, *America's First Cuisines* (Austin: University of Texas Press, 1994), 166.

9. *American Heritage Dictionary,* 2000.

10. Katz and Maytag, "Brewing an Ancient Beer," 26.

11. From Louis Pasteur's *Fermentation et Generations Dites Spontanees,* cited in Patrice Debre, *Louis Pasteur,* translated by Elborg Forster (Baltimore: Johns Hopkins University Press, 1998).

12. Leeuwenhoek cited in Daniel J. Boorstin, *The Discoverers: A History of Man's Search to Know His World and Himself* (New York: Random House, 1983).

13. Debre, *Louis Pasteur,* 95.

14. Justus Von Liebig's *Traite de Chemie Organique,* 1840, cited in Debre, *Louis Pasteur,* 92.

15. Louis Pasteur, *Oeuvres de Pasteur* 3:13, cited in Debre, *Louis Pasteur,* 101.

16. Jacob G. Lippman, *Bacteria in Relation to Country Life* (New York: The MacMillan Company, 1908), vii–viii.

17. Cited in Madeleine Parker Grant, *Microbiology and Human Progress* (New York: Rinehart & Co., 1953), 59.

CHAPTER 3. CULTURAL HOMOGENIZATION (pages 20 to 27)

1. Cocoa Research Institute.

2. "World's Chocolate Supply Threatened by Dread Diseases; Genetics May Help," *Tennessee Farm Bureau News* (November 2001): 6.

3. Mark Pendergrast, *Uncommon Grounds: The History of Coffee and How It Transformed Our World* (New York: Basic Books, 1999), 6.

4. McKenna, *Food of the Gods,* 186

5. International Coffee Organization, "Coffee Production 2000."

6. My primary source of historical information about the tea trade is Henry Hobhouse, *Seeds of Change: Five Plants that Transformed Mankind* (New York: Harper & Row, 1985), 95–137.

7. International Tea Commission.

8. McKenna, *Food of the Gods,* 185–86.

9. Hobhouse, *Seeds of Change,* 64.

10. Sidney W. Mintz, *Sweetness and Power: The Place of Sugar in Modern History* (New York: Viking, 1985), 46.

11. Ibid, 95.

12. This and most of my other historical information about sugar is culled from Mintz, *Sweetness and Power.*

13. Medicinally, sugar was mixed with unpleasant-tasting herbs to make them more palatable and applied topically to wounds. As a spice, sugar was grouped with the other varied and much-desired flavorings of the East, and it was used in combination with them in cooking, to spice up the monotonous and bland medieval European diet.

14. Sudarsan Raghavan and Sumana Chatterjee, "Slave Labor Taints

Sweetness of World Chocolate," *The Kansas City Star,* 23 June 2001.

15. Mintz, *Sweetness and Power,* 214.

16. José Bové, "Who Really Makes the Decisions about What We Eat?" *The Guardian* (London), 13 June 2001, excerpted from his book *The World Is Not for Sale: Farmers against Junk Food.*

17. Wendell Berry, *What Are People For?,* 1990, excerpted as "The Pleasures of Eating," *The Sun* (January 2002), 18.

18. Vandana Shiva, *Stolen Harvest: The Hijacking of the Global Food Supply* (Cambridge: South End Press, 2000), 127.

CHAPTER 4. CULTURAL MANIPULATION (pages 28 to 37)

1. Mikal Aasved, "Alcohol, Drinking, and Intoxication in Preindustrial Society: Theoretical, Nutritional, and Religious Considerations," unpublished Ph.D. dissertation, University of California, Santa Barbara, 1988, cited in Buhner, *Sacred and Herbal Healing Beers,* 73.

2. Mollison, *The Permaculture Book of Ferment and Human Nutrition,* 187.

3. Annie Hubert, "A Strong Smell of Fish?" *Slow* 22 (Summer 2001): 56.

CHAPTER 5. VEGETABLE FERMENTS (pages 38 to 56)

1. Cited by Ross Grant, "Fermenting Sauerkraut Foments a Cancer Fighter," *Health Scout News Reporter* (online), 24 October 2002.

2. William Woys Weaver, *Sauerkraut Yankees: Pennsylvania-German Foods and Foodways* (Philadelphia: University of Pennsylvania Press, 1983), 176.

3. Calvin Sims, "Cabbage Is Cabbage? Not to Kimchi Lovers; Koreans Take Issue with a Rendition of Their National Dish Made in Japan," *The New York Times,* 5 February 2000, C4.

4. Susun S. Weed, *Healing Wise* (Woodstock, N.Y.: Ash Tree Publishing, 1989), 96.

CHAPTER 6. BEAN FERMENTS (pages 57 to 72)

1. Frances Moore Lappé, *Diet for a Small Planet* (New York: Ballantine Books, 1971), 5.

2. Analects of Confucius, Scroll 2, Chapter 10, cited in William Shurtleff and Akiko Aoyagi, *The Book of Miso* (Berkeley: Ten Speed Press, 2001), 214.

3. Shurtleff and Aoyagi, *The Book of Miso,* 218.

4. Ibid., 25–26.

5. Weed, *Healing Wise,* 224.

CHAPTER 7. DAIRY FERMENTS (AND VEGAN ALTERNATIVES) (pages 73 to 91)

1. Susun S. Weed, *Breast Cancer? Breast Health! The Wise Woman Way* (Woodstock, NY: Ash Tree Publishing, 1996), 45.

2. Irma S. Rombauer and Marion Rombauer Becker, *Joy of Cooking* (New York: Signet, 1964), 486–87.

3. Dominic N. Anfiteatro, *Kefir: A Probiotic Gem Cultured with a Probiotic*

Jewel (Adelaide, Australia: self-published, 2001).

4. Burkhard Bilger, "Raw Faith," *The New Yorker*, 19 & 26 August 2002, 157.

5. Cited in Pierre Boisard, "The Future of a Tradition: Two Ways of Making Camembert, the Foremost Cheese of France," in *Food and Foodways* 4 (1991): 183–84.

6. Marlene Cimons, "Food Safety Concerns Drive FDA Review of Fine Cheeses," *American Society for Microbiology News*, 13 February 2001.

7. European Alliance for Artisan and Traditional Raw Milk Cheese, "Manifesto in Defense of Raw-Milk Cheese." Available online at www.bestofbridgestone.com/mb/nr/nr00/rmc.html

8. Jeffrey Steingarten, "Cheese Crisis", *Vogue*, June 2000, 269.

9. Cited in Bilger, *Raw Faith,* 157.

CHAPTER 8. BREAD (AND PANCAKES) (pages 92 to 109)

1. Michael Pollan, *The Botany of Desire: A Plant's Eye View of the World* (New York: Random House, 2001), 204.

2. Bruno Latour, *The Pasteurization of France*, translated by Alan Sheridan and John Law (Cambridge: Harvard University Press, 1988), 82.

3. For an in-depth discussion of the science of bread-baking, see Daniel Wing and Alan Scott, *The Bread Builders: Hearth Loaves and Masonry Ovens* (White River Junction, Vt.: Chelsea Green Publishing Co., 1999).

4. Ruth Allman, *Alaska Sourdough: The Real Stuff by a Real Alaskan* (Anchorage: Alaska Northwest Publishing Co., 1976).

CHAPTER 9. FERMENTED-GRAIN PORRIDGES AND BEVERAGES (pages 110 to 123)

1. Solomon H. Katz, M. L. Hediger, and L. A. Valleroy, "Traditional Maize Processing Techniques in the New World," *Science* 184 (17 May 1974).

2. Coe, *America's First Cuisines,*14.

3. www.members.tripod.com/~sekituwanation/index/recipes.html

4. Carol Kaesuk Yoon, "Genetic Modification Taints Corn in Mexico," *The New York Times,* 2 October, 2001.

5. Shiva, *Stolen Harvest,* 17.

6. Fedco Seeds 2002 catalogue, 7.

7. Fallon, *Nourishing Traditions,* 452.

8. Pitchford, *Healing with Whole Foods,* 184.

9. United Nations Food and Agriculture Organization, *Fermented Foods: A Global Perspective,* Agriculture Services Bulletin, 1999.

10. Elizabeth Meyer-Renschhausen, "The Porridge Debate: Grain, Nutrition, and Forgotten Food Preparation Techniques," *Food and Foodways* 5 (1991): 95–120.

CHAPTER 10. WINES
(pages 124 to 140)

1. Toussaint-Samat, *A History of Food,* 36.
2. Buhner, *Sacred and Herbal Healing Beers,* 67.
3. From the Web site of the Vegetarian Resource Group, www.vrg.org.
4. Ben Watson, *Cider, Hard and Sweet* (Woodstock, Vt.: The Countryman Press, 1999), 89.
5. Ibid., 25.

CHAPTER 11. BEERS
(pages 141 to 151)

1. Cited in Keith Steinkraus, ed., *Handbook of Indigenous Fermented Foods* (New York: Marcel Dekker, 1983).
2. Virginia Morell, "Empires Across the Andes," *National Geographic* 201, no. 6 (June 2002): 121.
3. Jeremy Geller, "Bread and Beer in Fourth-Millennium Egypt," *Food and Foodways* 5 (1993): 255–67.
4. Solomon H. Katz and Fritz Maytag, "Brewing an Ancient Beer," *Archaeology* (July/August 1991): 27.
5. Kathryn S. March, "Hospitality, Women, and the Efficacy of Beer," *Food and Foodways* 1 (1987): 367.
6. Buhner, *Sacred and Herbal Healing Beers,* 429.
7. Charlie Papazian, *The New Complete Joy of Home Brewing* (New York: Avon Books, 1991), 171.

CHAPTER 12. VINEGARS
(pages 152 to 157)

1. Emily Thacker, *The Vinegar Book* (Canton, Ohio: Tresco Publishers, 1996), 2.
2. Ibid., 6.
3. Terre Vivante, *Keeping Food Fresh: Old World Techniques and Recipes* (White River Junction, Vt.: Chelsea Green Publishing Co., 1999), 110.

CHAPTER 13. CULTURAL
REINCARNATION (pages 158 to 166)

1. Lippman, *Bacteria in Relation to Country Life,* 136–37.
2. Audre Lorde, *The Cancer Journals* (San Francisco: Aunt Lute Books, 1980), 16.
3. Walt Whitman, excerpt from "This Compost," *Leaves of Grass,* 1881.
4. J. I. Rodale, ed., *The Complete Book of Composting* (Emmaus, Penn.: Rodale Books, 1960), 44.
5. Justus von Liebig, *Chemistry and Its Application to Agriculture and Physiology* (Philadelphia: James M. Campbell, 1845), 69.

BIBLIOGRAPHY

Allman, Ruth. *Alaska Sourdough: The Real Stuff by a Real Alaskan.* Anchorage: Alaska Northwest Publishing Co., 1976.

Anfiteatro, Dominic N. *Kefir: A Probiotic Gem Cultured with a Probiotic Jewel.* Adelaide, Australia: self-published, 2001. Available online at www.chariot.net.au/~dna/kefirpage.

Boisard, Pierre. "The Future of a Tradition: Two Ways of Making Camembert, the Foremost Cheese of France." *Food and Foodways* 4 (1991): 183–84.

Brown, Edward Espe. *The Tassajara Bread Book* (25th Anniversary Edition). Boston: Shambala Publications, 1995.

Buhner, Stephen Harrod. *The Lost Language of Plants.* White River Junction, Vt.: Chelsea Green Publishing Co., 2002.

Buhner, Stephen Harrod. *Sacred and Healing Beers: The Secrets of Ancient Fermentation.* Boulder, Colo.: Siris Books, 1998.

Carroll, Ricki. *Home Cheese-making.* North Adams, Mass.: Storey Books, 2002.

Carroll, Ricki, and Phyllis Hobson. *Making Cheese, Butter, and Yogurt.* Pownal, Vt.: Storey Books, 1997.

Chamberlain, Lesley. *The Food and Cookery of Russia.* London: Penguin Books, 1982.

Ciletti, Barbara. *Making Great Cheese.* Asheville, N.C.: Lark Books, 2001.

Coe, Sophie D. *America's First Cuisines.* Austin: University of Texas Press, 1994.

Colbin, Annemarie. *Food and Healing.* New York: Balantine Press, 1986.

Coultrip-Davis, Deborah, and Young Sook Ramsay. *Flavors of Korea: Delicious Vegetarian Cuisine.* Summertown, Tenn.: Book Publishing Company, 1998.

Cresswell, Stephen. *Homemade Root Beer, Soda, and Pop.* Pownal, Vt.: Storey Books, 1998.

Dampier, William Cecil. *A History of Science.* Cambridge: Cambridge University Press, 1949.

Debré, Patrice. *Louis Pasteur*, trans. Elborg Forster. Baltimore: Johns Hopkins University Press, 1998.

Dirar, Hamid. *The Indigenous Fermented Food of the Sudan: A Study in African Food and Nutrition.* Oxford and New York: Oxford University Press, 1993.

Dorje, Rinjing. *Food in Tibetan Life.* London: Prospect Books, 1985.

Fallon, Sally, with Mary G. Enig. *Nourishing Traditions: The Cookbook That Challenges Politically Correct Nutrition and the Diet Dictocrats* (2nd Edition). Washington, D.C.: New Trends Publishing, 1999.

Garey, Terry A. *The Joy of Home Winemaking.* New York: Avon, 1996.

Geller, Jeremy. "Bread and Beer in Fourth-Millennium Egypt." *Food and Foodways* 5 (1993): 255–67.

Grant, Madeleine Parker. *Microbiology and Human Progress.* New York: Rinehart & Co., 1953.

Hagler, Louise, and Dorothy R. Bates, eds. *The New Farm Vegetarian Cookbook.* Summertown, Tenn.: Book Publishing Co., 1989.

Hobhouse, Henry. *Seeds of Change: Five Plants that Transformed Mankind.* New York: Harper & Row, 1985.

Jones, D. Gareth, ed. *Exploitation of Microorganisms*. London: Chapman & Hall, 1993

Katz, Solomon H., and Fritz Maytag. "Brewing an Ancient Beer." *Archaeology* (July/August 1991): 24–31.

Katz, Solomon H., M. L. Hediger, and L. A. Valleroy. "Traditional Maize Processing Techniques in the New World." *Science* 184 (17 May 1974): 765–69.

Kennedy, Diana. *The Cuisines of Mexico*. New York: Harper & Row, 1986.

Kurlansky, Mark. *Salt: A World History*. New York: Walker and Co., 2002.

Kushi, Aveline. *Aveline Kushi's Complete Guide to Macrobiotic Cooking*. New York: Warner Books, 1989.

Lappé, Frances Moore. *Diet for a Small Planet*. New York: Ballantine Books, 1971.

Latour, Bruno. *The Pasteurization of France*, trans. Alan Sheridan and John Law. Cambridge: Harvard University Press, 1988.

Leader, Daniel, and Judith Blahnik. *Bread Alone: Bold Fresh Loaves from Your Own Hands*. New York: William Morrow & Co., 1993.

Levi-Strauss, Claude. *From Honey to Ashes*, trans. John and Doreen Weightman. New York: Harper & Row, 1973.

Liebig, Justus von. *Chemistry and Its Application to Agriculture and Physiology*. Philadelphia: James M. Campbell, 1845.

Lippman, Jacob G. *Bacteria in Relation to Country Life*. New York: The MacMillan Company, 1908.

March, Kathryn S. "Hospitality, Women, and the Efficacy of Beer." *Food and Foodways* 1 (1987): 351–87.

Margulis, Lynn, and Karlene V. Schwartz. *Five Kingdoms*. New York: W. H. Freeman and Co., 1999.

McKenna, Terrance. *Food of the Gods: The Search for the Original Tree of Knowledge*. New York: Bantam, 1992.

Mesfin, Daniel Jote. *Exotic Ethiopian Cooking*. Falls Church, Va.: Ethiopian Cookbook Enterprise, 1994.

Metchnikoff, Elie. *The Prolongation of Life: Optimistic Studies*, trans. P. Chalmers Mitchell. New York & London: G.P. Putnam's Sons, 1908.

Meyer-Renschhausen, Elizabeth. "The Porridge Debate: Grain, Nutrition, and Forgotten Food Preparation Techniques." *Food and Foodways* 5 (1991): 95–120.

Miller, Dave. *Brewing the World's Great Beers*. Pownal, Vt.: Storey Books, 1992.

Mintz, Sidney W. *Sweetness and Power: The Place of Sugar in Modern History*. New York: Viking, 1985.

Mollison, Bill. *The Permaculture Book of Ferment and Human Nutrition*. Tyalgum, Australia: Tagari Publications, 1993.

Moosewood Collective. *Sundays at Moosewood Restaurant: Ethnic and Regional Recipes from the Cooks at the Legendary Restaurant*. New York: Fireside, 1990.

Papazian, Charlie. *The Home Brewer's Companion*. New York: Avon Books, 1994.

Papazian, Charlie. *The New Complete Joy of Home Brewing*. New York: Avon Books, 1991.

Pendergrast, Mark. *Uncommon Grounds: The History of Coffee and How It Transformed Our World*. New York: Basic Books, 1999.

Petrini, Carlo, with Ben Watson and Slow Food Editore. *Slow Food: Collected Thoughts on Taste, Tradition, and the Honest Pleasures of Food*. White River Junction, Vt.: Chelsea Green Publishing Company, 2001.

Pitchford, Paul. *Healing with Whole Foods*. Berkeley: North Atlantic Books, 1993.

Pollan, Michael. *The Botany of Desire: A Plant's Eye View of the World*. New York: Random House, 2001.

Reinhart, Peter. *Brother Juniper's Breadbook: Slow Rise as Method and Metaphor*. Reading, Mass.: Aris Books, 1991.

Robertson, Laurel, Carol Fliners, and Bronwen Godfrey. *Laurel's Kitchen Bread Book: A Guide to Whole-Grain Breadmaking*. New York: Random House, 1985.

Rodale, J. I., ed. *The Complete Book of Composting*. Emmaus, Penn.: Rodale Books, 1960.

Sacharoff, Shanta Nimbark. *Flavors of India: Vegetarian Indian Cooking*. Summertown, Tenn.: Book Publishing Co., 1996.

Sarnat, Richard, M.D., Paul Schulick, and Thomas M. Newmark. *The Life Bridge: The Way to Longevity with Probiotic Nutrients*. Brattleboro, Vt.: Herbal Free Press, 2002.

Shephard, Sue. *Pickled, Potted, and Canned: How the Art and Science of Food Preserving Changed the World*. New York: Simon & Schuster, 2000.

Shiva, Vandana. *Stolen Harvest: The Hijacking of the Global Food Supply*. Cambridge: South End Press, 2000.

Shurtleff, William, and Akiko Aoyagi. *The Book of Miso*. Berkeley: Ten Speed Press, 2001.

Shurtleff, William, and Akiko Aoyagi. *The Book of Tempeh*. Berkeley: Ten Speed Press, 2001.

Smith, R. E. F., and David Christian. *Bread and Salt: A Social and Economic History of Food and Drink in Russia*. Cambridge: Cambridge University Press, 1984.

Spence, Pamela. *Mad about Mead! Nectar of the Gods*. St. Paul: Llewellyn Publications, 1997.

Steinkraus, Keith, ed. *Handbook of Indigenous Fermented Foods*. New York: Marcel Dekker, 1999.

Stepaniak, JoAnne. *The Uncheese Cookbook*. Summertown, Tenn.: Book Publishing Company, 1994.

Terre Vivante. *Keeping Food Fresh: Old World Techniques and Recipes*. White River Junction, Vt.: Chelsea Green Publishing, 1999.

Thacker, Emily. *The Vinegar Book*. Canton, Ohio: Tresco Publishers, 1996.

Toussaint-Samat, Maguelonne. *A History of Food,* trans. Anthea Bell. Cambridge: Blackwell Publishers, 1992.

United Nations Food and Agriculture Organization. *Fermented Cereals: A Global Perspective*. Agriculture Services Bulletin #138, 1999.

Vargas, Pattie, and Rich Gulling. *Making Wild Wines and Meads: 125 Unusual Recipes Using Herbs, Fruits, Flowers, and More*. Pownal, Vt.: Storey Books, 1999.

Visson, Lynn. *The Complete Russian Cookbook*. Ann Arbor, Mich.: Ardis Publishers, 1982.

Watson, Ben. *Cider, Hard and Sweet*. Woodstock, Vt.: Countryman Press, 1999.

Weaver, William Woys. *Sauerkraut Yankees: Pennsylvania-German Foods and Foodways*. Philadelphia: University of Pennsylvania Press, 1983.

Weed, Susun S. *Breast Cancer? Breast Health!* Woodstock, N.Y.: Ash Tree Publishing, 1996.

Weed, Susun S. *Healing Wise*. Woodstock, N.Y.: Ash Tree Publishing, 1989.

Wing, Daniel, and Alan Scott. *The Bread Builders: Hearth Loaves and Masonry Ovens*. White River Junction, Vt.: Chelsea Green Publishing Co., 1999.

Wood, Ed. *World Sourdoughs from Antiquity*. Berkeley, Calif.: Ten Speed Press, 1996.

Ziedrich, Laura. *The Joy of Pickling*. Boston: The Harvard Common Press, 1998.

INDEX